Instrumental Music Guide

Instrumental Music Guide

A. Harold Goodman

Brigham Young University Press

Library of Congress Cataloging in Publication Data

Goodman, A   Harold, 1924–
  Instrumental music guide.

  1. Music—Bibliography—Graded lists. I. Title.
ML132.A2G66   016.78   77-7923
ISBN 0-8425-1525-9

Library of Congress Catalog Card Number: 77-7923
International Standard Book Number: 0-8425-1525-9
© 1977 by Brigham Young University Press. All rights reserved
Brigham Young University Press, Provo, Utah 84602
Printed in the United States of America
77 2.5M 18993

Contents

Preface

The instrumental musician has the incredible task of knowing not only the wealth of past music literature written for large and small ensembles as well as instrumental solo performance and study materials, but also current literature in this comprehensive field. Often this seems an impossible task. The success of a thriving instrumental program, however, is dependent to a large degree upon proper literature. Hence this resource guidebook has been prepared from years of performance experience at the elementary, junior and senior high school, higher education, and community levels.

Rather than a comprehensive listing of good and bad literature, only the best has been included in this work. My sincere hope is that this information will develop and enhance an even better instrumental music program in this nation's schools.

1

Selecting the Finest Music

The proper selection of literature for the band and orchestra or for the solo instrument is one of the most significant aspects of musical performance. More often than not, the average school band and orchestra will not perform representative samplings from the main periods of music history because these compositions may not be in the library. For an aesthetic experience, however, the best choice of music would still include literature that possesses intrinsic musical value.

The complete rehearsal or performance should evolve from this intrinsic value of the music itself, and if the major objective in teaching music is to develop a sense of appreciation and artistic taste, the relationship of music to human feelings and intellect must be discerned.

Form and style must be perceived and assimilated. Form in music is very important, because form gives intelligible meaning to all of the arts. Each main period of musical history also has a distinct style that will be inseparably related to any individual music composition from that period. If the conductor has properly chosen literature of each of the main periods, the distinctive qualities of each composition can be made manifest to the student through form, rhythm, melody, harmony, tone color, and other musical considerations.

The aesthetic values to be derived from musical performance must remain the fundamental essence of a rehearsal or concert. The conductor should know thoroughly the styles of performance practice in all periods of music literature. When a student can perform with the proper style, the music becomes more meaningful; and when the student begins to understand musical values, the conductor can spend more time—with less gyration—helping to mold the performance into an aesthetic experience.

The conductor should analyze and synthesize the music so that instead of mechanically following the definitions of musical symbols—repeat marks, *da capo*, *crescendo*, *ritard.,* and others—he/she can use these signs merely as a guide to achieve a valid interpretation of the music and thus keep to a minimum all nonmusical examples and terminologies, such as the following: "Would the members of the orchestra play the end of this composition as if a huge eagle with outspread wings were gradually and smoothly gliding to a permanent landing."

An effective approach is to explain to the students the rhythmic change in note values, the treatment of the melodic line, the harmonic structure, the tempo, the dynamics, and all other elements of the music that bring about a particular effect. For example, instead of merely explaining to a group that *da capo al fine* means repeating from the beginning and playing to the *fine* sign, the conductor should make the students aware also that they are repeating a previous theme as a concluding idea, and they should understand the manner in which it should be played. When the student realizes what the music itself expresses, without the conductor's having to shout musical symbols, a musical atmosphere that cannot be equaled by any other procedure should result. Musical learning should be the constant objective. And the better the literature, the more obvious the musical qualities will be.

With properly chosen literature, expectation, suspense, and the unexpected become tremendous factors in the proper interpretation and meaning of music. Whether it be tension created by a dominant seventh chord and its resolution, repetition of an idea until a change is expected, expectation treated by ambiguous elements in music, or other factors, the greater the buildup of suspense and tension, the greater the emotional release upon the resolution. Not only the conductor but also each group member should understand the evidence and significance of these qualities through the literature performed.

The ultimate purpose of any rehearsal is to be able to transform the printed note into the most expressive musical thought imaginable. If there is not expressiveness, or if the literature does not contain the fundamental qualities that would develop good taste and appreciation, the rehearsal is not giving the student full benefit. Music can assist the student to aesthetic awareness through his/her affective nature and can help the student live on a higher plane. The spirit of man needs to be fed, and music can assist in this function.

No conductor should ever be content with a mediocre performance of a group. One of the prime requisites for a better-than-mediocre performance is the very best literature, regardless of the level of difficulty. Band and orchestra students need incentive and challenge for a more perfect musical production. There must be a seriousness of purpose, a complete unanimity of discipline, and the possibility of a response greater than the students' own expectations. Psychologists theorize that the mind functions at about ten percent capacity. If this is true, conductors can demand and obtain greater proficiency from every member in the group. With the best literature and with essential understanding of that literature, aesthetic values to be derived from music can become the fundamental essence of a rehearsal.

And not only will the proper literature selection be the best experience for the student, but the audience at a concert will also become involved in an elevating musical adventure. Perhaps the following suggestions as criteria for the selection of music for instrumental organizations will be helpful.

CRITERIA FOR MUSIC SELECTION

In order to analyze, evaluate, and select the best of music literature, criteria need to be established that will best assist in determining the intrinsic musical values of a composition. The following outline was used in analyzing the instrumental music materials in this book and is recommended for further use by the music teacher.

1. Musical qualities
   a. Melodic
      (1) Does the arrangement provide as much melodic interest to all parts as is consistent with the style?
      (2) Did the arranger follow the natural tendencies of voice leading, even though the parts are primarily rhythmic?
      (3) Is the musical phrasing consistent with the limitations of the instrument and the performer (breathing, fingering, bowing and shifting, and tonguing)?
      (4) Are the individual parts idiomatic for their instrument?
   b. Harmonic
      (1) Is the harmony within the comprehension of the performer?
      (2) Is the selection in a harmonically consistent style?
      (3) Does the chord spacing give the proper texture?
   c. Rhythmic
      (1) Are the rhythmic complexities within the capabilities of the group?
      (2) Do the individual parts have rhythmic as well as melodic interest?
   d. Dynamic
      (1) Does the music offer an opportunity for the performer to use his/her dynamic range?
      (2) Are sustained extremes in dynamics avoided?
2. Instrumental characteristics
   a. Orchestration and instrumentation
      (1) Does the composition suit the medium used?
      (2) If a transcription, is the composition faithful to the composer's original intent, in both texture and form?
      (3) Does the arrangement use the instrumentation of the group effectively?
      (4) Are sufficient cross cues provided?
      (5) Are there passages for featuring solo instruments or sections?
   b. Range
      (1) Is the range in each part within the possible range of each player?
      (2) Do the parts consider the specific color possibilities of the instruments?
      (3) Is the register for each instrument comfortable?
      (4) Does the arrangement provide for occasional use of outside ranges?
3. Educational and functional values
   a. Is the music difficult enough to be challenging without being discouraging?
   b. Will the music be inspirational to the performers?
   c. Will it challenge the interest of both student and listener during the entire performance?
   d. Is the music of high quality?
   e. Will the composition contribute to a well-balanced library?
   f. Are there developmental values in the music?

4

4. Format

   a. Is there a full score?

   b. Are the following printing requirements met?

     (1) Suitable size

     (2) Print clear and not crowded

     (3) Good spacing

     (4) Good weight and quality of paper

     (5) Page turning at convenient places

   c. Does the editing provide the following?

     (1) Dynamic marks and tempo indications appropriately used

     (2) Phrasing, breathing, fingering, bowing, muting

     (3) Entrance cues

     (4) Numbered measures or rehearsal letters

     (5) Background information on the composer and arranger

     (6) Interpretive hints

     (7) For arrangements, the source of the original

     (8) Performing time

The literature in this book represents the best music of the main four periods of instrumental music history: baroque, classic, romantic, and contemporary. The annotated lists for band and orchestra include not only the title, composer/arranger, and publisher, but also the level of difficulty—I (easy) through VI (difficult). The items are listed in columns in this order:

Composer	Arranger	*Title*	Publisher	Level of diffi- culty

Please refer to the publisher's guide for complete references and addresses. The chamber music chosen is a sampling of each of the main periods of literature.

The materials for private study represent outstanding methods, studies, and solos for each orchestral and band instrument. The classification *I* is the elementary level; the highest classifications (*XI-XII*) are the graduate level.

The criteria in this chapter should serve as a basis for future selection of music. These materials are but a beginning and should be added to by the instrumental music teacher. Blank pages and parts of pages provide for an addendum by the teacher that will enhance this guide. As music is reviewed, analyzed, performed, and accepted, it should augment this collection.

Those composers, arrangers, and publishers that have made a major contribution to school music are presented by only a brief résumé and a sampling of recommended compositions. The instrumental music bibliography is a basic representation of books and pamphlets helpful to the instrumental teacher.

From time to time some of the selected literature in this guidebook may be out of print. Oftentimes the publisher will again make these quality compositions available. If not, perhaps a search of other band and orchestra libraries would be worth the effort.

2

The Orchestra

The good orchestral library should have the best music of the four major periods of music history, including a representation of musical forms from these periods. Form is the most intelligible aspect of all the arts and should be one of the educational thrusts of musical performance for both the listener and the performer. The literature in this section has been presented by music period with grade levels I and II (easy) primarily elementary school level, III and IV (medium difficulty) and occasionally V for high school level, and V and VI (difficult) for most college and university as well as community organizations. The annotation will be helpful to the conductor in ordering music, particularly on an approval basis from a reputable music dealer.

Since most of the compositions, other than symphonies and suites, require from four to six minutes to perform, the specific time of each composition is not included. Also, since the standard orchestral instrumentation prevails, the listing of parts (woodwinds in pairs, full brass complement, standard percussion, and full string section) seemed too repetitious.

In the elementary levels (I and II) music was selected with minimal rhythmic complexities, appropriate key signatures commensurate with the performance ability of elementary groups, and harmonic, melodic, dynamic, and instrumental considerations for this level of difficulty. As the literature becomes more challenging (III and IV), the above musical and technical factors are evaluated and presented accordingly. Only the most accomplished organizations should perform grades V and VI. Each conductor is encouraged to add compositions on the addendum page as he feels so motivated.

ELEMENTARY THROUGH COLLEGE
Grades I and II

BAROQUE PERIOD

| Arbeau | Rowley | *Pavane* | Mills | II |

Piano score. Interesting pizzicato part in cello and bass. Good discipline-type piece. Tone production and control required. Orchestrated in block style. Makes use of tone color and contrasting effects with the sections of the orchestra.

| Bach, J. S. | Coerre | *Gavotte and Musette from Third English Suite* | ODC | II |

Full score. Not technically difficult, with good voicing and movement. Tessitura reasonable in all parts.

| _____ | Jurey | *Musette* | CAR | II |

Full score. There are sixteenth-note passages that require exact articulation. Students must be guarded from rushing the staccato passages. Arrangement makes clever use of woodwind entrances. Excellent piece.

| _____ | Elliott | *Prelude, Passacaglia, and Fugue* | WN | I |

Three short pieces based on Bach chorale "Christus, Der ist mein Leben." Prelude arrangement for full orchestra. Fugue in three parts. Problem exists in counting measures and rests and making proper entrances. Piano score.

| _____ | | *Sixteen Chorales* | G. Schirmer | II |

For military band, woodwind ensemble, saxophone ensemble, brass ensemble, string ensemble, or ensemble of various instruments. Many parts doubled by other instruments. Good for elementary orchestra.

| _____ | Eller | *Two Bach Chorales* | SHB | I |

Piano score. No technical problems. Easy to play. Movement in every part. Written with interest.

| _____ | Gordon | *Chorale Prelude* | Bourne | II |

This is generally a II grade, but the advanced violin part is a grade III. Well cross-cued and equal distribution of parts. Parts are adequately marked dynamically; second violin has an independent part.

| Campra | Rowley | *Passepied* | Mills | II |

Full score. Arrangement uses much imitation in this piece. Enjoyable music. No difficult parts.

| (French Chant) | Jurey | *"Psalm of Praise"* | TOR | I |

Full score. Clarinets in low register. Melody in 2nd clarinet part. Adequate editing. Fully orchestrated. Enjoyable music.

Godard   Rowley   "Chanson de Florian"   Mills   II

Full score. This is mainly a string number with a small supporting part for woodwind and brass. Beautiful melody and nice treatment of woodwind entrances. No technical problems. Simple and interesting percussion part.

Gordon, P.   "Gothic Legend"   SHB   II

Full score. The "Gothic" melody is supported by half-note chords played by the accompaniment parts. The melody is repeated in different textures. Interesting to students.

Kindler, H.   Three 17th Century   CF   II
                              Dutch Tunes

Full score. High notes in first violin part. Tricky rhythms. Excellent selections.

(Old French) Rowley   "The Chase"   J. Williams   II

A lively number in 6/8 time. No real technical problems, except for speed or tempo. Fully edited, arranged, and adapted to the orchestra instruments.

Purcell   Jurey   March in G   Mills   I

Full score. Demands technical control. String sections have eighth-note passage which is difficult. Well edited. Interesting trumpet part.

CLASSICAL PERIOD

Couperin, Gluck,   Classical Dance Suite   G. Schirmer   II
Kerle, Grétry, Mattheson,
and Rameau.

Six dances well arranged for high school orchestra. Excellent suite for classic style. Well cued throughout. Full score.

Gluck   Woodhouse   "Che farò"   Bo. Hawkes   I

Piano score. No technical problems. Easy and beautiful melody. Excellent.

_____ Roberts   "Air de ballet"   CF   II

Graceful dance number. Not too technical. Nicely scored. Full score.

_____ Reibold   "Hymn to Diana"   CF   I

Full score. G major with sustained bowing material.

_____ Phillips   Cavatine from   Oxford   II
                            Semiramide

Full score. Could be used with strings only. Wind parts are flexible. Slow and short—three minutes in length. Predominantly first violins.

Goedicke, Powell,   Miniature Ancient Menuet   Birchard   II
Amani

Full score. Well orchestrated. Interesting parts. Few problem areas. Good literature.

Grétry   Reibold   Tambourin from   Fox   II
                            Cephale and Procris

Good classic number. Different bowings used. Not difficult in any part. Easy range and tessitura.

Handel   Page   Largo from **Xerxes**   ODC   II

Full score. Begins with the string section and gradually pyramids into full orchestra in the last 8 measures. Contains contrasting color of instruments. All parts not too difficult. Excellent number for concert.

_____ Woodhouse   *March from* **Scipio**   Bo. Hawkes   II

Full score. Third position for first violins. Scored for full orchestra.

Haydn   Woodhouse   *Melodies by J. Haydn*   Bo. Hawkes   II

Full score. Simplified version of Haydn's melodies. Adequate editing. Pleasant tunes. Good music for the young orchestra.

McKay   *Sinfonia No. 1*   Remick   I

Written in 20th century, in classic style. Easy composition, with few problems. Made up of (1) Prelude, (2) Dance, and (3) Finale. Good contrast.

Mozart, W. A.   Woodhouse   *"Ave verum corpus"*   Bo. Hawkes   II

Full score. Excellent tune for the orchestra. Appealing woodwind duet with string accompaniment. Second position introduced. Mostly sustained bowing required. Opportunity to develop full tone.

_____ Jurey   *Cavatina and Air*   CAR   II

Full score. Not demanding. Good use of instruments; similar to original. Editing is sufficient. Trumpet part goes to high F, also has some fast eighth notes. Requires delicate interpretation. Good learning experience for the students.

_____ Marcelli   *Minuet from* **Don Giovanni** CF   I

Well-known minuet. Easy and appealing to young people. Accurate style.

_____ Parry   *Two Waltzes*   Bo. Hawkes   II

Piano score. Two excellent tunes and artfully scored. First violin goes up to high D.

Piccinni   Johnson   **Didon** *Overture*   AMP   II

Full score. Fast passages and wide leaps; some technique required. A challenging number.

ROMANTIC PERIOD

Loesser   Isaac   *Songs from*   CF   II
                              Hans Christian Andersen

Modern composition in romantic style. Condensed score. Medley of five tunes. Attractive orchestration. No technical problems. Interesting parts.

Schubert   Gordon   *Allegretto grazioso*   SHB   II

Piano score. Good doubling and treatment of solo parts. Well scored for the elementary orchestra.

_____ Harris   *"Death and the Maiden"*   Bourne   II

Condensed score. Slow and legato style. Quite sustained, but easy.

———————— Perry   *Five Waltzes*   Bo. Hawkes   II

Full score. Medley of five wonderful waltzes. Excellent choice. Good orchestration.

———————— Page   *"Moment musical"*   ODC   II

Rhythmically stimulating and melodious. Each part quite easy. Tessitura good. Full instrumentation. Full score.

Schumann   Clark   *Schumann Suite*   G. Schirmer   II

Full score. Six pieces in a variety of styles and moods. Well orchestrated. Several difficult passages.

———————— Rowley   *Two Pieces*   Mills   II
               a. *"The Song of the Reapers"*
               b. *"Soldier's March"*

Full score. Lively movement in all parts. Second number has interesting descending passage. Lightly scored.

Weber   Jurey   *Waltz from* **Oberon**   TOR   I

Condensed score. Strings have long full bowing, easy fingering; clarinets kept in lower register. Melody will appeal to the students. An excellent number.

Whitney, Maurice   *Romantic Prelude*   Remick   II

Chordal. Easy orchestration. Ideal for less advanced high school orchestras. No runs in any of the parts.

MODERN PERIOD

Bartók   McKay   *Five Pieces for Younger Orchestra*   Remick   I

Full score. Transcriptions. Concise and extremely well orchestrated for the young group.

———————— McKay   *Six Pieces for Younger Orchestra, No. 2*   Remick   II

Condensed score. Transcriptions with modern treatment of harmony. Well-chosen combinations of instruments.

(Folk Tunes)   F. Muller   *Three Folk Tunes*   LUV   I

Full score. Technical difficulty found in rhythmic patterns. Familiar folk tunes children have sung in lower grades. Good sight reading and performance material.

Hansen, E.   *Little Norwegian Suite*   Bo. Hawkes   II

Full score. Three small, exciting numbers. Excellent contrast and moods. Second number has difficult rhythms.

Livingston   Matesky   *"The March of the Ill-assorted Guards"*   Remick   II

Full score. Difficult rhythms in the brass parts. Effective use of mutes in strings and brass. Offers variety, solo work. An appealing number.

Perry, H.   *"The Curtsy Minuet"*   Bo. Hawkes   II

Full score. Not too technical. Nice melody and good use of tone colors and instrument doublings. A good minuet.

Rebmann   Clark   *Elementary Orchestra*   G. Schirmer   I
                                      Series, No. 1

Full score. Four simple pieces. Interesting and colorful writing.

_____ Clark   *Elementary Orchestra*   G. Schirmer   II
                                      Series, No. 3

Full score. Contains numbers by J. Blockz, O. Hackh, and H. Sitt. Good selections of music and composers.

Reed, W.   *"March of the Prefects"*   Bo. Hawkes   II

Condensed score. A march written in three sections. No real technical problems. Good concert number.

Stone, David   *March, Interlude, and Jig*   Galaxy   II

Condensed score. March is very rhythmic. Open strings and double stops. Technically easy.

Walter, D.   *"Wayfaring Stranger"*   Berk   II

Full score. Largo tempo. Beautiful French horn solo. Demands playing with feeling. Some tricky rhythmic patterns.

Woodhouse, C.   *Three Welsh Melodies*   Bo. Hawkes   I

Piano score. No technical problems. Fine selections.

SPECIAL NUMBERS

Dedrick, A.   *"Blue Nocturne"*   Kend   II

Condensed score. Moderately slow piece in legato style. Contains different moods and effects. Some modern harmonies. Extremely interesting piece.

Gordon, P.   *"Greensleeves" (Fantasy)*   Chappell   I

Condensed score. Nice tune for young people. Allegro passage with accented notes in contrast to smooth and broad first section. Short, climactic coda. Good showpiece.

Jurey, E.   *"Dixie Showboat" (Old*   TOR   II
                                      Minstrel Song)

Full score, not too technical. Contains staccato, slurs, dynamic changes. Three distinct styles in one piece. An excellent show number.

Matesky, R.   *"Cowboy Rhapsody"*   EV   II

Full score. Offers a technical challenge to every player. Smooth and legato playing demanded. Good contrast created in the music. Extremely interesting to students.

_____   *"Military Salute"*   Chappell   II

Full score. Rhythms are familiar to students. Tunes are "Caissons," "Sailor's Hornpipe," and the "Marines' Hymn." Written in block style, with interesting countermelody.

Muller, F.   "Ol' MacDonald's Farm"   LUV   I

Full score. No technical problems. Pleasant music for young children; easy to see and understand. Artfully arranged.

_____   "The Concertmeister's   Robbins   I
                                         Serenade"

Opportunity for solo violin grade III level. Accompaniment varied in texture. A fine concert number.

Walter, D.   *Mother Goose Suite*   Berk   I

Full score. Contains "The Little Nut Tree," "Little Jack Horner," "Baa, Baa, Black Sheep." No technical problems. Music for fun. Choice trombone part and obbligato by strings.

Grades III and IV

BAROQUE PERIOD

Bach, J. S.   Damrosch   "A Mighty Fortress   *Witmark*   IV
                                   Is Our God"
                                   (Chorale Prelude)

Optional chorale finale; full instrumentation, easy range, full score.

_____   Clark   *Bach Suite*   G. Schirmer   IV

Master Series for Young Orchestras. Eight selections. Good cueing and editing. All parts interesting. Excellent selection. Full score.

_____   Marcelli   Chorale-Fugue, "All Glory   CF   IV
                                   Be to God on High"

All parts interesting, though not difficult. Good scoring. Could be played by most III groups. Full score.

_____   Demarest   *Fugue in G minor*   Remick   IV
                                   ("The Lesser")

Good instrumentation and cueing. Challenging, but not as difficult as the G minor Fugue ("The Greater"). Full score.

_____   Walter   "Jesu, Joy of   Berk   III-IV
                                   Man's Desiring"

Good use of brass section on chorale. First violin has triplet figure throughout. No full score.

_____   *Prelude in E minor*   Pro-Art   III

Condensed score. Fairly easy parts, with no rhythmic problems. Full instrumentation. Easy tessitura in all parts.

_____   Caillet   "Sheep May Safely Graze"   Bo. Hawkes   III

Full score. Instrumentation includes harp. Flowing melodic lines. Two solo violins. Not too difficult. Full sounding.

12

Gluck	Kahn	*Overture to the Ballet* **Don Juan**	G. Schirmer	IV

Selection may be performed according to original score or, with addition of optional parts by arranger, by full orchestra. Well edited. Full score.

Handel	Clark	*Handel Suite*	G. Schirmer	III-IV

Master Series for Young Orchestras, No. IV. Good melodic lines in all parts. Six different selections. Well edited and cued.

_____	Boss	*Largo from* **Xerxes**	ODC	III

Slow and sustained. Requires control. Originally orchestrated by Page. Full score.

_____	Kahn	**Water Music** *Selections*	G. Schirmer	IV

Eight selections from the suite. Uses original orchestra score with optional added instrumentation. Original trumpet part quite high in places, but optional simplified part is furnished. Full score.

_____	Anderson	*"Song of Jupiter"*	Mills	III

Aria "Where E'er You Walk," from oratorio *Semele*. Nicely scored. All parts interesting. Includes trumpet solo in first section. Also published for band. Full score.

Kirnberger	Scarmolin	*Little Baroque Suite*	Ludwig	III

Three selections, rather Handelian in style. Not difficult. Full score.

Lully	Murphy	*French Baroque Suite*	Witmark	IV

Six selections from *Le Bourgeois Gentilhomme*. Not heavily scored. Full score.

_____	Boss	*Gavotte in D minor*	ODC	III

Originally orchestrated by Page. Good selection. Full score.

Purcell	Rowley	*Air and Rondo*	Mills	IV

One part per wind instrument. Woodwinds and first violin predominant. First violin has melody throughout; other strings uninteresting. Full score.

_____	Barbirolli	*Chaconne in G minor*	CF	III

Full orchestration. Good melodic lines for all parts. Challenging in spots; good for expression and dynamics.

_____	Perry	*Trumpet Tune and Air*	Bo. Hawkes	III-IV

Not the famous "Trumpet Voluntary." Fine scoring in style of era. Not technically difficult, but trumpet part requires range and endurance.

Rameau	Stringham	*Suite for Orchestra from* **Dardanus**	MP	IV

From the opera. Four contrasting selections. Not technically difficult. May be purchased in original version, for small orchestra, or in arranged version, which retains spirit of original. Condensed score for the arranged.

Rebmann	Clark	*Suite No. 6*	G. Schirmer	III

Full score. First and second movements originally for 2 violins and cello. Generally III except for last movement, which is about a IV. Gigue has ornaments, and explanations of how to play them are in footnotes. The movements are: March from Sonata No. 2, Sarabande, Minuet from Sonata No. 4, Bourrée, Aria from *Rinaldo,* and Gigue.

CLASSICAL PERIOD

Bach, J. C.		*Sinfonia in D Major*	CFP	IV

Alfred Einstein, ed. Three movements. Good for small orchestra. Trumpets and horns in D. No clarinet, but part could be transcribed. Full score.

Beethoven	Sopkin	*Sonatina in G Major*	CF	III

Two movements, classical in concept and scoring. Exceptionally good use of strings and woodwinds. Full score.

Clementi	Sopkin	*Sonatina No. 1,* *op. 36, no. 1*	CF	IV

Well scored. Not too much melodic interest. Full score.

Dittersdorf	Schmid	*Symphony in F Major*	G. Schirmer	IV

Original score with optional supplementary parts used sparingly so as not to destroy original style. Not difficult. Full score.

_____	Kahn	*"Tournament of Temperaments"*	G. Schirmer	IV

May be performed in its original version or, by use of optional parts, with a more orchestral combination. Programmatic music. Full score.

Grétry	Barnes	**Lucile** *Overture*	Ludwig	III

Interesting tempo and style change in the middle section. Thinly scored. Full score.

Haydn		*Capriccio in A*	ODC	III

Full orchestration. Not too difficult. Full score.

_____	Clark	*Haydn Suite*	G. Schirmer	IV

_____	Rowley	*Moderato and Allegretto*	Mills	III

Scored lightly, but too much use of first violin for melody. Full score.

_____		*Symphony No. 45 in F-sharp minor*	AMP	IV

Second movement and adagio from last movement are playable in original form. Second movement scored for strings, 2 oboes, and 2 horns. Last 40 measures of last movement in 6 sharps for strings. If this key undesirable, use Adagio from the *Farewell Symphony,* arr. Rohner, pub. Ditson. Original but a half step higher. Full score.

_____	Isaac	*Andante from the Symphony in G Major*	CF	III

Second movement of Symphony No. 94 (*Surprise*). Very close to original, but simplified. Full score.

_____		*Symphony No. 94* **(Surprise)**	AMP	IV

Third movement of original. A minuet and trio which should appeal to students. Full score.

| | | *Toy* Symphony | Kalmus | IV |

Rather a curiosity piece. Scored for trumpet, drum, cuckoo, nightingale, rattle, triangle, first and second violins, and bass. Clever. Full score.

| | Stone | *Divertimento* | Bo. Hawkes | III |

Full score. Contains arrangements of three of Haydn's pieces: St. Anthony's Chorale, Menuetto, and Rondo. Very good piece in suite form. Any or all movements may be used.

| Mozart, W. A. | | **Così fan tutte** *Overture* | AMP | IV |

The original. Requires some 6th position in the violin part. Full score.

| | Rebmann-Clark | *Mozart Suite* | G. Schirmer | IV |

Master Series for Young Orchestras. Four selections. Good to have in the library. Full score.

| | | *Overture to* **The Impresario** | CF | IV |

Most of the instruments have melodious parts. Full orchestration. Piano conductor's score available through E. F. Kalmus Orchestra Scores.

| | Stringham | *Two Entr'acte Pieces from* **Thamos, King of Egypt** | MP | IV |

Score indicates which parts optional, added by arranger. May be played in original form by omitting these parts. Full score.

| Sammartini | Scarmolin | *Symphony in D Major* | Ludwig | IV |

Three movements. Some winds written with no key signature, sharps used as accidentals. Full scores.

| Steg, Paul | | *Symphony on Folk Songs* | Summy-Bir | IV |

Full score. The titles of the movements are: Sonata Allegro, Song and Dance, An Italian Minuet, and Rondo. A very interesting work in the classical style, but takes very good instrumentalists and some hard work to put it together.

ROMANTIC PERIOD

| Beethoven | Woodhouse | *Finale from the Fifth Symphony* | Bo. Hawkes | IV |

Simplified, yet not ineffective. Few technically difficult passages. Full score.

| Berlioz | Reibold | *"Marche Hongroise"* | Fox | III |

From *Damnation of Faust*. Difficult first violins, full score and good instrumentation.

| | Page | *"Rakoczy March"* | ODC | IV |

The stirring Hungarian march used by Berlioz in *Damnation of Faust*. Audience and student appeal. Full score.

| Bizet | Roberts | **Carmen** *Suite* | CF | IV |

Lively number with melodies from the opera. Good instrumentation. Condensed score.

| | Boss | *Intermezzo from* **l'Arlésienne** *Suite No. 2* | ODC | III | |

All parts interesting, but not continuously thickly scored. Several changes of style and tempo. Originally orchestrated by Page. Full score.

| Borodin | Schmid | *"On the Steppes of Central Asia"* | G. Schirmer | III |

Extremely melodious. Solo instruments. No great rhythmic problems. Folk songs set to music.

| Brahms | Seredy | *Hungarian Dances Nos. 3 and 6* | CF | III |

Rhythmically appealing. Few difficult passages. First violin playable in first position.

| Chabrier | | **España (Spanish Rhapsody)** | ODC | IV |

Full instrumentation. Delightful rhythmic setting of Spanish melodies. Demanding in spots but within the capabilities of a good high school orchestra.

| | | *"Marche joyeuse"* | Enoch | IV-V |

Full score. Technically not too difficult for strings. Makes extensive use of brass and woodwind sections. Interesting melodically.

| Chopin | Reibold | *"Polonaise militaire"* | Fox | IV |

Rhythmic and attack problems. Full orchestra throughout. Full score.

| Curzon, C. | | *"La gitane czardas"* | Bo. Hawkes | III |

Easy rhythm and melodies for all instruments. Majestic sound with lively action in dance. Full score.

| Delius | Beecham | *Intermezzo and Serenade from* **Hassan** | Bo. Hawkes | IV |

From incidental music. Intermezzo score includes harp and English horn. Serenade scored only for harp and strings. Not technically difficult. Thinly scored. Full score.

| | Beecham | *"The Walk to the Paradise Garden"* | Bo. Hawkes | III-IV |

Intermezzo from *A Village Romeo and Juliet*. Full score. Interesting rhythms. Harp. Not too difficult in range or tessitura. Lovely melodic lines.

| Franck | Johnson | *Gothic Suite from* **L'Organiste** | Kjos | IV |

Full score. Five selected pieces from 55 pieces for the organ composed during the last two years of Franck's life. Interesting orchestration. The five movements are: *Andante* (solo violin or flute), *Allegro poco maestoso*, *Moderato* (solo cello or bassoon or bass clarinet), *Andantino* (solo viola or clarinet), and *Maestoso con moto*. Well edited and bowed.

| German, E. | | *Three Dances* | G. Schirmer | III |

Piano score. These are three appealing dances done in a romantic style. Standard instrumentation, with the exception of the harp. The dances are very light.

| Grieg | Hoppin | *Christmas Music* | ODC | III-IV |

Unfamiliar music, not necessary to limit to Christmas season. Except for flute, not technically difficult. Unaccompanied flute solo in the middle. Full score.

| _____ | Clark | *Grieg Suite* | G. Schirmer | III |

Master Series for Young Orchestras. Five selections. Second movement has difficult section in E-flat minor which may be omitted. Good use of woodwinds in the third movement. Full score.

| _____ | Roberts | *"Wedding Day at Troldhaughen," op. 65, no. 6* | CF | IV |

Publisher intimates this adheres closely to original. Selection should have student appeal. No full score.

| Grundman, Clare | | *American Folk Rhapsody No. 1* | Bo. Hawkes | III |

Full score. No tuba part, otherwise full brass compliment. Several key changes, one to four flats. Frequent tempo changes. Equal distribution of wind parts. Good program material.

| Humperdinck | Isaac | **Hansel and Gretel** *Selection* | CF | III |

Potpourri of four melodies from the opera. No full score.

| Isaac | | *Russian Chorale and Overture* | CF | III |

Based on Tchaikovsky, op. 39, no. 34, and Russian folk tunes. Overture has rhythmic appeal, but not profound music. Not technically difficult. Full score.

| Mendelssohn | Muller | **Son and Stranger** *Overture, op. 89* | Kjos | IV |

Full score. Classical style overture, with slow introduction in 6/8 going into a faster *Alla breve.* Good wind and brass parts. Clarinets have lots of accidentals because of the key. The advanced violin part goes into fifth position quite often.

| Moussorgsky | Kindler | *Chanson Russe* | Mills | III |

Full score. Very slow introduction (*Andante con moto*) which is in B-flat. The faster part is in G Major. Interesting program contrasting piece.

| _____ | Kindler | *Love Music from* **Boris Godunov** | Mills | III |

Full score. Piano needed at letter D. Time signature a moderately slow 9/8; key is E-flat. There is an oboe solo and the first violin goes into fifth position. Dramatic music, good for teaching feeling and expression.

| Nicolai | | **Merry Wives of Windsor** *Overture* | CF | IV |

Very moving melodic number. Technical bowings and long slurs for strings. Good brass parts. Full score.

Offenbach   Isaac   **Ballet Parisien**   CF   IV

Suite of 5 selections from three of Offenbach's most popular operas. Rhythmic. Attractive but not profound.

Saint-Saëns   Isaac   **Danse macabre**   CF   III

Simplified, but retains flavor of original. Score includes harp. String fingerings well marked where necessary. No full score.

Schubert   Weaver   *Menuetto from the Fifth Symphony*   Mills   IV

Somewhat Mozartean in style. Weaver retained classic flavor of score. Not difficult. Excellent music. Full score.

————————   Douglas   **Rosamunde** *Ballet Music Nos. 1 and 2*   Bo. Hawkes   IV

Doesn't include overture. Nicely scored. No. 1 has woodwinds predominant throughout. Some overlapping of selections with Schubert Suite.

————————   Weaver   **Rosamunde** *Overture*   Mills   III

Recommended, usable. Not difficult. All strings first position except advanced violin (optional).

————————   Clark   *Schubert Suite*   G. Schirmer   III-IV

Master Series for Young Orchestras. Six selections, most originally orchestral. One of the best of this series. Full score.

————————   Dasch   *Sinfonietta*   SIB   IV

Adapted from Sonatina, op. 137, for violin and piano. Three movements, second and third especially good. Excellent selection. Full score.

————————   Perry   *Waltzes*   Bo. Hawkes   IV

Three waltzes. No full score, but appears to be well scored. Includes waltz popularly known as "Valse sentimentale."

————————   Johnson   *Overture in D Major*   Kjos   IV

Good overture in classical style; well edited. Full score.

Strauss R.   Perry   *Melodies from* **Der Rosenkavalier**   Bo. Hawkes   III

Score includes alto and bass clarinets. Otherwise scored for small instrumentation, considering composer: 2 trumpets, 2 horns, 1 trombone. Good selection for high school group with limited technical ability.

Svendsen   Dasch   "Zorahay da Legend"   CF   IV

A colorful number. Full conductor's score and instrumentation. Fairly challenging. Short biography of composer and foreword about composition.

Tchaikovsky   Clark   *Tchaikovsky Suite*   BS   IV

Master Series for Young Orchestras. Not his most popular works (one exception: "None but the Lonely Heart"), but most of the five selections are worth doing. Full score.

Wagner   *Prelude to* **Lohengrin**   Broude   IV

Full orchestra. Many fine passages for strings. Contains passages for woodwinds and brass, but not many. Not difficult, but requires good sustained tone. Short but effective.

Weber   Clark   *Weber Suite*   G. Schirmer   III-IV

Master Series for Young Orchestras. Six of Weber's most popular works, most originally scored for orchestra. Recommended. Full score.

CONTEMPORARY PERIOD

Bartók   Serly   *Bartók Suite*   SMC   IV

Four sections. Interesting. Should appeal to students. Contemporary idiom. No full score.

Britten   Stone   *Five Courtly Dances from* **Gloriana**   Bo. Hawkes   IV

Full score. Interesting parts, including percussion. Well edited. One of the most interesting orchestra compositions.

Copland   *"Prairie Night" and "Celebration Dance" from* **Billy the Kid**   Bo. Hawkes   IV

Arranged for small orchestra by the composer. "Prairie Night" slow and legato; "Celebration" rhythmic. All parts interesting. Trombone and bassoon use some tenor clef, viola some treble. Excellent. Full score.

—————————   *Waltz from* **Billy the Kid**   Bo. Hawkes   IV

Solos in various parts, including trombones and bassoon. Trombone and bassoon use some tenor clef, viola some treble. Easy tempo, not a fast waltz. Full score.

—————————   *"John Henry"*   Bo. Hawkes   III

Interesting piece about the folk hero John Henry. Needs 3 tympani and an anvil effect. Also considerable string technique for special effects. Full score.

—————————   *"Letter from Home"*   Bo. Hawkes   III

Full score. An earlier score revised for a smaller orchestra. A nice modern piece. A number of solo passages for woodwinds and brass, but very few extreme technical demands.

Curzon, C.   *"The Capricious Ballerina"*   Bo. Hawkes   IV

Not junk, as a glance at the title might indicate. Emphasis on strings and woodwinds, brasses uninteresting. Score includes harp. Thinly scored. Change of style in .middle section with the sustained, easy cello solo.

Debussy   Guenther   *Mazurka*   Marl   III

Rather easy but interesting, not typical of Debussy's works; piano conductor's score. Full orchestration. Interesting melodies in all instruments.

_____ Urban   *"Reverie"*   Mills   III

For strings and piano only (optional piano part). Can be used for string quartet. Not too difficult.

Demarest   **Sunrise at Sea**   Witmark   III
                  (Tone poem)

Full tonal color. Good dramatic tone poem. Parts in good range and tessitura.

Fine, I.   *Diversions for Orchestra*   Mills   IV

Full score. Three short movements. Contemporary in style. First movement is polyrhythmic, with string glissandos and interesting percussion parts. Second movement has English horn solo and special string effects. Well suited to good high school orchestras.

Gillis, D.   *"January, February, March"*   Mills   IV

Smashing sound, with challenging parts for each section. Particularly technical brass parts. Large percussion section solo.

Glière   Cohn   *Cortège from the*   EV   IV
                              Red Poppy

Interesting. Not slow throughout, but gains motion toward end. Good use of percussion and brass. Full score.

Grofé   Isaac   *Mississippi Suite*   Feist   IV

Piano conductor's score (4 lines). Breathing problems in flute; most of other parts not too difficult.

Hadley, P.   **The Enchanted Castle**   CF   IV
                    Overture

Condensed piano score, written for school orchestra. Full orchestration, including harp. All instruments have a chance at melody.

Hanson, H.   *"Elegy"*   CF   IV

Contemporary. Not too difficult. A quiet, unassuming piece.

Holmes, A.   *"Three Archaic Dances"*   SW   IV

Contemporary idiom. Scored for strings, woodwinds, and horns. Should sound well with small orchestra. Not too difficult.

Holst, G.   *A Somerset Rhapsody*   Bo. Hawkes   IV

Typically Holst. Contemporary but not extremely dissonant. All parts interesting. Good selection.

Ingalls, A.   *"Song of Peace"*   Kjos   III

This composition was the winner of the NSOA composition contest in 1960. It has a full score. Opens with interplay between the 1st oboe and 1st violin. Interesting rhythms with changes from 5/4 to 3/4 and back again. Dynamics well marked, with some bowings. Viola goes into treble clef.

Ketèlbey, A.   *"In a Persian Market"*   Bos   III-IV

Condensed score: full instruments include harp and male chorus. Very thematic, with motifs for different characters and events in the market. Tessitura good range.

Kindler, Hans — *Three 17th Century Dutch Tunes* — CF — III

Effectively scored in full-sounding style. All parts interesting. Not difficult. Full score.

Kirk, T. — *"Vignettes"* — Mills — III-IV

Contemporary idiom. Suite of three movements. Not difficult technically. Full score.

Klauss, N. — *Prelude for Orchestra* — Pro-Art — III

Full score. Award-winning composition—Pennsylvania Music Educators Association orchestra composition contest. Technically not too difficult. Most hard part would be to try to maintain a clean triplet pattern, used extensively throughout. Many accidentals.

Kodály — *Intermezzo from* **Háry János** — Bo. Hawkes — IV

Full score. Very conservative, but does display a modernistic taste. Instrumentation regular, except for the piano or cembalo.

Lecuona — Jenkins — *Andalucia Suite* — Marl — III-IV

Six selections, some of which are not performed very often. Effective full scoring for this style. Attractive but not profound. No full score.

Maganini, Q. — *"Americanese"* — EM — III-IV

Suite on three early American pieces, of differing moods. Not too contemporary in sound. Second movement is scored for 1st and 2nd violin, flute, and bass. Full score.

McKay, G. F. — *Symphonette in D* — Galaxy — III

Full score and piano score. Composed in 1952 and played by an all-city junior high orchestra. Piano necessary. Good rhythms and syncopation. No bow markings.

Riegger, W. — *Suite for Younger Orchestras, op. 56* — AMP — III

Five selections, one of which is polytonal. Full score not arranged in conventional manner. Scoring also unconventional. Excellent selection.

Suolahti, H. — *Sinfonia piccola* — Bo. Hawkes — IV-V

Full of accidentals. Difficult orchestration. Ideal for advanced high school or college orchestras. Many rests. Transposed parts for clarinet and trumpet are available.

Verrall, J. — *Symphony for Young Orchestras* — Bos — III

Contemporary idiom. Three movements. Third movement shifts back and forth from 3/4 to 2/4. Not technically difficult. Excellent selection; full score.

Washburn, R. — *St. Lawrence Overture* — Bo. Hawkes — III-IV

Full score. Interesting rhythms and good woodwind parts. Needs a good oboe, but is cued in the clarinet. Good program music.

Weinberger, J. — *"Dance of the Children,"* from **The Beloved Voice** — AMP — IV

Czech flavor by a noted Czech composer. Changes mood from lively to lyric. Appealing melody and rhythm. Good selection. Full score.

Whear, P.   *"Catskill Legend"*   EV   IV

Full score and no piano part. Winner of the 1962 NSOA composition contest. Very rhythmical and interesting. Contrasting middle, with horn solo that is not cued. Good clarinet, brass, and oboe solos, none of which are cross-cued. Needs some bowing changes.

Whitney, M.   *Chaconne*   Witmark   IV

Full score. Good imitation of the old masters' writing of the Chaconne form. Good for teaching this form to high school groups. Not too difficult. Interesting reeds and brass sections alone.

Grades V and VI

BAROQUE PERIOD

Bach, J. S.   *Concerto No. 1 in F*   Broude   VI

3 oboes, bassoon, 2 horns, violin solo, strings (combined). Excellent training material for strings, woodwinds, and horn, but too difficult or demanding on the three oboists.

———————————   *Fugue in G minor*   Witmark   V
                             ("The Great")

Difficult number for strings only. Full score. Requires advanced strings.

———————————   *Overture (Suite) No. 1*   AMP   IV-VI
                             in C Major

2 oboes, bassoon, and strings. Quite long and demanding for the oboists. The Courante, Gavotte, Forlana, Minuett, and Bourrée may be played by grade IV and V groups. Fine string materials.

———————————   *Overture (Suite) No. 2*   AMP   IV-VI
                             in B minor

Flute, strings, and cembalo. The Rondeau, Sarabande, Bourrée, Polonaise, and Minuet are much easier than the overture. Requires very fine flutists.

———————————   *Overture (Suite) No. 3*   AMP   IV-VI
                             in D Major

3 trumpets, 2 oboes, timpani, strings, and continuo. Transpositions for trumpets in B-flat are included, as well as a simplified version. Requires good trumpets if original version is used. Air, Gavotte, and Bourrée are much easier.

———————————   *Overture (Suite) No. 4*   AMP   IV-VI
                             in D Major

3 trumpets, 3 oboes, timpani, strings, and cembalo. Transpositions for trumpets available, as well as simplified versions. Requires fine winds. Bourrée, Gavotte, and Minuett easy.

——————— Stokowski   *Passacaglia and Fugue*   Broude   VI
                             in C minor

Excellent 20th-century orchestration of Bach. Stokowski did not score as full of instrumentation throughout the composition as he generally does.

| | Stokowski | *Toccata and Fugue in D minor* | Broude | VI |

A colorful present-day orchestration of Bach. Some may feel this has been overly orchestrated.

| Corelli | Muller | *Adagio and Allegro* | Ludwig | V |

Subjective, nice contrasts between sections (brass, woodwinds, strings); interesting mixing of colors and timbres. Excellent string writing.

| Couperin | Milhaud | *Overture and Allegro from **La Sultane*** | Broude | V |

Opening overture slow and sustained. Chorale style. Allegro makes composition more difficult.

| Frescobaldi | Kindler | *Toccata* | Broude | V |

Outstanding full orchestra setting that all orchestras will want to play, particularly advanced high school groups.

| Handel | | *Concerti Grossi, op. 3* | Broude | V-VI |

No. 1, B-flat Major—2 violins, 2 oboes, 2 flutes, 2 bassoons, 2 violas, and basso continuo.

No. 2, B-flat Major—4 violins, viola, 2 celli, 2 oboes, and basso continuo.

No. 3, G Major—3 violins, viola, 2 oboes, bassoon, and basso continuo.

No. 4, F Major—2 violins, viola, 2 oboes, bassoon, and basso continuo.

No. 5, D minor—2 violins, viola, cello, 2 oboes, and basso continuo.

No. 6, D Major—2 violins, viola, cello, 2 oboes, bassoon, and basso continuo.

All of these concerti grossi are excellent training materials for woodwinds and strings. This edition is unedited.

| | | *Concerto Grosso in C Major (**Alexander's Feast**)* | Broude | V-VI |

4 violins, viola, cello, 2 oboes, and basso continuo.

| | | *Four Concerti Grossi* | Broude | V-VI |

The first three are written as oboe concerti with strings, and No. 2 includes 2 horns. No. 4 is a violin concerto, with strings and two oboes.

| | Harty | **Water Music** *Suite* | Broude | V |

One of the better suites of this period. Should be in every orchestra library. Demanding on the horns.

| | Beecham | **The Faithful Shepherd** *Suite* | Broude | V-VI |

A full orchestra transcription for present-day orchestras. This suite should be in all libraries.

| | Harty | **Royal Fireworks** *Music* | Broude | V |

Good program music, as well as excellent training material for the orchestra, particularly the strings and woodwinds.

_____ Jacob   *Overture,* **Theodora**   Mills   V

Colorful, full, contrapuntal in spots. Must have good horns.

_____ Kindler   *Prelude and Fugue*   Mills   V
in D minor

Sonorous; wide, grandiose orchestration, not technically difficult except in concluding part, written by arranger. High school students will particularly enjoy this composition.

Purcell   Lambert   **Comus** *Suite*   Broude   V
(From the ballet)

Beautiful color and texture. Fine suite for orchestra libraries.

Rameau   Mottl   *Ballet Suite*   Broude   V

Good writing for strings. Not quite as outstanding as some of the suites written during this period.

CLASSICAL PERIOD

Beethoven   *Symphony No. 1 in C*   Broude   V-VI
Major, op. 21

Excellent editing and printing. Both original and transposed parts available. Somewhat Haydnesque in style. Interesting woodwind passages.

_____ *Symphony No. 2 in D*   Broude   V-VI
Major, op. 36

(Same comments as Symphony No. 1.) Second movement outstanding. Spirited and harmonious in faster movements; reflections of humor.

_____ *Symphony No. 3 in*   Broude   V-VI
*E-flat Major (***Eroica***), op. 55*

Both original and transposed parts available. Lengthy and complex sonata allegro form (1st movement); famous funeral march in 2nd movement; 4th movement a theme and variations.

_____ *Symphony No. 4 in*   Broude   V-VI
B-flat Major, op. 60

Both original and transposed parts available. Possesses a gentleness and tranquil beauty that has sometimes been overshadowed by the fiery grandeur of its companion symphonies.

Boccherini   *Symphony in B-flat*   Broude   V
Major, op. 22, no. 1

One of the many Boccherini symphonies that are excellent orchestra material. Particularly good material for string section.

Cimarosa   Carse   **The Impresario** *Overture*   Broude   V

2 flutes, 2 oboes, 2 clarinets, 2 bassoons, 2 horns, 2 trumpets, timpani, and strings. A good piece for small orchestra, exciting and clean.

Dittersdorf   Carse   *Symphony in C Major*   Broude   V

2 oboes, 2 horns, and strings. An intellectual interweaving of a small group of instruments; needs outstanding players to achieve the proper sound.

Donizetti — *Sinfonia Concertante in D Major* — Broude — V

Flute, 2 oboes, 2 clarinets, 2 bassoons, 2 horns, 2 trumpets, and strings. Delightful piece for chamber orchestra.

Gluck — Weingartner — **Alceste** *Overture* — Broude — V

Typical carriage of classical style—not too light, not too heavy.

——————— — **Iphigenia in Aulis** *Overture* — Broude — V

Bright orchestration; top three string parts demand dexterity. Also available as arranged by Wagner from AMP.

Haydn — *Symphony No. 104 in D Major (***London***)* — Broude — V-VI

This choice is merely one of the 104 authenticated symphonies of this prolific composer. All are good material for orchestra. The middle movement may be used by grades IV and V. Broude Bros. publish all but a few of Haydn's earlier works.

Jacob, G. — *Suite No. 1 in F Major* — Mills — V

Good editing and printing, written in classical manner by a contemporary composer. (May also be listed under "Contemporary.") Contains: overture, air, gavotte and musette, march.

Mozart, W. A. — **Don Giovanni** *Overture, K. 527* — Broude — V

Not as popular as some of Mozart's other overtures, but well written and serves as good reading material.

——————— — **Impresario** *Overture, K. 486* — Broude — V

Excellent training material for intermediate orchestras. (May be done in grade IV—or at least read.)

——————— — *Symphony No. 40 in G Minor, K. 550* — Broude — VI

All of Mozart's (41) symphonies are excellent. This one was listed because of popularity. Grades IV and V might include the middle two movements and some of the first movements.

——————— — **The Marriage of Figaro** *Overture, K. 492* — Broude — VI

This might appear to be grade V, but if played up to tempo it would fall into the category of grade VI. Exciting music, especially for the strings.

——————— — Beecham — *Symphony No. 29 in A Major, K. 201* — Bo. Hawkes — V

Full score. Two oboes, two horns, and strings. Score well marked.

Pleyel — Carse — *Symphony in C Major* — Broude — VI

Good training material for orchestra, excellent string writing.

Sammartini, G.   *Symphony in C Major*   Broude   V

2 oboes, 2 bassoons, timpani, strings. Average symphony of classic era.

Stamitz   Carse   *Symphony in G Major,*   Broude   V
                                          op. 3, no. 3

One of the many fine symphonies written by Carl Stamitz, excellently conceived for classical orchestra.

———————— Kindler   *Symphony in E-flat Major*   EV   V

Full conductor's score. Fairly easy in parts. For flutes, oboe, bassoon, horns, timpani, and strings only. Large tutti passages.

ROMANTIC PERIOD

Beethoven   **Egmont** *Overture, op. 84*   Broude   V-VI

A standard overture that every good orchestra should have in its library.

————————   *Coriolanus Overture,*   Broude   VI
                                          op. 62

Both original and transposed parts available. A standard number that should be in any good library.

————————   *Leonore Overture,*   Broude   VI
                                          No. 3, op. 72b

Most popular of the three Leonore overtures, bright and exciting.

————————   **Prometheus** *Overture,*   Broude   VI
                                          op. 43

Exemplary music for the orchestra to know.

————————   *Symphony No. 5 in*   Broude   VI
                                          C minor, op. 67

Excellent editing and printing; both original and transposed parts available. A symphony of dramatic tension.

————————   *Symphony No. 6 in*   Broude   VI
                                          F Major, op. 68
                                          (Pastoral)

Both original and transposed parts available; very melodious and nostalgic. A display for woodwinds; challenging horn work.

————————   *Symphony No. 7 in*   Broude   VI
                                          A Major, op. 92

Both original and transposed parts available. One of the most energetic and highly spirited of Beethoven's works.

————————   *Symphony No. 8 in*   Broude   VI
                                          F Major, op. 93

Warm string texture, well into the romantic style.

| | | *Symphony No. 9 in D minor, op. 125* **(Choral)** | Broude | VI |

The climax to all of the nine symphonies; demands highly skilled chorus; should not be attempted by less than mature and skilled orchestra.

| Berlioz | | *Roman Carnival Overture, op. 9* | Broude | VI |

Colorful, dramatic, lots of brass and woodwind work. Strings well orchestrated and outstanding in color.

| | | **Symphonie Fantastique,** *op. 14* | Broude | VI |

Requires more than standard instrumentation especially in percussion. Five movements in symphony, a very dramatic work. Lots of peculiar instrumental combinations and ranges. Takes mature and talented players to play successfully.

| | | *"Hungarian March,"* from **The Damnation of Faust** | Broude | VI |

A Hungarian war song. Typical Berlioz dynamic contrasts and color.

| Bizet | | **L'Arlésienne** *Suite No. 1* | Broude | V |

Lively, dynamic, and exciting; offers full brass work.

| | Langey | **L'Arlésienne** *Suite No. 1* | G. Schirmer | V |

Colorful, challenging; some of the "spark" may have been lost through the arrangement and revision. Students enjoy playing these themes; a good "opener."

| | | **l'Arlésienne** *Suite No. 2* | Broude | V |

The pastorale is one of the finest pieces in either of the suites.

| | Langey | **L'Arlésienne** *Suite No. 2* | G. Schirmer | V |

Interesting to play; colorful contrast in sections; not so demanding but can be polished in minimal length of time.

| | | *Symphony No. 1 in C Major* | AMP | VI |

Movements other than the last may be done by grade V orchestras of better than average ability. This symphony should be performed, as it has almost fallen into oblivion.

| Borodin | | *"Polovtsian Dances,"* from **Prince Igor** | Broude | V-VI |

No. 8 and No. 17 especially colorful and interesting. Nice style of orchestration. Woodwinds used well.

| | | *Symphony No. 2 in B minor* | Broude | VI |

Well orchestrated. All parts seem to be idiomatic and interesting. Borodin is a master of "orchestral build-ups" of dynamics rather than the inferior standard method of using dynamic markings.

| Brahms | | *Academic Festival Overture* | Broude | VI |
| | | *Overture, op. 80* | | |

Contains familiar folk tunes. A very exciting and colorful piece. Good brass workout. Full string sound.

| ——————— | | *Tragic Overture, op. 81* | Broude | VI |

An exciting thematic piece that students enjoy playing. Brilliant orchestration.

| ——————— | | *Symphony No. 1 in* | Broude | VI |
| | | *C minor, op. 68* | | |

Both original and transposed parts available. Demands excellent players, fine solo spots for horn, oboe, etc. Beautiful texture in orchestration.

| ——————— | | *Symphony No. 2 in* | Broude | VI |
| | | *D Major, op. 73* | | |

Excellent editing and printing. Both original and transposed parts available. Very thematic. Outstanding string parts.

| ——————— | | *Symphony No. 3 in* | Broude | VI |
| | | *F Major, op. 90* | | |

This is the shortest of the Brahms symphonies, also the most romantic and picturesque.

| ——————— | | *Symphony No. 4 in* | Broude | VI |
| | | *E minor, op. 98* | | |

A definite climax in the works of Brahms; mature and formal. Last movement is the famous passacaglia, a tremendous feat for the whole orchestra. Should not be attempted without the best of college orchestras.

| Bruckner | | *Symphony No. 1 in* | Broude | VI |
| | | *C minor* | | |

Any of the nine Bruckner symphonies are challenging and may be too much for college orchestras. The first and fourth symphonies seem to be the most popular. Lengthy and heavy in style, exploited orchestration, dissonant.

| Chausson | | *Symphony in B-flat* | Broude | VI |
| | | *Major, op. 20* | | |

A romantic symphony with audience appeal. Requires organ.

| Chopin | Sopkin | *Polonaise in A-flat* | Mills | V |

Transcribed for orchestra in C by Henry Sopkin. Complete instrumentation. Interesting parts distributed throughout entire orchestra. Challenging rhythmically.

| Debussy | | **Prelude to the Afternoon** | Broude | VI |
| | | **of a Faun** | | |

3 flutes, 2 oboes, English horn, 2 clarinets, 1 bassoon, 4 horns, 2 harps, strings, and percussion. An outstanding piece of program music. Subtle but thrilling woodwind writing. Excellent coloring and texture.

| ——————— | | **La Mer** | EV | VI |

Exploits orchestral devices. Shimmering and colorful. Difficult in most parts. Lots of harp.

| | | Nocturnes | Broude | VI |

Impressive and pleasant. Requires good harpist.

| Delius | | **North Country Sketches** | Broude | VI |

Excellent editing and printing. Very descriptive music.

| | Beecham | "Summer Evening" | Mills | V-VI |

Pleasant, almost pastoral. Challenging woodwinds.

| Dukas | | **The Sorcerer's Apprentice** | Broude | VI |

Descriptive. Popular, especially with young audience. Nice passages of small and different instrumental combinations. Woodwinds kept busy.

| Dvořák | | Symphony No. 9 in E minor (**From the New World**) (Formerly No. 5) | Broude | VI |

Might be done by good grade V orchestra. Contains popular "composed" folklike tunes. Easy to comprehend, delightful and dynamic themes. Excellent orchestration; especially bright spots for flute and strings. Horn section must be secure, second movement mostly for English horn solo. Brass has opportunity to perform. Other four symphonies are also fine.

| | | Carnival Overture | Broude | VI |

Full orchestra; harp. Good contrasting sections. No really difficult problems, except in the strings.

| | | Symphony No. 8 in G Major | Broude | V |

Full orchestra; augmented percussion. Requires good woodwinds and brass; winds have good solo passages. Themes and movements create colorful contrasts.

| | | Slavonic Dances | Bo. Hawkes | VI |

Full orchestra; some dances require augmented sections. Difficult rhythms.

| Elgar | | **Enigma** Variations | Broude | VI |

A thorough treatment of 14 variations.

| Enesco | | Rumanian Rhapsody No. 1 | Broude | VI |

Might be used by outstanding grade V group. Colorful and "frilly." Challenging clarinet and oboe passages; lavish string sound. Popular and thrilling.

| | | Rumanian Rhapsody No. 2 | Bo. Hawkes | V |

Not as well known as No. 1, but equally effective, though in a simpler style.

| Flotow | Dasch | **Stradella** Overture | CF | V |

Rich, sonorous, but not too heavy. Considerable contrast.

| Franck | | Symphony in D minor | Broude | VI |

One of the first great symphonies built on a cyclical form. Beautiful themes, harmonies, and textures. Interesting work in the lines of the lower instruments. Violin part difficult with considerable shifting of positions. Choice woodwind and brass colors.

| Glière | | "Dance of the Russian Sailors," from **The Red Poppy** | Broude | V |

An exotic and colorful piece. Interesting to play and pleasing to hear.

| Goldmark, K. | | "Sakuntala" | SCH | V-VI |

Full score. Two celli solo in parts. Chordal in structure. Thick in texture, especially in bass. Parts written high above staff.

| Gounod | Moses | Ballet Music from **Faust** | CF | V |

Delightful, but only melodically interesting to play.

| Grieg | | **Peer Gynt** Suite No. 1 | Broude | IV-VI |

A varicolored and exotic suite based on Nordic folklore. Simple harmonies and pleasing melodies. Outstanding parts include flute, lower strings, and oboe. Delicate violin lines in slow sections.

| ———————— | | **Peer Gynt** Suite No. 2 | Broude | V-VI |

A continuation of style and ideas of Suite No. 1.

| Griffes | | "The White Peacock" | Broude | VI |

An American impressionistic piece. Requires céleste and two harps.

| Humperdinck | | Overture to **Hansel and Gretel** | Broude | V |

A delightful, appealing piece, particularly good for voice leading.

| Ippolitov-Ivanov, M. | | **Caucasian Sketches,** op. 10 | Broude | VI |

An unusual programmatic piece. Requires good viola, oboe, English horn, piccolo, and bassoon. Very colorful.

| Jarnefelt, A. | | "Praeludium" | Broude | VI |

A melodic program selection for small orchestra.

| Kalinnikov, V. | | Symphony No. 1 in G minor | Kalmus | V-VI |

Full score. Requires a harp. All parts display technical passages. Interesting melodically. Rated above average.

| Lalo, E. | | **Le Roi d'Ys** Overture | Kalmus | VI |

Interesting in color contrast. Melodic; both orchestra and audience will enjoy this composition.

| Liszt | | **Les Préludes** | Broude | VI |

A difficult, thematic, symphonic poem. Lower instruments must have good technique.

| ———————— | | Symphonic Poem No. 6 (**Mazeppa**) | Broude | VI |

Full orchestra; augmented woodwinds, brass, and percussion. Requires a good orchestra. Contains many runs, arpeggios, and difficult rhythms.

MacDowell   *Second Indian Suite,*   Broude   VI
                                 op. 48

This suite has been listed mainly to acquaint orchestra members with more of Mac-
Dowell's music besides the *First Indian Suite* and the *Woodland Sketches.* Typical
MacDowell, nothing revolutionary.

Mascagni   *Prelude and Siciliana*   Broude   V

Considerably less known than some of Mascagni's other pieces. Contrasting tone coloring in the siciliana. Prelude just average.

Mendelssohn   *Symphony No. 4 in*   Broude   VI
                                 A Major, op. 90
                                 (**Italian**)

Energetic work. Fourth movement difficult. Fast passages with simple rhythms. Full
score. Good melodic lines in parts. Brass parts fairly simple.

———————————   *Symphony No. 5 in*   Broude   VI
                                 D Major, op. 107
                                 (**Reformation**)

The last of Mendelssohn's symphonies, and a climactic achievement.

———————————   *Hebrides Overture*   Broude   V
                                 ("Fingal's Cave")

Melodic, programmatic. Requires good cello section.

Moussorgsky   Reibold   *"The Great Gate*   G. Schirmer   V
                                 of Kiev"

Dynamic, full of colorful orchestration and thick textures. Demands tone control.
Other parts of *Pictures at an Exhibition* are suitable for grade V.

———————————   Sopkin   **A Night on Bald**   CF   VI
                                 Mountain

Descriptive and colorful. Difficult woodwind parts. Eulenburg edition better than CF, if
possible to obtain the original.

Offenbach   Dorati   **La Vie Parisienne**   Mills   V
                                 Overture

Light, spirited, takes perseverance and a controlled, light technique. Familiar and
bright.

———————————   Wersen   **Orpheus in the Under-**   CF   V
                                 world *Suite*

Good solos for clarinet, oboes, harp, and violin. High positions for first violins. Multiple stops for strings. Full score.

Respighi   **Pines of Rome**   B&C   VI

A most dynamic and colorful symphonic poem, tremendous brass display. Difficult in
most parts; especially high woodwinds, violins, violas. High in range much of time.
Sometimes called the "sequel" is the *Fountains of Rome,* which is in the same style
and extremely colorful.

| Rimsky-Korsakov | | *Le Coq d'or* Suite | Broude | VI |

Not performed as often as *Capriccio espagnol* and *Scheherazade,* but equally well written.

| —————————— | Woodhouse | *Polonaise from* **Christmas Night** | G. Schirmer | V |

Full, colorful, difficult.

| Rossini | | **La gazza ladra** (**The Thieving Magpie**) *Overture* | Broude | V-VI |

Opening *maestoso,* full and powerful. The *allegro* is typical of Rossini's light, fast movements.

| —————————— | | **The Barber of Seville** *Overture* | Broude | V-VI |

Strictly a romantic overture that may be performed quite easily by average groups.

| —————————— | | **L'Italiana in Algeri** *Overture* | Broude | V-VI |

A typical Rossini overture that is not too challenging.

| Schubert | | Overture to **Rosamunde** | Broude | V |

Popular to audiences, standard in general.

| —————————— | | *Symphony No. 8 in B minor* | CF | VI |

The famous *Unfinished,* broad and sonorous. No part outstandingly difficult, but requires mature players.

| Smetana | | *"The Moldau"* | Broude | VI |

Descriptive of the great Moldau river. Difficult flute parts. Perhaps more demanding than warranted by musical results.

| —————————— | | *Overture to* **The Bartered Bride** | Broude | VI |

Excellent edition, the most popular of Smetana's overtures, light and delightful. Violin parts lie well.

| —————————— | Riessenfeld | *Three Dances from* **The Bartered Bride** | G. Schirmer | V |

Suitable to be programmed as separate selections. Violin parts lie well—very little shifting from first position.

| Steg, P. | | *Symphony on Folk Songs* | SUM | VI |

Includes English, French, French-Canadian, Irish, Italian, Jewish, and American folk themes. Written in a classical and romantic style. Folk tune idea seems more important than good symphonic form.

| Strauss, J. | | **Die Fledermaus** *Overture* | Broude | VI |

Popular overture of light nature; nothing profound, but a standard.

| | Sopkin | *"Perpetuum mobile"* *("Musical Humoresque")* | CF | V |

Humorous number, every instrument having a solo. Has a different orchestral effect. Ends suddenly in the middle of a phrase. Conductor's score has biography of composer, also a forward about the work.

| Strauss, R. | *"Don Juan,"* op. 20 | Broude | VI |

An excellent symphonic poem, but should be performed by professional orchestras. Very few college orchestras could play it well.

| | ***Der Rosenkavalier*** Suite | Broude | VI |

Excellent light concert material. Requires good horn section. Insightful string writing.

| Tchaikovsky | ***Capriccio italien,*** op. 45 | Broude | VI |

Might be done with very fine grade V orchestra, but presents technical problems. Excellent "opener"; beautifully colored, especially in the strings. Cello in singing style. Full brass ensemble. Climactic.

| | *Symphony No. 6 in B minor, op. 74* (***Pathétique***) | Broude | VI |

All of Tchaikovsky's symphonies are popular with audiences, particularly Nos. 4, 5, and 6. Demanding in all sections of orchestra in range and rhythm. Good strings absolutely essential.

| | ***Romeo and Juliet*** *Overture* | Broude | VI |

Enjoyable and popular; not a profound composition.

| Wagner | Introduction to ***Die Meistersinger,*** Act 3, *"Dance of the Apprentices"* and *"Procession"* | Broude | VI |

Outstanding orchestration. Every instrument sensitive. Brass and strings demand complete control.

| | *Prelude and Love Death from* ***Tristan and Isolde*** | Broude | VI |

Dynamic and contrasting. Outstanding orchestration. Beauty of line and harmonies. Takes persistent control of strings and woodwinds.

| | *Overture to* ***The Flying Dutchman*** | Broude | VI |

Exciting, moving, many different string techniques involved. A workout for brass.

| | *Prelude to* ***Die Meistersinger*** | Broude | VI |

Probably the most popular of all the Wagner preludes and overtures. Typical Wagnerian orchestration and sound; extreme brass range.

Light orchestration—brass represented with only 2 horns and 1 trumpet. Contains interesting melodies. Excellent horn and oboe solo passages.

Weber	Overture to **Der Freischutz**	AMP	V-VI

Outstanding training material for high school and college orchestras. A bright and serious piece, takes good horn section.

_____	Overture to **Oberon**	Broude	V-VI

A popular "old standard"; all orchestras should have this in their libraries.

Wolf-Ferrari	*Scherzo and Finale*	Broude	VI

An interesting piece in the early style; fairly standard orchestration.

CONTEMPORARY PERIOD

Benjamin, A.	*"Jamaican Rumba"*	Broude	V-VI

An exciting, rhythmical, colorful, and complex dance. An excellent short encore selection.

Bartók	*Concerto for Orchestra*	Broude	VI

Treatment of single instruments in a concertant, or soloistic, manner. Specifically: fugato development of the first movement (brass); mobilelike passages of the principal themes in the last movement (strings). Written in five movements.

_____	*Rumanian Folk Dances*	Bo. Hawkes	V

1 flute, 2 clarinets, 2 bassoons, 1 horn, and strings. One of the outstanding folk compositions of this outstanding twentieth-century composer.

Barber	**First Essay for Orchestra**	G. Schirmer	VI

Good printing and editing. Demanding on small instrumentation of the orchestra. Thrilling composition of modern idiom.

Britten	**Matinées musicales**	Broude	V-VI

Interesting to perform and pleasant to listen to. Continuation of the *Soirées Musicales*. This is the second suite.

_____	**Soirées musicales**	Broude	V-VI

Same as above. First suite from Rossini: March, Canzonetta, Tirolese, Bolero, and Tarantella.

Chadwick	*"Jubilee"* and *"Noel,"* from **Symphonic Sketches**	Broude	VI

Excellent orchestra writing, with only moderate modern idioms.

Copland	*"An Outdoor Overture"*	Broude	VI

Demanding for the musical results obtained.

| | *Appalachian Spring* | Bo. Hawkes | VI |

Requires additional xylophone, harp, and piano. One of Copland's better symphonic works. Written in 1945.

| | "John Henry" | Bo. Hawkes | V |

Clever program selection, with audience appeal. Demands considerable string technique.

| | *Four Dance Episodes* from **Rodeo** | Bo. Hawkes | VI |

"Buckaroo Holiday," 7 minutes; "Corral Nocturne," 3½ minutes; "Saturday Night Waltz," 4 minutes; "Hoe Down," 3½ minutes. Fine group of modern and original dances.

| | **A Lincoln Portrait** | Bo. Hawkes | VI |

Outstanding modern patriotic selection with narrative.

| | **El salón México** | Bo. Hawkes | VI |

Full orchestra; augmented woodwinds and brass. Based on a popular Mexican folk song. Good melodic passages; many intricate, rhythmic passages, multimetric.

| Cowell, H. | *Hymn and Fuguing Tune No. 3* | AMP | V-VI |

Written in 1944. Performance time: 8 minutes.

| Creston, P. | *Dance Overture, op. 62* | Templeton | VI |

Written in 18/16 or 9/8 meter; rhythmical; awkward string writing.

| | **Lydian Ode** | Ricordi | V |

Full orchestra; piano. Composed in lydian mode. Not difficult, except for modern harmonic idiom.

| Dello Joio, N. | **New York Profiles** | CF | VI |

Written in 1952. Performance time: 20 minutes.

| Gershwin | **An American in Paris** | Broude | VI |

A program composition with a jazz flavor. A bit more difficult than orchestra players like to think.

| | **Rhapsody in Blue** | Broude | VI |

Written as a piano solo with orchestra accompaniment. Requires a good pianist. A light program selection.

| Giannini, V. | *Symphony No. 2* | Chappell | VI |

Commissioned for the 50th anniversary of the MENC. Written in three movements.

| Goeb, R. | *American Dances 4 and 5* | Amer. Comp. Alliance | VI |

Written in 1952. Performance time: 6 minutes.

| Gould, M. | "Fall River Legend," from *Ballet Suite* | Chappell | VI |

May require more technical and performance skill than is worth the effect musically.

	"Serenade of Carols"	Chappell	V

Full score. In four movements for small orchestra. Extremely thin in parts and very contrapuntal. Would require good solo wind players and a lot of study to put it together. Carols are not evident, but must be carefully studied to make them sound.

Hanson, H.	*Love Duet from* **Merrymount**	Harms	V-VI

Printing not too good. Typical orchestral sound of Hanson. Good for short program selection.

	Symphony No. 1 (**Nordic**)	Broude	V-VI

An easier symphony that young groups like to perform.

	Symphony No. 2 (**Romantic**)	Broude	VI

The C. C. Birchard edition is also good. Not too modern, with great rhythmic and melodic appeal. The third symphony has not been as popular as the first two.

Holst, G.	**The Planets** *(Suite)*	G. Schirmer	VI

Excellent editing and printing, but extremely difficult. Mars, the Bringer of War; Venus, the Bringer of Peace; Mercury, the Winged Messenger; Jupiter, the Bringer of Jollity; Saturn, the Bringer of Old Age; Uranus, the Magician; and Neptune, the Mystic.

Hovhaness, A.	*Prelude and Quadruple Fugue, op. 128*	AMP	VI

This is an excellent example of good prelude and fugue writing in the modern idiom.

Irvine	*"Romantic Overture,"* *op. 2 (1932)*	MSS, Univ. of Wash.	V
	Symphonic Poem, **Printemps,** *op. 4 (1934)*		
	"Traume," for Soprano and Orchestra, op. 5 (1934)		
	Serende, op. 8 (1944)		

Ives, C.	*Symphony No. 3*	Arrow	VI

Written in 1911; won the Pulitzer Prize in 1947. Performance time: 17 minutes.

Jacob, G.	*Fantasia on the Alleluia Hymn*	Mills	V

An interesting composition for the young student. Contemporary orchestration with contrasting colorful sections. All instruments kept busy.

Kay, U.	*Suite from* **The Quiet One**	Amer. Comp. Alliance	VI

American Black composer. Written in 1948. Performance time: 16 minutes. In manuscript. All movements are grade VI.

Kechley, G.	Bright Variations on an Original Theme	MSS, Univ. of Wash.	V
	Prelude and Allegro for Small Orchestra		
	Music for Oboe and Strings		
	Interlude for String Orchestra		
Kubik, G.	Symphonie Concertante	Chappell	VI

Performance time: 24½ minutes.

| Larsson, L. | Pastoral Suite (Pastoralsvit) | Mills | V-VI |

Interesting lines in all parts, romantic orchestration, tonal and pleasing.

| Mahler | Symphony No. 10, op. posth. | Broude | VI |

All ten symphonies are extremely difficult and may be best reserved for professional groups. However, some of the movements individually would not be too challenging.

McKay, G.	Allegretto Scherzando from Sinfonietta No. 1	CF	V
	Symphonie Miniature	Birchard	V
	Suite on Fiddler's Tunes	J. Fischer	IV-V
	Variants on a Texas Tune	G. Schirmer	V
Mennin, P.	Sinfonia	Hargail Music	VI

Written in 1946 and in manuscript. Performance time: 10 minutes.

| _____ | Symphony No. 6 | CF | VI |

Full orchestra. Contemporary idiom; generally quite difficult. Good tutti passages are frequent.

| _____ | Concertato for Orchestra (**Moby Dick**) | CF | VI |

Full orchestra; augmented woodwinds. Many intricate rhythms. Good sound.

| Menotti, G. | Suite from **Sebastian** | Ricordi | VI |

Written in 1947. Performance time: 25 minutes.

| Moore, D. | **Farm Journal** Suite | CF | IV-V |

Written in 1950. Performance time: 13-15 minutes.

| Piston, W. | Sinfonietta | Bo. Hawkes | V-VI |

Requires only horns of the brass. Written in 1942. Performance time: 17 minutes.

| Prokofiev | **Classical** Symphony, op. 25 | Broude | V-VI |

Relatively modern composition that is just moderately difficult. Delightful and interesting.

| _____ | *Peter and the Wolf* | Broude | VI |

A must for children's programs, and could be used on lighter programs just as well.

| Rózsa, M. | **The Jungle Book** *Suite* | Broude | VI |

An excellent descriptive suite based on Rudyard Kipling's *Jungle Books*.

| _____ | "The Vitner's Daughter" | Broude | VI |

Twelve variations on a French folk song.

| Schuman, W. | *Circus Overture* | G. Schirmer | VI |

Full orchestra; augmented woodwinds and percussion. "Showy" composition, programmatic—depicting circus events. Contains difficult rhythms.

| Shostakovich | *Symphony No. 5, op. 47* | Broude | VI |

Full orchestra; augmented winds and percussion. More romantic than most works of this composer. Difficult passages for all instruments; intricate rhythms. Requires good orchestra.

| _____ Stokowski | *Prelude in E-flat minor* | Broude | V |

Full orchestra. A very short composition, but contains exciting tension. Sustained, full, vibrant tone essential.

| Sibelius | "Valse triste," op. 44 | Broude | V |

Beautiful, melodic, short program selection, mostly for the string section.

| _____ | *Symphony No. 2 in D Major, op. 43* | Broude | VI |

This has been the most popular of Sibelius's eight symphonies, even though all are excellent works. Colorful and interesting.

| Villa-Lobos | *Sinfonietta No. 2* | SMC | V |

Full orchestra; augmented with céleste and piano. Modern idiom may present problems. Some difficult passages.

COMMUNITY ORCHESTRA

The community symphony orchestra generally has personnel that can play more advanced literature but because of a few limitations may not be able to give the best performance of the most difficult compositions. For this reason the following compositions are recommended for the review of the conductor. These compositions are of the highest musical quality, yet playable for most civic organizations. Since the conductor will know the literature, this list is given without annotation and will serve as possible concert program selections that will appeal to the orchestra personnel, conductor, and audience.

Albéniz, Isaac (1860-1909) "Fête-Dieu à Seville," from the suite **Iberia** (Transcribed for orchestra by E. Fernandez Arbos)

Arensky, Anton Stepanovich (1861-1906) *Variations on a Theme by Tchaikovsky* (for string orchestra), op. 35A

Bach, Carl Philipp Emanuel
(1714–88)

Concerto for Stringed Instruments in D Major
(Transcribed for orchestra by Maximilian Steinberg)

Bach, Johann Sebastian
(1685–1750)

Brandenburg Concertos
Chaconne (Transcribed for orchestra by A. Walter Kramer)
Chorale-Prelude ("Credo") (Transcribed for orchestra by Leopold Stokowski)
D minor Partita
Passacaglia and Fugue (Transcribed by Leopold Stokowski)
Passacaglia in C minor (Transcribed for orchestra by Ottorino Respighi)
Prelude and Fugue in B minor for Organ (Transcribed for orchestra by Dimitri Mitropoulos)
Three Chorale-Preludes (Transcribed for orchestra by Ottorino Respighi)
Toccata and Fugue in D minor (Symphonic transcription by Leopold Stokowski)

Balakirev, Mily Alexeievitch
(1837–1910)

"Islamey," Oriental Fantasy (Transcribed for orchestra by Alfredo Casella)
Overture to **King Lear**
Russia, *Symphonic Poem*
Tamara, *Symphonic Poem*

Barber, Samuel (1910–   )

Adagio for String Orchestra, op. 11
"Essay for Orchestra"
Overture to **The School for Scandal**
"Second Essay"
Symphony in One Movement

Bartók, Béla (1881–1945)

Concerto for Orchestra
Music for Strings, Percussion, and Celesta
Two suites for orchestra

Beethoven, Ludwig van
(1770–1827)

Grand Fugue in B-flat Major, op. 133 (Transcribed for orchestra by Felix Weingartner)
Overture, "Consecration of the House"
Overture, "Coriolanus," op. 62
Overture to **Egmont,** *op. 84*
Overture, "Leonore," No. 2, op. 72a
Overture to **Prometheus,** *op. 43*
Symphony in C Major, No. 1, op. 21
Symphony in E-flat Major, No. 3 **(Eroica),** *op. 55*
Symphony in B-flat Major, No. 4, op. 60
Symphony in C minor, No. 5, op. 67
Symphony in F Major, No. 6 **(Pastoral),** *op. 68*
Symphony in A Major, No. 7, op. 92
Symphony in F Major, No. 8, op. 93
Symphony in D minor, No. 9, with final chorus on Schiller's "Ode to Joy," op. 125

Benjamin, Arthur (1893–1960)

"Jamaican Rumba"
"Overture to an Italian Comedy"
Orchestra Suite, **Cotillon**
"Prelude to a Holiday"
"Romantic Fantasy"
Symphony No. 1

Bergsma, William (1921–   )

Paul Bunyan Suite
Symphony No. 1

Berlioz, Hector, (1803–69)

Excerpts from the dramatic legend **The Damnation of Faust,** op. 24
Orchestral Excerpts from the Dramatic Symphony **Romeo and Juliet,** op. 17
Overture to **Benvenuto Cellini,** op. 23
Overture, "Le Carnaval Romain" ("The Roman Carnival"), op. 9
Overture, "Le Corsaire"
Overture, "King Lear"
Symphonie Fantastique, op. 14A

Bernstein, Leonard (1918–   )

Overture to **Candide**
Suite from the ballet **Fancy Free**
Symphony, **Jeremiah**

Bizet, Georges (1838–75)

L'Arlésienne Suites Nos. 1 and 2
Excerpts from **Carmen**
Overture, "Patrie"
Symphony in C Major
Symphonic Suite, **Roma**

Bloch, Ernest (1880–1959)

"America"
"Evocations"
"Israel"
"Three Jewish Poems"
Concerti Grossi Nos. 1 and 2

Borodin, Alexander (1833–87)

Excerpts from **Prince Igor**
Orchestral sketch, **On the Steppes of Central Asia**
"Polovtsian Dances"
Symphony in B minor, No. 2, op. 5

Boyce, William (1710–79)

12 overtures
8 symphonies
Suite in A Major

Brahms, Johannes (1833–97)

Academic Festival Overture, op. 80
Hungarian Dances
Symphony in C minor, No. 1, op. 68
Symphony in D Major, No. 2, op. 73
Symphony in F Major, No. 3, op. 90
Symphony in E minor, No. 4, op. 98
Tragic Overture, op. 81
Serenades, op. 11, 21

Britten, Benjamin (1913-)	*Matinées musicales* *Simple Symphony for string orchestra* *Sinfonia da Requiem, op. 20* *Soirées musicales* *A Young Person's Guide to the Orchestra* "Four Sea Interludes," from *Peter Grimes*
Bruckner, Anton (1824-96)	*Overture in G minor* *Symphony in E-flat Major, No. 4 (Romantic)* *Symphony in E Major, No. 7* *Symphony in D minor, No. 9*
Busoni, Ferruccio (1866-1924)	*Second Orchestral Suite, Geharnischte (Armor), op. 34A* "Sarabande" and "Cortège," studies for *Doktor Faust, op. 51*
Carpenter, John Alden (1876-1951)	Symphony No. 2 *Skyscrapers, "A ballet of American life"*
Castelnuovo-Tedesco, Mario (1895-1968)	*Overture, King John*
Chabrier, Emmanuel (1841-94)	*España, Rhapsody for Orchestra*
Chadwick, George Whitefield (1854-1931)	6 overtures 3 symphonies Symphonic poems: **Angel of Death** **Aphrodite** **Cleopatra** **Tam o' Shanter** "Jubilee" and "Noel," from **Symphonic Sketches**
Chausson, Ernest (1855-99)	*Symphony in B-flat Major, op. 20*
Chávez, Carlos (1899-)	*4 symphonies*
Cherubini, Luigi (1760-1842)	*Overture to the ballet opera Anacreon* *Overture to The Water Carrier*
Cimarosa, Domenico (1749-1801)	Overture to **A Secret Marriage** *Three Brother Overture*
Clementi, Muzio (1752-1832)	*Symphony in D Major, No. 2 (Revised by Alfredo Casella)*
Coates, Eric (1886-1957)	*London Suite*
Copland, Aaron (1900-)	*A Lincoln Portrait* *El salón México* Orchestral suite from **Appalachian Spring** An Outdoor Overture **Rodeo** Suite **Billy the Kid** Suite Symphony No. 3

Corelli, Arcangelo (1653-1713)

*Concerto Grosso in G minor, op. 6, no. 8 (**Christmas** Concerto) **Fatto per la notte di natale***
Suite for String Orchestra

Couperin, Francois (1668-1733)

*Prelude and Allegro from **La Sultane** (Transcribed for orchestra by Darius Milhaud)*

Cowell, Henry (1897-1965)

8 hymn and fuguing tunes
6 symphonies
Tales of Our Countryside

Creston, Paul (1906-   )

Dance Overture, op. 62
Pastorale and Tarantella
Symphony No. 2, op. 35

Debussy, Claude (1862-1918)

Iberia: Images pour orchestre, *No. 2*
La Mer (The Sea)—*Three Symphonic Sketches*
Prelude to the Afternoon of a Faun
Sarabande (Transcribed for orchestra by Maurice Ravel)
Two nocturnes: "Nuages" ("Clouds"), "Fêtes" ("Festivals")
"Six épigraphes antiques," arranged by Ansermet

Delius, Frederick (1862-1934)

"A Song of Summer"
Brigg Fair
"Fantastic Dance"
*Intermezzo, "The Walk to the Paradise Garden," from the opera **A Village Romeo and Juliet***
"Irmelin" (Prelude)
"Paris, a Night Piece" ("The Song of a Great City")
North Country Sketches
Sea-Drift

Dello Joio, Norman (1913-   )

Joan of Arc
Variants on a Medieval Tune

Demuth, Norman (1898-1968)

6 symphonies

Diamond, David (1915-   )

4 symphonies
Rounds for String Orchestra

Dittersdorf, Karl Ditters von (1739-99)

115 symphonies
Tournament of the Temperaments

Dohnányi, Ernst von (1877-1960)

3 symphonies
Ruralia Hungarica
Suite for Orchestra, op. 19
Variations on a Nursery Air, for Orchestra with Piano Obbligato, op. 25

Dukas, Paul (1865-1935)

*Scherzo, **L'Apprenti sorcier** (**The Sorcerer's Apprentice**)*

Dvořák, Anton (1841-1904)

6 overtures
5 symphonic poems

"Ein Heldenlied" ("A Hero's Song")
"Carnival," Overture for Grand Orchestra, op. 92
Symphony in D minor, No. 7, op. 70
Symphony in G Major, No. 8, op. 88
*Symphony in E minor, No. 9 (**From the New World**), op. 95*

Elgar, Edward (1857-1934)	**Falstaff:** *A Symphonic Study for Orchestra* *Overture, "Cockaigne" ("In London Town"), op. 40* *Variations on an Original Theme (**Enigma**), op. 36*
Enesco, Georges (1881-1955)	*3 symphonies* *Overture to the Opera **Oedipe*** *Rumanian Rhapsody in A Major, op. 11, no. 1*
Falla, Manuel de (1876-1946)	*Suite from the ballet pantomime **El Amor Brujo (Love the Sorcerer)*** *Three Dances from the Ballet **The Three-Cornered Hat (El sombrero de tres picos)***
Fauré, Gabriel (1845-1924)	*Pavane* *"Fileuse"* **Pelléas et Mélisande** **Shylock** *Suite, Nocturne*
Foote, Arthur (1853-1937)	*Suite for String Orchestra in E Major, op. 63*

Franck, César (1822-90)	*Symphony in D minor*
	Symphonic Poems
	   1. **Les Eolides**
	   2. **Le Chasseur maudit**
	   3. **Les Djinns**
	   4. **Psyché**

Gershwin, George (1898-1937)	**An American in Paris** **Rhapsody in Blue** *Selections from **Porgy and Bess***
Giannini, Vittorio (1903-66)	*Symphony No. 2* *Symphony in One Movement*
Gillis, Don (1912-)	*8 symphonies* **A Symphony for Fun** *(No. 5½)* *"January, February, March"* *"The Man Who"*
Glazounov, Alexander (1865-1936)	*6 overtures* *6 suites* *8 symphonies* *Symphonic Poem, **Stenka Rasin***
Glière, Reinhold Moritzovich (1875-1956)	*3 symphonies* *"March of the Red Army"* *Victory Overture* *"Marche héroïque," op. 71* *The Ballet **Red Poppy***

Glinka, Mikhail Ivanovitch (1804-57)	*"Jota Aragonesa," Caprice brilliant* *Overture to* **Russlan and Ludmilla**
Gluck, Christoph Willibald (1714-87)	*11 symphonies* **Orfeo and Euridice** *Suite* *Overture to the opera* **Alceste** *Overture to* **Iphigenia in Aulis**
Goldmark, Karl (1830-1915)	**Rustic Wedding** *Symphony*
Gould, Morton (1913-)	*American Symphonette No. 2* *"Jericho"*
Grainger, Percy (1882-1961)	*"Irish Tune from County Derry"* *"Shepherd's Hey"* *"Suite in a Nut Shell"*
Grieg, Edvard (1843-1907)	*Overture in Autumn* **Peer Gynt,** *Suite No. 1, op. 46, and Suite No. 2, op. 55* *Symphonic Dances*
Griffes, Charles Tomlinson (1884-1920)	**The Pleasure Dome of Kubla Kahn** **The White Peacock**
Grofé, Ferde, (1892-1972)	**Grand Canyon** *Suite* **Mississippi** *Suite*
Hadley, Henry (1871-1937)	**The Enchanted Castle** *Overture* *Overture, "In Bohemia," op. 28* *4 symphonies*
Halvorsen, Johan (1864-1935)	*Dance Scenes from* **Queen Tamara** *"Triumphal Entrance of the Boyars"* *9 orchestral suites* *3 symphonies*
Handel, George Frederick (1685-1759)	**Fireworks** *Music* *Prelude and Fugue in D minor* *Suite from the Opera* **Il pastor fido (The Faithful Shepherd)** *(Arranged by Sir Thomas Beecham)* **Water Music** *Suite (Arranged by Sir Hamilton Harty)*
Hanson, Howard (1896-)	**Nordic** *Symphony* **Merrymount** *Excerpts* *Symphony No. 2* **(Romantic)** *Symphonic Prelude* *Symphonic Legend* *Symphonic Rhapsody*
Harris, Roy (1898-)	*7 symphonies* *Folksong Symphony* *"When Johnny Comes Marching Home" Overture*
Haydn, Joseph (1732-1809)	*104 symphonies* *Symphony in D Major (Breitkopf and Hartel No. 13)*

Symphony in F minor, No. 49 (**La Passione**)
Symphony in D Major, No. 10 (B. and H. No. 86)
Symphony in G Major (B. and H. No. 88)
Symphony in G Major, No. 92 (**Oxford**)
Symphony in D Major, No. 93 (Salomon No. 2)
Symphony in C Major (B. and H. No. 97) (Salomon
    No. 1)
Toy Symphony

Hérold, Louis Joseph Ferdinand (1791–1833)	**Zampa** Overture
Hindemith, Paul (1895–1963)	**Noblissima visione** (Suite from the ballet, also called **St. Francis**) Overture, "Cupid and Psyche" Symphony, **Mathis der Maler (Matthias the Painter)** Symphonic Metamorphosis on Themes of Carl Maria von Weber Symphonic Dances
Holst, Gustav (1874–1934)	**Egdon Heath,** op. 47, no. 1 **Hammersmith** Fugal Overture **St. Paul's Suite** for string orchestra **The Planets,** op. 32
Honegger, Arthur (1892–1955)	"Pacific 231," orchestral movement 5 symphonies Concerto da camera
Humperdinck, Engelbert (1854–1921)	Overture to **Hansel and Gretel**
Ibert, Jacques (1890–1962)	**Escales (Ports of Call)**
Inghelbrecht, Désiré-Emile (1880–1965)	**Automne** (Symphonic Sketch) **El Greco,** Evocations symphoniques
Ippolitov-Ivanov, Mikhail (1859–1935)	**Caucasian Sketches**
Janáček, Leos (1854–1928)	Sinfonietta **Taras Bulba**
Kabalevsky, Dmitri (1904–)	Overture to the opera **Colas Breugnon** 4 symphonies Symphony No. 2, op. 19
Kalinnikov, Vassily Sergeivich (1866–1901)	Symphony No. 1
Kern, Jerome (1885–1945)	Scenario for Orchestra on Themes from **Showboat**
Khatchaturian, Aram (1903–)	"Dance with the Sabers," from the ballet **Gayaneh** 2 symphonies

Kindler, Hans (1892–1949)	*17th-Century Dutch Tunes* *Toccata by Frescobaldi*
Kodály, Zoltán (1882–1967)	***Dances of Galánta*** *Suite from* **Háry János**
Lalo, Edouard (1823–92)	*Overture to the Opera* **Le Roi d'Ys (The King of Ys)**
Larsson, Lars Erik (1908–)	*3 overtures* *3 symphonies*
Liadov, Anatol (1855–1914)	*Eight Russian Folk Songs, op. 58* ***Kikimora***, *Legend for Full Orchestra, op. 63* **Le Lac enchanté (The Enchanted Lake)**, *Legend for Orchestra, op. 62*
Liszt, Franz (1811–86)	***Dante*** *Symphony* ***Faust*** *Symphony* *12 Symphonic Poems, including* **Les Préludes** *(After Lamartine)*
Lully, Jean-Baptiste (1632–87)	*Ballet Suite,* **Les Noces de village**
MacDowell, Edward (1861–1908)	*Suite No. 2 in E minor (**Indian**), op. 48* **Woodland Sketches,** *op. 51*
Mahler, Gustav (1860–1911)	*Symphony in D Major, No. 1* *Symphony in C minor, No. 2, for Orchestra, Soprano, and Alto Solos, and Mixed Chorus* *Symphony in G Major, No. 4 (with soprano solos)* *Symphony No. 5 in C-sharp minor* *Symphony No. 9, in D minor*
Massenet, Jules (1842–1912)	*Ballet music from* **Le Cid**
McDonald, Harl (1899–1955)	*4 symphonies* *"Rhumba"* *Symphonic Poem,* **Bataan**
McKay, George Frederick (1899–1970)	*4 sinfoniettas* *Suite on Old Fiddler's Tunes* *Symphonette in D*
Mendelssohn, Felix (1809–47)	*Excerpts from the Music to* **A Midsummer Night's Dream** *Overture, "The Hebrides" ("Fingal's Cave"), op. 26* *Overture, "The Legend of Fair Melusina," op. 32* *Overture, "Ruy Blas," op. 95* *Overture to the Opera* **The Wedding of Camacho** *Symphony in A minor, No. 3 (**Scotch**), op. 56* *Symphony in A Major, No. 4 (**Italian**), op. 90* *Symphony in D Major, No. 5 (**Reformation**), op. 107*
Mennin, Peter (1923–)	*Folk Overture* *Symphonies*

46

Menotti, Gian-Carlo (1911-) — *Overture to the opera* **The Old Maid and the Thief**
Suite from the ballet **Sebastian**

Milhaud, Darius (1892-1974) — *8 symphonies*
Suite symphonique, from Paul Claudel's play **Protée (Proteus)**
Suite provençale
Suite française

Moussorgsky, Modest (1839-81) — **A Night on Bald Mountain,** *Fantasy for Orchestra*
Pictures at an Exhibition *(Transcribed for orchestra by Maurice Ravel)*
Prelude to the Opera **Khovanschina**

Mozart, Wolfgang Amadeus (1756-91) — *Overture to* **Idomeneo**
Overture to **Don Giovanni**
Overture to **The Magic Flute**
Overture to **The Marriage of Figaro (Le Nozze di Figaro)**
Serenata notturna (Serenade No. 6) in D Major for Two Small Orchestras (K. 239)
Sinfonia concertante for Violin, Viola, and Orchestra in E-flat Major (K. 364)
Symphony in G minor, No. 25 (K. 183)
Symphony in C Major, No. 34 (K. 338)
Symphony in D Major, No. 35 **(Haffner)** *(K. 385)*
Symphony in E-flat Major, No. 39 (K. 543)
Symphony in G minor, No. 40 (K. 550)
Symphony in C Major, No. 41 **(Jupiter)** *(K. 551)*

Nicolai, Otto (1810-49) — *Overture to* **The Merry Wives of Windsor**

Piston, Walter (1894-) — *Suite from the ballet* **The Incredible Flutist**
Symphony No. 2

Poulenc, Francis (1889-1963) — **The History of Babar the Elephant**

Prokofiev, Serge (1891-1953) — **Classical** *Symphony in D Major, op. 25*
Excerpts from the ballet **Romeo and Juliet,** *op. 64*
Lieutenant Kije, *Orchestral Suite, op. 60*
Peter and the Wolf, *Orchestral Fairy Tale for Children, op. 67*
Summer Day *Children's Suite for Little Symphony, op. 65B*
Symphony No. 5, op. 100
The Love for Three Oranges

Purcell, Henry (1659-95) — *"Prelude and Death of Dido," from* **Dido and Aeneas** *(Arranged by Dimitri Mitropoulos))*

Rachmaninoff, Sergei (1873-1943) — *Symphony in E minor, No. 2, op. 27*
Symphony in A minor, No. 3, op. 44
Symphonic Dances for Orchestra, op. 45
Symphonic Poem, "Die Toteninsel" ("The Isle of the Dead")

Ravel, Maurice (1875-1937)	**Daphnis et Chloé,** Ballet in One Act—Orchestral Excerpts "La Valse," A Choreographic Poem Pavane for a Dead Princess **Ma Mère l'Oye (Mother Goose),** Five Children's Pieces **Rhapsodie espagnole** Suite for Orchestra, **Le Tombeau de Couperin (The Grave of Couperin)**
Respighi, Ottorino (1879-1936)	**Roman Festivals** **The Fountains of Rome** **The Pines of Rome**
Riegger, Wallingford (1885-1961)	Finale from **New Dance** "Dance Rhythms"
Rimsky-Korsakov, Nicholas (1844-1908)	**Capriccio espagnole,** op. 34 Overture, "The Russian Easter," op. 36 Scheherazade, Symphonic Suite after **The Thousand and One Nights,** op. 35 Suite from the opera **Tsar Saltan**
Rossini, Gioacchino (1792-1868)	Overture to **L'Italiana in Algeri (The Italian Woman in Algiers)** Overture to **Semiramide,** melodramma tragico in two acts Overture to **The Barber of Seville,** opera buffa in two acts **Overture to La gazza ladra (The Thieving Magpie)** Overture to **Il Signor Bruschino**
Roussel, Albert (1869-1937)	**Bacchus et Ariane,** Ballet Suite No. 2, op. 43 Symphony in G minor, No. 3, op. 42
Rowley, Alex (1892-1958)	Orchestral Compositions for Children
Saeverud, Harald (1897-)	Symphonies Overtura Appasionata Passacaglia **Suite Lucrezia** Symphonic Dance
Saint-Saëns, Charles Camille (1835-1921)	Bacchanale from **Samson and Delila** **Carnival of the Animals,** Piano Duo Symphonic Poem, **Danse macabre,** op. 40 Symphony in C minor, No. 3, op. 78
Schönberg, Arnold (1874-1951)	Theme and Variations for Orchestra in G minor, op. 43b "Verklaerte Nacht"
Schubert, Franz (1797-1828)	Music from **Rosamunde** Symphony No. 2 in B-flat Major Symphony in C minor, No. 4 (**Tragic**)

Symphony in B-flat Major, No. 5
Symphony in C Major, No. 7
Symphony in B minor, No. 8 (Unfinished)

Schuman, William (1910-)

American Festival Overture
Symphony No. 3
William Billings Overture

Schumann, Robert (1810-56)

Concerto for Piano and Orchestra in A minor, op. 54
Overture to Byron's Manfred, op. 115
Symphony in B-flat Major, No. 1, op. 38
Symphony in C Major, No. 2, op. 61
Symphony in E-flat Major, No. 3 (Rhenish), op. 97
Symphony in D minor, No. 4, op. 120
Symphony in C minor

Scriabin, Alexander (1872-1915)

Prometheus: The Poem of Fire, op. 60
Poem of Ecstasy, op. 54

Shostakovich, Dmitri (1906-75)

Festive Overture
Prelude, Polka, and Dance from the ballet The Golden Age, op. 22
Symphony No. 1, op. 10
Symphony No. 5, op. 47
Symphony No. 6, op. 54
Symphony No. 7, op. 60
Symphony No. 8, op. 65
Symphony No. 9, op. 70

Sibelius, Jean (1865-1957)

Finlandia, Tone Poem for Orchestra, op. 26, no. 7
Nightride and Sunrise, op. 55
Pohjola's Daughter, op. 49
Symphony in E minor, No. 1, op. 39
Symphony in D Major, No. 2, op. 43
Symphony in C Major, No. 3, op. 52
Symphony in A minor, No. 4, op. 63
Symphony in E-flat Major, No. 5, op. 82
Symphony in D minor, No. 6, op. 104
Symphony in C Major, No. 7 (in one movement), op. 105
The Bard, op. 64
The Oceanides, op. 73
The Swan of Tuonela, Legend from the Kalevala, op. 22, no. 3
"Valse triste," op. 44

Siegmeister, Elie (1909-)

"Prairie Legend," A Midwestern Set

Smetana, Bedrich (1824-84)

Overture to the opera The Bartered Bride
Three Dances from The Bartered Bride
Symphonic Poem, "Vltava" ("The Moldau"), from the cycle Má vlast (My Fatherland)

Stamitz, Karl (1745-1801)

70 symphonies

Still, William (1895-)	***In Memoriam: The Colored Soldiers Who Died for Democracy*** ***Plain Chant for America,*** *based on a poem by Katharine Garrison Chapin* Poem for Orchestra Symphonic Poem, ***Old California***
Strauss, Johann (1825-99)	*Overture to the Operetta **Die Fledermaus (The Bat)*** *"Treasure" Waltz from **Der Zigeunerbaron (The Gypsy Baron)***
Strauss, Richard (1864-1949)	***Don Quixote*** *(Introduction, Theme with Variations, and Finale), "Fantastic Variations on a Theme of Knightly Character," op. 35* *Rondo, **Till Eulenspiegel's Merry Pranks,** op. 28* ***Symphonia domestica,** op. 53* *Tone Poem, **Don Juan,** op. 20* ***Ein Heldenleben (A Hero's Life), op. 40***
Stravinsky, Igor (1882-1971)	*Fair Scenes from the Ballet **Petrouchka*** ***Feu d'artifice (Fireworks),** A Fantasy for Orchestra, op. 4* *"Four Norwegian Moods"* ***Ode** in three parts, for orchestra* *Suite from **L'Oiseau de feu (The Firebird)*** *"Circus Polka"*
Taylor, Deems (1885-1966)	*Fantasy, **Circus Day,** op. 18* *Suite, **Through the Looking Glass***
Tchaikovsky, Peter Ilyitch (1840-93)	*"Elegy" and "Waltz" from the Serenade for Strings in C Major, op. 48* *"Francesca da Rimini," Fantasia for Orchestra (after Dante), op. 32* *Marche slave, op. 31* *Overture Fantasy, **Romeo and Juliet*** *Overture, 1812, op. 49* *Suite from the ballet **Le Lac des cygnes** (Swan Lake)* *Suite from the ballet **The Nutcracker,** op. 71A* *Symphony in C minor, No. 2, op. 17* *Symphony in F minor, No. 4, op. 36* *Symphony in E minor, No. 5, op. 64* *Symphony in B minor, No. 6 (**Pathétique**), op. 74* *"Theme and Variations" from Suite No. 3 in G, op. 55*
Thompson, Randall (1899-)	*Symphony in E minor, No. 2*
Thomson, Virgil (1896-)	*Symphony on a Hymn Tune*
Toch, Ernst (1887-1964)	*"Pinocchio," "A Merry Overture"*
Vaughan Williams, Ralph (1872-1958)	***A London Symphony*** ***Pastoral Symphony*** *Symphony in F minor ("No. 4")*

Symphony in D Major ("No. 5")
Symphony in E minor ("No. 6")

Verdi, Giuseppe (1813-1901)
*"Dance of the Nubian Slaves," from **Aida***
*Overture to **La forza del destino (The Force of Destiny)***
*Overture to **Luisa Miller***

Villa-Lobos, Heitor (1881-1959)
6 symphonies
Symphonic poems

Vitali, Tommaso Antonio (1665-1735)
Chaconne (Transcribed for strings and organ by Alfonso Gibilaro)

Wagner, Richard (1813-1883)
A Faust Overture
A Siegfried Idyll
*"Bacchanale" from **Tannhäuser***
*Preludes to Act I and Act III of **Lohengrin***
*Prelude to **Die Meistersinger***
*Prelude and Love Death from **Tristan und Isolde***
*Overture to **The Flying Dutchman***
*Overture to **Tannhäuser***
*Excerpts from **Götterdämmerung***

Walton, William (1902-   )
Overture, "Portsmouth Point"
"Scapino," A Comedy Overture

Weber, Carl Maria von (1786-1826)
*Overture to the opera **Euryanthe***
*Overture to the opera **Der Freischutz***
Overture, "Jubel" ("Jubilee")
*Overture to the opera **Oberon***
Invitation to the Dance

Weinberger, Jaromir (1896-1967)
*Polka and Fugue from the opera **Schwanda***

BOWING TECHNIQUES

Many woodwind, brass, and percussion teachers would like to do a better job of teaching stringed instruments and conducting orchestras. The following four basic classifications of bowing, with examples and descriptions, will strengthen the basic stringed instrument weaknesses and provide a good bowing technique. Abbreviations: ⊓ —down bow; ∨ —up bow; UH—upper half; LH—lower half; WB—whole bow; M—middle; LM—lower middle; UM—upper middle; F—frog; P—point.

1. Legato ⊓ and ∨

   a. All *slurred,* smooth strokes on any part of the bow.

   Example 1:

This may be executed with the whole bow, upper half (UH) or lower half (LH), or middle of the bow (M), depending on the tempo of the passage and the number of notes to be played. In a faster tempo more notes are usually played in one bow than in a slower tempo.

b. Portato—slurred but slightly and smoothly separated strokes on any part of the bow.

Example 2:

This may be executed with the whole bow (WB), upper half (UH) or lower half (LH), or middle of the bow (M), depending on the tempo of the passage and the number of notes to be played. There is a slight separation between the notes. The notes themselves are not too short; otherwise, a staccato effect would be the result.

c. Detaché strokes on all parts of the bow.

Example 3:

Each note is played with either a down or up bow. The notes may be executed on any part of the bow, but the most convenient place in fast tempo is between the point and the middle.

d. Tremolo—very fast, short strokes at the point of the bow. The arm must not tighten. Because of the speed of this stroke, the movements are small and are done entirely by fingers and hand from the wrist.

Example 4:

2. Staccato and ∨

a. Martelé—the bow does not leave the string. Possible on any part of the bow, but preferred on UH.

Example 5:

This is a fast stroke, like the detaché, but with pauses between strokes. Each note is played on a separate bow. It is of the utmost importance that the bow be drawn very fast on each note and that the pauses between the notes be long. It is not necessary to press the bow very strongly on the string. The natural arm weight of the relaxed arm plus a good contact between bow hair and string, through the feeling of the index finger on the bow stick, should be sufficient to produce a well-sounding strong tone. (Note section 5b under "General Remarks," below, discussing the correct point of contact between bow and string.) This stroke gives the impression of energy and vigor. The most convenient place on the bow for the execution of this stroke is the upper half.

b. Firm staccato—possible on any part of the bow, but preferred on UH.

Example 6:

These are short, interrupted notes, with the bow moving in the same direction. Since the notes in this stroke are very short, and the bow expenditure on each note very small, the index finger, moving from its knuckle on the bow stick, is the main power behind each note. The most convenient part of the bow for the execution of the firm staccato is UH to LM. The bow does not leave the string between notes.

c. Flying staccato—the bow leaves the string between notes (bounces).

Example 7:

This is similar to the firm staccato, except that the bow leaves the string between the notes. Because the bow in this stroke is bouncing, the flying staccato has a somewhat lighter character than the firm staccato. In contrast to the firm staccato, very little arm weight is used in the flying staccato. Bow expenditure on each note is very small, the index finger being the main power behind each note, as in the firm staccato. The bow hair is very elastic, and the bow, not being held down on the string by too heavy an arm weight, has a tendency to bounce off the string between notes. The bow is very slightly raised after the first staccato note and bounces back to the string for the following note. This slight impact is usually sufficient to set the bouncing motion for the duration of the entire stroke. Great skill and perfect coordination are required for this stroke to keep the critical bouncing of the bow and the horizontal arm movement directing the stroke in good proportion. Otherwise the stroke sounds uneven. A common fault is that the bow bounces too high off the string. The most convenient part of the bow for execution of this stroke is the upper middle.

d. Picchietato

(1) Heavy

Example 8:

This consists of short, fast, heavy down-bow strokes. The bow is lifted after each down bow and brought back to the frog.

(2) Light

Example 9:

If a lighter tone is desired, this stroke is executed at the lower middle of the bow, using only up bows.

3. Spiccato ⊓ and V

a. Thrown, detached strokes (bouncing off the string, *only in moderate speed*).

Example 10:

This is produced by a small rocking motion of the relaxed arm, allowing the middle of the bow to touch the string at the lowest point of this motion, producing a short note.

 Motion of bow string

This stroke must be practiced very slowly on the A or D string at first, since it is easiest to acquire a well-balanced feeling of the bow arm in a more or less horizontal position. When the stroke becomes faster, the arc of the rocking motion becomes flatter and shorter.

slow   faster   fast

However, the tempo should never exceed the speed in which the player would have to tighten up his arm to execute these movements. At such a speed he would have to change into the springing stroke (3b, below) for the same sound effect. The most convenient place on the bow is the middle when playing moderately loud, the upper middle when playing softly, and the point when playing very softly.

b. Springing, detached strokes (*only in fast speed*).

Example 11:

This is a small detaché with very little bow, executed in the place on the bow where the stick vibrates. The bow hair does not leave the string. This stroke is applied only in fast tempo. The vibrating point of each bow stick varies somewhat but is usually around the middle of the bow.

4. Arpeggio ⊓ and ∨

a. Broken chords across two, three, or four strings, slurred.

Example 12:

A continuous stroke across the strings is always executed with little expenditure of bow. The level of the entire arm changes from string to string. This is done from the shoulder. The most convenient place for execution is the middle of the bow, as in this place all arm movements from the shoulder are kept at a minimum.

b. Passages as above and similar, but off the string.

Example 13:

This is the same as the slurred arpeggio, but executed with a bouncing bow.

General Remarks

1. All strokes must be executed with *minimum effort.*

2. Very often the tempo and the character of the music to be played present the only clues as to the choice of the correct stroke. This is because our notation is limited, and often passages in a fast, light piece of music are notated in the same way as in a slow movement.

Example 15:

Example 14 is in a fast tempo. The character is cheerful and light, and the stroke would be executed with the middle part of the bow bouncing off the string.

Example 15 is slower in tempo, and the sound effect should be somewhat heavier. This stroke would be executed with more expenditure of bow, the bow kept on the string. The dots over the notes are only an indication of a separation between the notes. Both passages are notated in the same manner; the difference lies in the tempo indication and, of course, the general character of the composition. Only *adequate musical background, a good conception of the different styles in music,* and *good taste* will help the player to choose the right stroke.

3. Limitation of space precludes the description of all the possible combinations of different strokes, but a well-calculated and proportioned distribution in the expenditure of the bow is very important in all mixed strokes. For example, *slurred and detached notes:*

   a. Fast tempo

   Example 16:

   b. Slow tempo

   Incorrect bow distribution will always result in either unmusical accents or bad tone.

4. Sharp attacks (SFZ or Fp) are done by pressing the bow on the string *before* commencing the stroke. At the beginning of the stroke, pressure is released and simultaneously the bow is drawn lightly, as described above:

5. Strength and softness of tone, i.e., *forte* and *piano,* are determined by three factors: (1) point of contact between bow hair and string (varying between bridge and fingerboard); (2) speed of bow; (3) arm weight. The arm weight on the bow must be in the right proportion to the speed of the bow, and the point of contact in turn depends upon the bow speed. It is very hard to establish rules here, and experimenting in the right direction will usually give the desired sound effect, but the following rules should be taken as basic principles.

   a. Slow *forte* strokes (slow-moving bow) should be played in the neighborhood of the bridge. The string can withstand more bow pressure in this place, thus producing a strong tone without suppressing the vibrations of the string.

b. Fast *forte* strokes with the whole bow (fast-moving bow) should be played in the neighborhood of the fingerboard. The bow moves fast and the pressure on the string is light. Fast *forte* strokes with half bow (fast-moving bow) are played around the central point, i.e., between the end of the fingerboard and the bridge.

The more tone conscious a player is, the more he/she will experiment with the point of contact, arm weight, and speed of the bow, until finding the desired sound effect. This is a simple introduction to tone production. For further study refer to the excellent book dealing with this specific problem, entitled *The Problem of Tone Production,* by Professor Carl Flesch, published by Carl Fischer, New York.

(This article, on "Bowing Techniques," appeared earlier under the title "How to Use the Bow," in *Orchestra News,* vol. 14, no. 2 [March 1975], pp. 4-5, 15. Used here by permission of the publisher.)

ADDENDUM

Elementary through College and Community Orchestras

3

The Band

Many band libraries in the public schools lack representative literature of the main periods of music history as well as an adequate sampling of the major forms of compositions. The following recommendations contain only the best of literature and are classified for elementary bands (I-II, easy), with appropriate key signatures, rhythmic complexities, and harmonic, melodic, dynamic, and instrumental considerations; junior and senior high school bands (III-IV, medium difficulty), more complex musically and technically (some better high school bands could play grade V literature on occasion); and college, university, and community organizations, most of whom will select the difficult compositions (V-VI).

Although most of the baroque and classic music periods are represented with arrangements, they are tastefully done and highly recommended. Most compositions will take from four to seven minutes for performance. The standard band instrumentation is used throughout these recommendations. Each conductor is encouraged to add compositions on the addendum page as he feels motivated.

ELEMENTARY THROUGH COLLEGE
Grades I and II

BAROQUE PERIOD

| Bach, J. S. | Nowak | Aria ("When Thou Art Near") | Big Bells | II |

A melodic, legato composition that gives the young band an opportunity to produce singing, expressive phrasing. The vital bass line is easy to play in tune, yet is dignified and stately. No particularly exposed parts.

| | Tolmage | *"Come Blessed Peace"* | Sta | II |

Good tonal use of woodwinds. Dynamic variation. Effective for limited instrumentation.

| | Eller | *Three Bach Chorales* | SHB | II |

Full score. Time about 3¾ minutes. No. 1: "Take Courage Now, My Feeble Soul." No. 2: "Then unto God the Lord." No. 3: "O Sacred Head Now Wounded." Well-written arrangement of Bach chorales for young bands. Offers excellent material for chorale style of playing and tuning.

| | Erickson | *Two Marches for Band* | Bourne | II |

Easy keys. No technical problems. Helpful addition for young bands of this style period. Full score.

| | Finlayson | *"Sleepers, Wake"* | Marks | I |

Condensed score. Duration: 2½ minutes. An excellent-sounding Bach chorale arrangement for young bands. Good moving low brass parts.

| Carter, C. | | *Three Pieces in Antique Style* | CF | II |

Consists of motet, canon, and madrigal. Suitable for young bands. Contemporary harmonies in baroque style. Appropriate modal melodic line. No full score.

| Clementi | Johnson | *Passacaglia and Fugue* | CF | II |

Easy, melodious program number for period literature. Good dynamic contrasts. It will challenge a grade II band.

| | Isaac | *Sonatina, op. 36, no. 1* | CF | II |

This piano work makes good material for band. All parts active and challenging for younger bands. Can develop good musicianship and good habits in listening. Has three contrasting movements: *Allegro, Andante, Vivace.* Time: 4½ minutes. No full score.

| Corelli | Gordon | *Sarabande and Gavotte* | Bourne | II |

Colorful and easy. Full score. Good training material.

| Couperin | Gordon | *March from Little Baroque Suite* | CF | I |

Good material. Well edited. Full score.

| Gluck | Gordon | *Two Opera Selections* | EV | II |

These selections are well chosen from *Alceste* and from *Iphigenia in Aulis* ("Chorus"). Both are stately, in moderate tempo, giving no technical problems. Traditional harmonies with many diatonic melodies. Duration: 6¼ minutes. No full score.

| Gordon, Phillip | | *Italian Masters Suite* | Marks | II |

1. "Harvest Echoes" from *The Seasons,* by Vivaldi

2. "Slow Dance," by Corelli

3. "Country Round," by Scarlatti

The Italian melody permeates this suite, taken from the baroque masters. Rhythmic vitality throughout.

| Handel | Beeler | *Air and Bourrée* | Ru | II |

From the *Water Music*. Excellent for junior high band. Interesting moments in all parts. Key changes twice; also tempo changes from *Andante* to *Allegro vivo*.

| _____ | Conley | *"The Harmonious Blacksmith"* | Kend | II |

Virtually no problems in this familiar music arranged for young bands. Short passages for brass and woodwinds, otherwise scored *Tutti*. Full score. Performance time: 3½ minutes.

| _____ | Gordon | *Music for Saint Cecilia's Day* | Mills | II |

Minuet and March, with contrast in color. Interest in all parts. Variety in articulation and tempo. Time: 2¼ minutes.

| _____ | Gordon | *Little Handel Suite* | Remick | II |

Excellent. Three-movement suite for young band (fast, slow, fast). Second movement colorful. Good trumpet section needed. Third movement in staccato style. Full score.

| _____ | Harris | *Larghetto from Concerto Grosso* | Bourne | II |

Good for intermediate level. Interesting parts for all, especially low brass and percussion. Ending rather abrupt. Articulation problems for clarinets. Full score.

| Karg-Elert | Hastings | *Two Chorales* | Witmark | II |

Good chord progressions, with excellent suspensions. Equally good warm-up, developing ensemble balance.

| Lasso | Gardner | *"Echo Song"* | Sta | II |

Scored for band with an "echo" choir of three trumpets to twelve performers. Parts are simple, yet need careful study for balance, intonation, and rhythmic accuracy. Time: 2 minutes. No full score.

| Lawes | Gordon | *Sarabande from Little Baroque Suite* | CF | I |

English dance tune. Generally well arranged, but scored a little thin. Full score.

| Monteverdi | Irons | *"Let Death Now Come"* | Ru | II |

From opera *L'Arianna*. Muted brass. No technical problems. Four-line score.

| Morley | McLinn | *Two Madrigals* | Pro-Art | II |

Simple but clever. Characteristic English folk songs set in the manner of a fugue. Rhythmic problems, but remains choice composition. Condensed score.

| Palestrina | Harvey | *"Adoramus te"* | EV | II |

Emphasis on tone quality and interpretation. Challenging because all trombone ranges are a little high. Few technical problems. Full score.

Purcell   Gordon   *Airs from the Theatre*   SHB   II

Five-line conductor's score. A well-arranged band number of Purcell's music. Well suited for junior high students; offers good training material from this period of musical composition.

_____   Gordon   *"Song of Victory"*   Bourne   II

Well edited. Interesting for all. Clear three-part form. Colorful, marchlike. Challenging. Outstanding. Full score.

Rameau   Gordon   *Two Courtly Dances*   Bourne   II

Thinly scored; remains interesting for all. Third clarinet does not have to play above the break. Full score.

Susato   Gordon   *Rondo from Little Baroque Suite*   CF   I

Dance tune from baroque period. Full score.

Telemann   Gordon   *"Beau Galant"*   SHB   II

Colorful and interesting. Excellent for use of dynamics, phrasing, and tempo changes. Full score.

CLASSICAL PERIOD

Cherubini   Landes   *"Lacrimosa" from Requiem Mass in C minor*   II

A good study in attacks, releases, and dynamic control. Also good for correct breathing and intonation. Tempo slow and unvarying, but exciting because of the sudden changes in harmony. Time: 2½ minutes. Full score.

Haydn   Kiser   *Minuet from* **Surprise** *Symphony*   LEO   II

Most voices move with good interest, except bass and percussion. Will sound well with a band of medium instrumentation. A safe selection, if moving eighth notes have already been introduced.

_____   North   *Minute and Trio from* **Surprise** *Symphony*   Bo. Hawkes   II

No technical difficulties. Good orchestration.

Jackson   *"Three Classic Miniatures"*   War   II

Good arrangement of pieces by Haydn, Telemann, and Purcell. Opportunity for brass and woodwind choirs to work separately. Good introductory literature for the classic style.

Mozart, W. A.   Beeler   *Adagio and Allegro from Viennese Sonatina*   Han   II

Good, easy piece for grade II band.

_____   Phillips   *Andantino*   Wn   I

This arrangement may be used in the following ways: (1) flute solo with band accompaniment; (2) featuring flute section with band accompaniment; (3) as a straight band arrangement. A fine piece for the young flutist, yet plenty of activity for the entire band.

| | Beeler | *Menuetto and Trio from Symphony No. 36 in C* | Ru | II |

A good introduction into the classical era. Mozart's graceful melodies, direct harmony, and perfect form will enlarge the musical scope of the players. All parts well within the range of first- or second-year players.

| | Lake | *Minuet in E-flat* | ODC | II |

Good cross-cueing. Technically easy. Good piece for elementary or junior high.

| | Taylor | **The Magic Flute** *Selections* | CF | II |

Three melodies from the opera. A good arrangement for this age level. Not too thick, and technically easy.

| Telemann | Gordon | "Beau Galant" | Summy-Bir | II |

Harmonically reserved: special opportunities for phrasing and articulation. Lower parts for reeds and brass interesting and not too active. Time: 2½ minutes.

ROMANTIC PERIOD

| Beethoven | Tolmage | "Hymn of Brotherhood" | Sta | II |

From Beethoven's Ninth Symphony. No technical problems. Good for elementary or junior high, but overbandstrated.

| | Finlayson | "Moonlight" | Bo. Hawkes | II |

From the first movement of the *Moonlight* Sonata. A good piece for junior high. Well edited, with a solid sound and not too much doubling.

| | North | *Two Songs by Beethoven* | Bo. Hawkes | II |

"Love Song" and "Creation's Hymn." No technical difficulty. Good, solid sound. Full chords. Junior high or elementary.

| Grieg | Sears | "Heart Wounds" | FR | II |

Good material for phrasing, tuning, and expressive playing. The lovely melody is scored in full, rich sounds. The percussion includes timpani and cymbals. Time: 4½ minutes. Full score.

| Mendelssohn | Gordon | *Three Mendelssohn Chorales* | Bourne | II |

Full score. No. 1: "To God on High Be Thanks and Praise." No. 2: "Cast Thy Burden upon the Lord." No. 3: "O Thou, the True and Only Light." Well arranged for band, with good cross-cueing so it can be played by small bands with limited instrumentation.

| | Gordon | *Three Mendelssohn Chorales* | Bourne | II |

Sturdy, vital harmonization. Not chromatically or contrapuntally active. First and third chorales from *St. Paul* oratorio; second from *Elijah*. Condensed score.

| Offenbach | Beeler | *Barcarolle from* **Tales of Hoffman** | CF | II |

Well arranged for young bands. Appealing melodic material. Good training material for legato and staccato style. Time: 2¼ minutes.

| Saint-Saëns | Stouffer | *"Alleluia"* | Belwin | I |

From *Christmas Oratorio.* Easy, flowing music, with interesting dynamics.

| Stravinsky | Wilson | *Berceuse from* **Firebird** *Suite* | TP | II |

Effectively scored for the instruments that best express the mood of the *Firebird.* Therefore, tubas, trombones, and lower cornets have little and drums do not play. Good for rest of band. Time: 2 minutes. Full score.

CONTEMPORARY PERIOD

| Abbot, G. | | *"Elmira," Concert March* | CF | II |

Traditional march form. Very melodic. Rather thick, but worth playing. Three-line score.

| Akers, H. | | *Allegro, Adagio, Alleluia* | CF | I |

Melodically easy and interesting. Good training material for young band. Three-line score.

| _____ | | *"Snow Mountain"* | Kjos | I |

Traditional overture style and form, well bandstrated. Good use of band's sonorities. Not thickly scored. Four-line score.

| Bartók | Gordon, P. | *From* **The Children's Album** | EV | II |

Two short movements, each with identical style and tempo. Almost no dissonance. Scoring light and delicate. Exciting dialogue between contrasting instruments.

| Bennett, D. | | *Palomar Overture* | Mills | II |

Uses timpani to good advantage. Easy progression. Good contrasting color. Full score. Time: 3 minutes.

| Berryman, J. | | *"Colonel McCain"* | BS | II |

A very easy 2/4 march, with two repeated trios. The counter-melody is strong and the woodwinds are given quick tempo. Time: 2 minutes.

| Birstahler, E. | | *Deep Water Overture* | PAU | I |

Traditional form. Very melodic and well arranged. Takes good flute section for this level, and above average musical value. Five-line score.

| Britten | Barnes | *"Danish Patrol"* | SHB | II |

Eight-line conductor's score. Written in march style, based on Danish folk songs. Good program number.

| Buchtel, F. | | *Tampico Overture* | Kjos | II |

A light overture in three movements: *Maestoso, Beguine,* and *March.* Well balanced in its difficulty. Time: 3 minutes.

March form. Good use of the idiom. Not too thick. Some nice effects, as mutes and glissando. Rhythm is in the jazz idiom. Unusual use of the form. Three-line score.

_____   *"La Nuit" ("The Night")*   Witmark   II

Quite melodic: Three movements. Good band series music. Time: 2½ minutes. Full score.

Caneva, E.   *Suite España, "La Favorita"*   Leonard   II

Interesting Spanish rhythm (habanera). Good full sound. Band will enjoy performing this selection.

Conley, L.   *"Abendlied" ("Bedtime*   Kend   II
                                       Story")

Melodic concert piece for young band; good variety in sound; scoring safe; some meter changes. Time: 2¼ minutes.

Dalby, J. P.   *"Islands of the Coronados"* Summy-Bir   I

Overture form. Requires strong flute section. Melodic line is good, as is the arrangement. Four-line score.

Davis, A.   *Welsh Folk Suite*   Ludwig   II

Three movements. Simple scoring, but requires careful balancing. Good use of the idiom. Chimes required for second movement. Careful articulation needed in last movement. Three-line score.

Erickson, F.   *"Legendary Air"*   Bourne   I

Well written for band idiom. Interesting contrasts of dark brass color with bright color. High musical value.

Eyman, D.   *"Dance Duo"*   PAU   II

Waltz style. Beguine rhythm in second section. Well scored for band. Avoids stylistic clichés. Average musical value. Three-line score.

Finlayson, W.   *"Little Prelude"*   Bo. Hawkes   I

Scored with alternated woodwind and brass colors. Nice use of sonorities at this level. Melodically interesting.

Gillette   *Legende Overture*   Kjos   II

Condensed score. Well-written overture, with two principal themes developed throughout the work. Good material for junior high bands, with few technical problems, but yet offers fine training and developing of musicianship through playing good quality, easy music.

Gordon, P.   *"Bright Dawn"*   Han   I

Traditional overture form. Fresh treatment of material; very playable. Four-line score.

_____   *Canticle for Band*   Mills   II

A little waltz that offers a slightly bigger challenge. Full instrumentation. Passages that move are based on scales. The large instruments are less active. Time: 1⅔ minutes.

| | | "Prelude on an Odd Rhythm" | Bourne | II |

In 5/4 meter, catchy, and designed to unusual rhythm. Time: 2½ minutes.

| Grundman, C. | "Diversion" | Bo. Hawkes | II |

A delightful number, with interesting parts for everyone. Fanfare—exchange between high brass, woodwinds, and low brass.

| Isaac, M. | "Festival Holiday" | CF | II |

Traditional overture form. Thickly scored, with some interesting harmonies in last section. Average musical value. Full score.

| Jackson, L. | *Little English Suite* | War | II |

Suite in three movements: *Con moto, Andante,* and *Moderato.* Good for octave intonation between woodwinds and low brass. Section for cornet duet. Last movement good for development of accents and staccato styles.

| Kepner, F. | "Medieval Tournament" | SCH | II |

Very challenging musically. Meter interesting: 7/4. Some use of modal harmonies. Brass section must be adequate. Unusual work for this level. Three-line score.

| Kinyon, J. | *Creole Suite* | Bourne | I |

Thin texture, but interesting scoring. High melodic value. Last movement vigorous and harmonically interesting. Three-line score.

| Minelli, C. | *Ballad for Winds* | Bourne | II |

Big sounds, chords, and a great challenge for the players. Many tempo changes will keep the student alert. He will have to watch the conductor. Condensed score.

| Morrissey, J. | "Little Sports Car" | Han | I |

Harmonically in the modern idiom. Rhythmically monotonous. Fills a need for program material on this level of difficulty. Full score.

| Nyquist, M. | "Parade Precision" | Sum | II |

A 6/8 march for modified instrumentation. Single parts, written *divisi,* are provided for horns and trombones. Good material for parade or football. Time: 2¾ minutes.

| Osterling, E. | "Jolly Cobbler" | Ludwig | I |

Skillfully orchestrated. Solo cornet must be adequate. Good articulation study. Basically program music.

| Peterson, T. | "Lament" | Kend | I |

Easy baritone solo. Harmonically interesting and well written, with long phrases. Three-line score.

| Prokofiev | Parker | *Two Pieces from Summer Day Suite* | Leeds | II-III |

No full score. Two pieces are "Morning" and "March" from *Summer Day* Suite. This arrangement keeps the style of Prokofiev and is well scored for band. Some delicate spots, but well within average second-year band's ability. Good training material for light, delicate style of playing.

Reed, A.   *Chorale Prelude in*   Han   II
                                E minor

Slow, sustained work. Good use of tone colors. Pleasing melodic style. Some doubling could be omitted. Excellent training material. Three-line score.

Thomas, P.   *"Festival Day"*   Ru   I

Cornet solo in slow section. Traditional overture form. Harmonically uninteresting, but melodically good. Rhythms are easy; sections are too short. Four-line score.

Verrall, J.   *"Holiday Moods"*   CF   I

Modern treatment of material. Interesting modulatory passages. Short contrapuntal sections very interesting. Three-line score.

Whitney, M.   *Ceremonial March*   Marks   II

Duration: 1⅔ minutes. Evokes image of a stately processional. Broad sonorities and strong melodic pulse demonstrate the best qualities of a concert march. Excellent for young bands of limited experience.

Grades III and IV

BAROQUE PERIOD

Bach, J.S.   Land   *Air from Suite in*   Law-Gould   III
                                D Major

Good editing. Would require careful interpretation. Trombone parts should have been given to baritone. Color combinations excellent. Full score.

_____   Bennett   *"Bach Bouquet"*   CF   III

Four light compositions. Good melodic lines. Interesting to all. Simple but effective harmonies. Well suited for the band. No full score.

_____   Goldman-   *Fantasia in B Major*   Mercury/   III
                Leist   Presser

Grade V music but completely playable by grade III group. Requires little technical skill and only average ranges, but will demand the utmost in musicianship and style. No full score.

_____   Whitney   *"In Thee Is Gladness"*   Kend   IV

In two parts. Technically difficult. Part I used for development of tone. Part II in fugal style. Interesting treatment of parts. Three-line score.

_____   Moehlmann   *Prelude and Fugue in*   Remick/WB   IV
                                B-flat Major

Interesting for high school band. Articulation problems. Challenging for all. Full score.

_____   Moehlmann   *Prelude and Fugue in*   FitzSimons IV
                                B-flat minor

Excellent. Well edited. Colorful treatment of individual parts and sections. Full score.

| | Conley | *Prelude and Fugue in E-flat Major* | Kend | III |

Worthwhile band music for group of average ability. Rare example where fugue is easier than prelude. Makes maximum use of instruments. Suitable contest or concert material. Full score. Time: 5 minutes.

| | Moehlmann | *Prelude and Fugue in G minor* | Remick/WB | IV |

Demanding in articulation and clarity of rhythm. Excellent. Full score.

| | Gillette | *Short Classics for Band: Sarabande* | CF | III |

Well edited. Could be played by class II band.

| Crüger | Caillet | *"Now Thank We All Our God"* | Bo. Hawkes | IV |

Arrangement published for chorus, band, and orchestra, combined or separate. Little editing. Thin but colorful score. Full score.

| Frescobaldi | Johnson | *Galliard and Courante* | Ru | III |

Proper instrumentation needed for result to be colorful and expressive. Parts move in blocks, with enough melodic contrast to keep interest. Three-line score.

| Handel | Osterling | *An Occasional Suite* | Ludwig | IV |

Three numbers from the *Occasional Oratorio*. Excellent for growth and development of tone quality and interpretation. Fugue in third part. Full score.

| | Anderson | *Baroque Suite* | Pro-Art | III |

Three selections taken from the *Water Music*. Few editorial guides. Good for introduction of baroque literature. Technically difficult and challenging. Six-line score.

| | Leidzen | *"Care Selve," from* **Atalanta** | AMP | IV |

Written in G-flat. Effective use of woodwind unison.

| | Mairs | *Prelude and Fugue in D minor* | Marks | IV |

From Concerto No. 5. Simplified edition, but very effective. Rhythmic problems in prelude. Technical ability required. Good woodwind color combinations. No full score.

| | Gillette | *Short Classics for Band: Gavotte* | CF | III |

Excellent, well edited. Full score.

| | Anderson | *"Song of Jupiter"* | Mills | III |

Aria "Where E'er You Walk," from oratorio *Semele*. Good version for easy high school or upper junior high. Might be used for program and period music. No full score.

| Kirnberger | Osterling | *Baroque Suite* | Ludwig | III |

Delightful music of the late 18th century. Rhythmically refreshing. Time: 3½ minutes. Full score.

| Latham | | "Il Pasticco" | CF | IV |

In the form and style of the Italian overture of the early 18th century. Three movements. A patching together of arias from different operas. Well written, colorful, moving, and interesting for all. No full score.

| Marcello | Gillette | Short Classics for Band: "Psalm 18" | CF | III |

Title suggests sacred theme, but piece more like a march. No technical difficulties, but interpretation necessary. Rich in tone color. Full score.

| Palestrina | Harvey | "Sanctus" | EV | IV |

Included with "Adoramus Te." Tessitura high for woodwinds. Full score.

| _____ | Gordon | Three Hymns | Bourne | III |

Parts independent and interesting. Rich contrasting tone colors. Use of five parts. Based on church modes. Full score.

| Purcell | Gordon | Air and March | Bourne | III |

Problems for lower brass. Thick scoring in some parts. Meter and tempo changes. In manner of English folk songs. Full score.

| _____ | Gardner | Fanfare and Rondo | Sta | III |

Well edited. Delightful and impressive—woodwinds dominate. Three-line score.

| _____ | Walker | Suite from **Dido and Aeneas** | Kjos | IV |

Three movements: (1) Overture; (2) Prelude for the Witches; (3) Echo Dance. First two movements technically within reach of good high school band. Third movement, "Echo Dance," has rapid 16th-note passages, but these are mostly scalewise and can be worked out. Would be an interesting musical experience for high school band members.

| Rameau | Mattis | Rigaudon from **Dardanus** | CF | III |

Excellent study in contrapuntal style. Interpretation requires attention. Contrasting program number, reminiscent of Bach in style but themes are less restricted. Full score.

| Tenaglia | Gillette | Short Classics for Band: Aria | CF | III |

Melodic, interesting for all; well edited, legato and appealing. Full score.

CLASSICAL PERIOD

| Beethoven | | Ecossaise | AMP | III |

Written for band in 1810. No technical difficulties. Almost same as Polonaise.

| _____ | Revelli | Military March in D | G. Schirmer | IV |

A good piece, well edited. No tempo marks in the music, but the full score has a paragraph explaining the music and gives ideas how to perform it as originally done.

| | Leidzen | *Polonaise* | AMP | III |

Easy composition, originally written for band in 1810. No technical difficulties except for trill in clarinet, which would be played as eight 16th notes in moderate time. Strongly recommended for junior high and class C high school.

| Beethoven and Bach, J.S. | Erickson | *Two Marches for Band* | Bourne | III |

No technical difficulties. Frequent dotted 8th- and 16th-note passages. Full score.

| Duncombe, W. | | *Early English Suite* | Bo. Hawkes | III |

Contains "Trumpet Minuet," "Sonatina" (which features high woodwind parts—not difficult), "Minuet" for woodwind choir, and "Hunting Jig," which is typical and uses full group. Would be very interesting. Full score.

| Haydn | Logan | *Introduction and Minuetto* | SCH | III |

An easy arrangement from Symphony No. 102.

| | | *Largo and Minuetto from Symphony No. 88* | Bourne | IV |

Can sound more difficult than it is because of 16th-note runs that are easily executed. No high notes for clarinet or trumpet.

| | Riley | *March for the Prince of Wales* | CF | III |

Full score. An original march written by Haydn for wind band. This edition taken directly from photostats of original manuscript. Harmonies not altered, but parts reconstructed and others supplied to fit the instrumentation of the modern band.

| | De Rubertis | **Orlanda Paladino** *Overture* | Remick | IV |

Sixteenth-note triplets. Good editing. Some rhythmic problems. A good high school number.

| Jadin, L. | Schaefer | *Symphony for Band* (1974) | Shawnee | IV-V |

Basically in the style of Mozart. Single movement, original band piece reconstructed for symphonic band. Good parts for all voices. Very worthwhile addition to the library.

| Mozart | Barnes | *"Alleluia"* | Ludwig | IV |

Arranging excellent. Score thin enough to express delicacy of original soprano solo.

| | Moehlmann | **Cosi fan tutte** *Overture* | FitzSimons | IV |

Technically easy. Watch interpretation of grace notes.

| | Tolmage | *"Hymn of Praise"* | Sta | III |

Technically simple. Good for elementary and junior high.

| | Barnes | **The Impresario** *Overture* | Ludwig | IV |

The editing has not changed the piece. Horns have syncopation that needs to be watched seriously. Some articulation problems for cornet. Full score.

| | Barnes | **La finta giardiniera** *Overture* | Ludwig | IV |

Eighth-note runs. Keep low woodwinds busy with 16th- and 32nd-note patterns. Over-edited. Full score.

Needs careful blend, balance, and dynamic control. Choice music in every respect. Ideal learning material. Deeply in demand to fill need for simple, expressive, melodic material in band literature. Time: 6⅓ minutes. Full score.

ROMANTIC PERIOD

Brahms   Guenther   *Two Choral Preludes*   Summy-Bir   III

1. "A Lovely Rose in Blooming"

2. "O God, Thy Holy God"

Originally written for organ. Challenging rhythms; interesting horn part. No full score, but provides director notes.

D'Indy   Powell   *Themes from **Symphony** on a French Mountain Air*   Pro-Art   III

Full score. Here is an impellingly beautiful and stirring composition which is highly representative of the later French romantic period. The band arrangement keeps much of the original flavor and has all of the principal themes.

Gallon   Fayesille   *"Deux pièces pour musique d'harmonie"*   Ludwig   III

Modern composition in romantic style. Two short, descriptive, impressionistic pieces. There are dissonances, such as major 7ths and 11ths and minor 9ths. Melodically expressive and romantic. Voice leading easy; ranges not extreme. Unusual combinations of instruments and new color. Time: 4¾ minutes.

Grief   Davis   *"Notturno"*   Alexander   III

Sensitive music, nicely scored for band. Hard fingering combinations for upper reeds. Expressive styling with rubato. Condensed eight-line score only. Time: 2½ minutes.

Kistler   Barr   *Prelude to Act Three of the Opera **Kunihild***   Ludwig   III

Somewhat Wagnerian in style, with slow, sustained chromatic lines building to dramatic climaxes. Beautiful, expressive melodies throughout.

Mendelssohn   Shepard   *Ruy Blas Overture*   Pro-Art   IV

A good high school group could play and enjoy this fine literature. Would require solid clarinet section with facility and stamina to handle violin transcriptions.

_____ Barnard   *Symphony No. 3* (Scotch)   Ru   IV

Interesting and challenging work. Lies within comfortable tessitura of instrumentation. Rhythmic challenge. Lacks full score.

Meyerbeer   Lake   *"Coronation March"*   CF   IV

Well-scored work; challenging in phrasing.

Moussorgsky   Buehlman   *Coronation Scene from **Boris Godunov***   Ru   IV

Dramatic and powerful, with optional extra parts for antiphonal brass quartets or choirs. Upper woodwinds must move with facility; good strength required in baritones, trombones, and basses. Frequent rhythm and meter changes, with both staccato and legato playing. Eight-line score provided. Time: 6 minutes.

| | Eyman | *"Great Gate of Kiev"* | Belwin | III |

Condensed eight-line score. Approximate playing time: 4¼ minutes. A fine transcription that lends itself well to the band. Well arranged for band, and offers few technical problems for average junior high band. Written with good full sound that offers excellent tonal development.

| Puccini | Cacavas | **Madame Butterfly** *Suite* | Fox | III |

A concert suite for band. Scored well; would give students a chance to become acquainted with opera and like it.

| Ravel | Gray | *Extracts from* **Mother Goose** *Suite* | EV | III |

An effective transcription of the "Lullaby of the Sleeping Beauty" and the "Enchanted Garden." Requires full, mature tone from flutes and oboes. Other parts easy. Impressionistic style. Time: 4½ minutes.

| Rimsky-Korsakov | Clay | *Coronation Scene from* **Ivan the Terrible** | Marks | III |

Rich and powerful scoring. Gives low brass good opportunity to be heard to advantage. Firm and full throughout.

| Saint-Saëns | Lake | *"March militaire française"* | CF | III |

Interesting and colorful work. Would be challenging for average high school band.

| Schumann | Vitto | *"Evening Song"* | HD | IV |

Extremely short selection. Might cause intonation and phrasing problems because of slow, sustained, expressive lines. No full score.

| Strauss, J. | Duthoit | *"Acceleration Waltz"* | Chappell | IV |

Contrasting rhythms, but difficult as a waltz. Uninteresting horn part. No full score. Time: 8½ minutes.

| Strauss, R. | Thomas | *Themes from* **Thus Spake Zarathustra** | J. W. Pepper | III |

Only brief statements from original, but dramatic and effective program material. Melodic line sustained; requires good breath support and mature tone quality.

| Tchaikovsky | Cheyette | *"A Legend"* | Fox | III |

Easy, but effective. Full of melody. Brings out legato and staccato playing with variety of rhythmic patterns. Time: 2¼ minutes.

| | Gardner | *"Andantino Marziale"* | SUM | III |

Challenging work. Uses muted trumpets and trombones. Interesting and colorful selection. No full score.

| | Gates | *"Humoresque"* | TP | III |

An old tune, safely scored and in a good key, with audience and player appeal. Time: 2¾ minutes. No full score.

| Wagner | Moore | *Wagner Showcase: March from **Tannhäuser; Rienzi** Overture; "Evening Star" from **Tannhäuser;** Prelude to **Die Meistersinger*** | Mercury | III-IV |

Good, challenging study in dynamics, phrasing, and musical interpretation. Challenging horn parts. Lacks full score.

| Weber | Leidzen | *"Trauersinfonie" (Funeral music on themes from Euryanthe)* | AMP | III |

Easy, colorful moving parts. Arranged well within tessitura.

CONTEMPORARY PERIOD

| Addison, J. | | *"Reach for the Sky"* | Mills | IV |

A noisy march fantasy that employs both 3/4 and 4/4 meter in fast grand march style. Requires better than average band—better than a quick look at the score would imply. A dramatic and exciting ending. Time: 3 minutes.

| Akers, H. | | *"The Showman March"* | CF | III |

Written very much in style of best Alexander marches, even to choice of A-flat and D-flat for concert keys. Good break strain and powerful last trio demand good technique. Time: 2 minutes.

| Anderson, L. | | *"Pyramid Dance"* | Mills | IV |

Uses many chromatic passages. Not recommended for easy music, since it requires a fairly good band. Uses accidentals rather freely throughout. Time: 3 minutes.

| Antonini | Cacavas | *"World's Fair March"* | Bourne | IV |

Rousing concert march. Solo passes through upper and lower voices. Interesting rhythmic figures and good dynamic contrasts; scored for interest in all parts.

| Bartók | Leidzen | *"An Evening in the Village"* | AMP | III |

A quiet medley, dissonant and descriptive. Requires graceful and careful interpretation which emphasizes balance and blend. Time: 2¾ minutes.

| _____ | Leidzen | *"Bear Dance"* | AMP | IV |

Excellent program material plus good arrangement. Gives unique opportunities for study of proper accents irrespective of bar lines and for experience in playing without key signatures. Time: 2 minutes.

| Bennett, R. R. | | *"March of Might"* | Chappell | III |

A concert march taken from NBC's *Nightmare in Red.* Has overwhelming power and tonal depth. Not at all difficult. Time: 3½ minutes.

| Cacavas, J. | | *"Burnished Brass"* | CF | III |

A concert march. Brass feature set in 6/8 with interesting contemporary band sound. Appealing to band and audience.

72

"The Gallant Boulevardier"   Bourne   III

Work features all the instruments in the band; provides opportunities for musical shading. Excellent concert or contest material. Time: 4 minutes.

Praeludium for Band   Bourne   III

Contrapuntal sections are alternated with modern chordal sections. D-flat key signature in middle section will offer some problems. Technique simple; balance and phrasing emphasized. Will require much practice, but worthwhile for programming.

Carter, C.   *Introduction and Caprice*   Bar   III

Attractive and appealing tonal composition, with two contrasting movements that are not challenging in technical demands or tessitura. Audiences enjoy this refreshing band sound.

Motet for Band   Han   IV

Polyphonic; emphasis on blend and moving voices. Requires good intonation, tone quality, and balance. Range and technique are easy. Good practice material for high levels. No full score.

Overture for Winds   Bourne   IV

ABA form; takes good technique in woodwinds. Full score.

Symphonic Overture   CF   IV

Of considerable rhythmic interest; ABA form, with flute introducing second theme. Both contrapuntal and homophonic textures, in a contemporary setting.

Coates, Duthoit   "The Dam Busters"   Chappell   III

More than the usual staccato brass playing; excellent countermelodies for trombones and baritones. Has a powerful and impressive close. Time: 4 minutes.

Conley, L.   "Antiphony"   Kendor   III-IV

Relatively easy contemporary; antiphonal interplay between woodwind and brass sections. Mood is meant to be religious. Horn solo imitating Gregorian chant style. Three sections.

Davis   Werle   "Carol of the Drum"   Ludwig   III

Easy melodic line progressing through all instruments; good Christmas or holiday piece. No full score. Time: 2 minutes, 25 seconds.

Welsh Folk Suite   Ludwig   III

1. "Jenny Jones"
2. "All through the Night"
3. "Men of Harlech"

Challenge in phrasing, technique, and balance. Each tune requires different style. Range in brass challenging—trumpet A, trombone G. But not difficult. Good program material.

Dello Joio, N.   *Scenes from* **The Louvre**   Marks   IV

Full score; five scenes. Original scoring; program notes. Solo work throughout, and a very interesting percussion part. Challenging, but could be performed by a good junior high band.

	Variants on a Medieval Tune	Marks	IV

Tune is "Good Christian Men, Rejoice." A distinctive addition to serious band repertoire. Take grade V for detail. Calls for bass trombone. All parts carry equal musical and technical challenge. Five percussion parts require timpani, bass drum, snare drum, cymbals, glockenspiel, chimes, xylophone, and tam-tam. Five contrasting variations. Full score. Time: 11½ minutes.

Erickson, F.	*Balladair*	Bourne	III

Technique easy. Slow, with emphasis in melodic and countermelodic lines. Harmony modern, using jazz progressions in spots. Performance requires control and endurance for class III.

	Fantasy for Band	Bourne	IV

Antiphonal effects throughout require thoughtful balance. Parallel harmonies offer modern style effect. Technical requirements easy for class IV.

	Festive Winds	Summit	III

There is more sophistication in harmony in this composition than in many of Erickson's works. Choice program music. Many passages quite subdued and not dramatic. Contrasting meters.

	First Symphony for Band	Bourne	IV

Highly modal in flavor. Slightly dissonant, melodic, and appealing. Has frequent shifts of mood and tonal centers. Worthwhile music. Full score. Time: 9⅔ minutes.

	"Presidio" (Symphonic March)	Belwin	III

Contemporary idiom with interesting sound. Repeated background of quartet could take interest out of lower brass parts. Some rhythmic challenges in upper parts. Modified nine-line condensed score, all in concert pitch.

Eyman, D.	*Beguine for Band*	PAU	IV

Difficult rhythm; good melodies; interesting horn part. No full score.

Farrell, K.	*"Thunder West" March*	Belwin	III

Brilliantly scored, with equal melodic and harmonic interest. A good piece for concert or contest. Time: 3¼ minutes.

Forsblad, L.	*"Edifice Structure for Band"*	Bar	III

A tone poem that stays within moderate range for band, that students appreciate and enjoy. Voice leading superb, and symphonic sound attractive.

Giannini, V.	*Fantasia for Band*	Colombo	III

Full score. An original work for band that has many rich and beautiful textures not often heard in band music. Not a difficult piece technically, but requires sensitive musicianship and control of tone and balance. Should be playable by groups from good junior high band level on up; offers really interesting tonal experience in new and out-of-the-ordinary harmonies. A worthwhile piece of music for band.

Gillis, D.   *The Land of Wheat*   Kjos   IV

Work is in six sections, each published separately. Parts are included for contrabass clarinet, alto oboe (English horn), harp, and piano. Overall time of the suite: 21½ minutes. Six sections include "The Land and the People," "The Planting," "The Fields in Summer," "The Lazy Days," "Thrashing Bee," and "Harvest Celebration."

_____   *Symphony No. 5½*   Bo. Hawkes   IV

A good exercise in tone, balance, and control for entire band. Key signature of five flats gives interesting reading. Technique easy. Program interest only in showing contrasts of tone quality.

Giovannini   Robinson   *Fanfare, Chorale, and Fugue* SMC   IV

Variety in form and refreshing scoring for band makes this composition a must. Sounds more difficult than it really is. Contrasts in coloring, dynamics, moods, and form make this selection not only educationally sound but good for concerts.

_____   Robinson   *Overture in B-flat*   Fox   IV

Contemporary harmony and rhythm; one tempo throughout. Opening has energetic brass fanfares answered by legato woodwinds. Contrasting sustained melodic section most expressive.

Gordon, P.   *"Ceremony at Margate"*   CF   III-IV

A new and pleasing grand march. An appealing melodic line. Here is a new way to eliminate the old standby "Pomp and Circumstance." Time: 3 minutes.

_____   *"Merry England Fantasy"*   SUM   III

Emphasis on balance; technique easy. Based on two *not* well known English folk songs. Charming, well bandstrated. Good program material for grade III.

_____   *"Prelude on an Odd*   Bourne   III
                            Rhythm"

Technique easy, emphasis upon playing 5/4 time. Most measures built on an alternating count of two, then three. Antiphonal effects offer opportunity to emphasize balance as section answers choir. Percussion featured throughout. Would make a novel addition to program.

Grainger   Kent   *"Irish Tune from County*   CF   IV
                        Derry" and "Shepherds Hey"

First section, on "Irish Tune," offers some beautiful sustained brass choir work, followed by woodwind choir. "Shepherds Hey" much more demanding technically and rhythmically. Good woodwind section required. Important solos in oboe, alto sax, etc. Because of very little doubling of parts, every section must be strong enough to carry its part.

Grundman, C.   *American Folk Rhapsody*   Bo. Hawkes   IV
                        No. 1

Full score. Based on American folk songs. Offers good opportunities for development of solo performance by first chair players.

_____   *"The Black Knight"*   Bo. Hawkes   III

Presents tone picture with contrasting moods. Full scoring, with interplay of reeds and brass. Does not require full instrumentation. Melodic line for horns good. Exceptional percussion parts. Time: 3 minutes, 10 seconds.

| ——————— | Fantasy on American Sailing Songs | Bo. Hawkes | III |

Condensed and full scores. Several key and meter changes. Dedicated to the Michigan School Band and Orchestra Association. Folk suite written in B-flat concert. Has an easy range.

| ——————— | "Harlequin" | Bo. Hawkes | IV |

Piece has wide skips, interesting variations. Jovial, happy, full sound. Rather serious novelty number.

| ——————— | *Interval Town* | Bo. Hawkes | III |

Suite with sections as follows: (1) "2nd St. and 7th Ave." (built mostly on intervals of 2nds and 7ths); (2) "3rd St. and 6th Ave." (built mostly on 3rds and 6ths); (3) "4th St. and 5th Ave." (etc.); (4) "Octave Circle" (etc.). Wonderful ear-training material; can be used at almost any level. Technically simple and colorful enough for performance.

| ——————— | "Kentucky—1800" | Bo. Hawkes | III |

Built upon three early American folk songs. Harmony often modal. Interesting parts for all instruments. Technique and range easy. Emphasis upon melodic and counter-melodic flow. Colorful material. Full score.

| ——————— | Little Suite for Band | Bo. Hawkes | III |

Excellent composition for junior high. Technique easy. Emphasis on balance and overall color. First movement offers rich, modern sound, requiring thoughtful balance between sections. Second movement required good intonation and careful listening. Features muted brass. Effective program number. Full score.

| ——————— | "Music for a Carnival" | Bo. Hawkes | IV |

Complex rhythms at a bright tempo require much accuracy. Music atonal and colorful. Emphasis on balance, as melodies skip from voice to voice. Three-versus-two rhythm at ending will require much work. A colorful program piece.

| Hansen, J. | "Valdres" | Bo. Hawkes | IV |

A fascinating march that offers a number of instrumental improvements and parts for American groups. Optional antiphonal trumpet parts for dramatic staging. One of the better marches. Condensed score. Time: 3⅓ minutes.

| Herbert, F. | "Sea Chantey" | Belwin | IV |

Colorful program fare built around two sea songs, one obscure, the other well known. Excellent orchestration, challenging rhythmically to all. Modern harmony versus modal harmony. Simple melodic statements versus involved melodic shifting, all well combined.

| Hermann, R. | Ballet for Young Americans | EMS | IV |

Technically difficult for clarinet; good for development of runs in first movement. Third movement good for intonation. Should be interesting for teenagers. No full score.

Hill, C.   *"Northern Legend"*   Mills   IV

A choice concert piece. Uses many chromatic passages and triplets and is a good piece for developing technique and tonguing. Time: 5 minutes.

Johnson, C.   *Passacaglia and Fugue*   CF   III

Time of performance: 3 minutes. Full score. Adheres to the forms of the title but has many sections of dramatic and romantic interest. An easy number from the standpoint of tone and technique, which maintains a fine quality of musical interest. Every section participates in the melodic line. An appealing way to introduce the fugue style to young bands.

Kenny, G.   *"Coat of Arms"*   Summy-Bir   IV

Condensed score. Some good woodwind obbligato parts. Comfortable range. An enjoyable selection. Some fingering problems in clarinets. Rhythmic problem, sixteenth notes against triplet eighths.

Kinyon, J.   *Appalachian Suite*   Bourne   IV

A collection of folk tunes, including "Tooytoodum" and "Green Sleeves." The several key and meter changes offer a challenge for a young band. Trumpets never go above D.

Koepke, P.   *"Stella polaris"*   Ru   III

A concert march patterned after the grand marches of Wagner. A wide range in the trio. Melody in the woodwinds is of modest range. Technical demands not too difficult. Time: 2½ minutes. No full score.

Latham, W.   *Court Festival Suite*   SUM   III

Written in form and style of 16th and 17th centuries. Fresh, appealing, and authentically demonstrates early musical forms. Simple technically and requires accurate adherence to style. Charming program music. No full score.

Lillya, C.   *Two Etudes*   CF   IV

1. Etude No. 30 ("Rose") for clarinet section in unison—IV

2. Etude No. 11 ("Arban") for cornet section in unison—V

Piece has novelty program value. Accompaniment parts uninteresting. Easy technique in clarinet etude, but requires precision. Optional parts provided for "non-virtuoso" clarinetists and cornetists. Trumpet etude much harder; wide leaps, although range is simple. Good motivation for "inner part" players, who here can "play the melody," as it were.

Logan, R.   *"El chaco"*   Sta   III

A Spanish-flavored 2/4 march. Contains good melodies, assigned to various sections of the band. Strong countermelodies. Maracas and claves required. Time: 2 minutes. No full score.

Lo Presti, R.   *Pageant Overture*   Bo. Hawkes   IV

Contemporary work, complete with rhythmic figures and meter changes. More melodic interest than many contemporary works. The unusual entrances would be a good device for teaching careful counting. Sudden dynamic changes.

Loewe-Lerner   Leidzen   ***Brigadoon*** Selections   Fox   IV

Well-chosen selection of tunes from this great show. Transitions well done. Some difficult keys. Excellent quality. Three score.

———————————   Bennett   ***My Fair Lady*** Selections   Chappell   IV

Effective scoring; technically challenging. Broadway flavor. Three score.

Luke, R.   "Sonics and Metrics"   Ludwig   III

Somewhat of an experimental composition, with unique sounds and various meters. Even though musically there are some inadequacies, compositionally and educationally it is worthy of consideration.

Maxwell, E.   "Herald Trumpets"   SUM   III

Concert march, featuring trumpets in easy triads in ornamentation. Chromatic harmonies are in three-part chords. Snare drum and cymbal prominent throughout. Good show piece. Time: 3 minutes. Full score.

McBeth, F.   "Chant and Jubilo"   SMC   IV

Early church music style organum. Should be done in a very sensitive manner, with the jubilo contrasting with its explosive lower brass and percussions. Full score.

———————————   "Joyant Narrative"   SMC   IV

Colorful tonal patterns in opening passages require good discipline in intonation. A driving rhythmic quality that is appealing, energetic, and demanding. This composition is typical of McBeth's rhythmic tension and excitement.

———————————   "Masque"   SMC   IV

A dramatic, impelling, rhythmic opening that requires good percussion and brass. There is a tendency to cover the woodwinds, so brass and percussion have to play softer than dynamics indicate. Contrasting sustained middle section offers good variety and interest.

McBride, R.   Yoder   "Fugato on a Well-   Mills   IV
                                 Known Theme"

Takes fine players in all sections. Rhythmically and harmonically very interesting; technically challenging, yet flattering to the band.

McKay, G.   ***The Plainsman:*** Symphonic   Boston   III
                         Suite for Band

Approximate time: 9½ minutes. No full score. Excellent contemporary band music for young bands. Dissonant harmonies and tonalities give this number something new and special from the ordinary music for young bands. Contrasting movements and rhythms skillfully written to give several contrasting moods.

Mitchell, R.   Introduction and Fantasia   Marks   IV

A one-movement composition with frequent tempo and mood changes. Impressive rhythmic accentuations, yet not too difficult. Worthy of being in any band library.

Moore, D.   "March Chalumeau"   SHB   III

A snappy, exciting concert march with full instrumentation. Written with good range for all instruments in mind.

| | "Marcho Poco" | Mills | III |

A lively concert march: strong dynamic contrast. Good program music. No full score. Time: 2½ minutes.

| | "Marcho Scherzo" | Mills | IV |

Condensed score only. Playing time 3⅓ minutes. A 6/8 march with several duple rhythms inserted within the triple meter. Some bands may experience many rhythm problems with this march. Mixing of duple and triple rhythms offers good rhythmic development.

| Morrissey, J. | "An American Weekend" | Witmark | IV |

An exciting symphony in four movements, the last a little more difficult. A nice exchange of melody among the parts. Clarinet has a solo in part II, percussion in part III. No full score.

| | "Music for a Ceremony" | Witmark | III |

Good for graduation processional. Drum and trumpet fanfare introduction. Full sound. Requires repeated 16th notes in tempo. Brass sections featured a couple of times.

| Nicholls | Leist | "The March of the Herald" | Mills | III |

Full brass triads and frequent unison octave melodies in the brass. Ranges for clarinet and trumpet are high.

| Olivadoti, J. | Ensenada Overture | Ru | III |

A Spanish overture with interesting and varied Spanish rhythms. Enjoyable to junior high school band.

| | "Hall of Fame" | Ru | III |

Condensed score. Concert march that offers good material for young band. Key of trio section may be a problem for young bands. Good upper and low brass section required on ending.

| Overgard, G. | Ballade—Bravura | Kjos | III |

Technique challenging for junior high musicians. Brass range high in a few spots, but possible for them to play. Should provide valuable experience in playing in fanfare style. Interesting parts for each section. Due to length, may tax the endurance of a program, but would do as an overture or graduation-type presentation. No full score.

| Persichetti, V. | Serenade for Band | EV | IV |

Five Movements: Pastoral, Humoreske, Nocturne, Intermezzo, and Capriccio. Grade deceptive, as excellent, mature musicianship demanded for effective performance. Full score. Good as entire selection, or may be used as individual numbers.

| Rodgers and Hammerstein | Sound of Music Selections | Chappell | III |

Baritone plays quite high along with trumpets. Good rhythm changes make it interesting. Fine program material.

| Schmidt, W. | "The Natchez Trace" | Av | IV |

A concert march completely different from the run-of-the-mill march atonally and rhythmically. Complex and charming. Woodwinds' range becomes extreme near the end. Only other technical problems are in many accidentals. Should prove tonally and rhythmically exciting program material. No full score.

Smith, F.   *Canzone for Band*   Bourne   IV

Rhythmically challenging; atonal and antiphonal. Technique easy for all. Full score.

Smith, L.   *"The Traveler"*   Bandland   IV

Rousing march, with power, originality, and style. Should be played by a better-than-average group for a real challenge. Lower brass and percussions particularly striking. Trumpets busy most of the time. Time: 3½ minutes.

Steck, A.   *"Piccadilly"*   Bo. Hawkes   IV

Fast tempo march in 6/8 that has much flavor of circus march. Scored in style of early Sousa marches. Trombones, horns, and often trumpets use after-beats. Time: 3¼ minutes.

———————————   *"Path of Glory" March*   Bo. Hawkes   III

A quick tempo. Range for first trumpets and trombones slightly high. Parts not written for F horn. Time: 3 minutes.

Tatgenhorst, J.   *"Tanglewood"*   Bar   III

Has some tonal characteristics of Persichetti. Beautiful tonal introduction is compelling. Second portion rhythmic and driving. Some contrapuntal feeling. No technical facility problems.

Thielman, R.   *Chelsea Suite*   Luds   III

Three movements: *Intrada, Canzone, Allegro.* Good workout for percussion. Contemporary band sound.

Thompson, D.   *Intermezzo for Band*   Bourne   IV

Strong emphasis on modern harmony. Melodic fragments tossed from voice to voice. Syncopation throughout, requiring exact counting and repeating difficult entrances. Strong horn section a must. Percussion parts extremely challenging. Much use of the xylophone and glockenspiel. Full score.

Vaughan Williams   *English Folk Song Suite* Bo. Hawkes   IV

Full score. A well-known suite popular for performer and audience alike. An oboe solo in second movement. Any or all movements could be programmed effectively.

Ward, R.   Dragon   *"America, the Beautiful"* Fox   IV

Full score. Performance time approximately 3 minutes, 18 seconds. Well-written arrangement of a patriotic song. Major problems are the runs in the woodwinds and the key. Goes into G-flat major concert key, which is a problem for most bands. Cornets have fanfare-type ending that requires triple tonguing. Has audience appeal and may serve well as a mass or combined band number for a festival-type concert.

———————————   *Prairie Overture*   Galaxy   IV

Good contribution for band, with much rhythmic strength. Ranges moderate; uses all instruments with melodic importance in horns, sax basses, and low reeds. In a bright tempo. Full score. Time: 6¼ minutes.

Washburn, R.   *"Pageantry"*   Bo. Hawkes   IV

Full score. Excellent band number, written in style of grand march, with two basic tempo changes. Well written for all sections, with excellent solo sections for trombone, baritone, and horn section. Some dissonance of harmony, but always returns to more conventional sound. Good concert number that should have much appeal to performers and audience.

Whear, P.   *Czech Suite*   Ludwig   III

First part requires legato phrasing and attention to dynamic markings. Second part requires much expressive playing. Third part is the well-known "Festival Dance," a lively 4/4 dance reminiscent of the polka. Ends with a grand climax.

————————   *Introduction and Invention*   Ludwig   IV

One movement, two-section design, with fantasia and tight fugal treatment. Excellent scoring, percussion unusually interesting and important. Offers good ear training to students. Full score. Time: 4½ minutes.

————————   *Jedermann* Overture   Leeds   III

Opening very vigorous. Second part slow and allows for expression. Ending broad and majestic. Has universal appeal. *Jedermann* is a German adaptation of the early sixteenth-century English miracle play entitled *Everyman*. Good full score. Time: 5 minutes.

Whitcomb, K.   *"Cavalcade"*   G. Schirmer   III

ABA form: fanfare, slow march, fanfare. Strongly reminiscent of Holst: typical English march sound. Clarinets to high F on ending, but other range and technique easy. Occasional three-versus-two rhythmical patterns should provide challenge. Suitable as a concert march. Chief musical value lies in producing a good musical sound and broad tone.

White, D.   *Miniature Set for Band*   Shawnee   IV

Flute solo and trumpet-and-French horn dialogue included in five-movement set. Voted "outstanding contribution in '58" by CBDNA. Time: 11½ minutes.

Whitney, M.   *"Dramatic Episode"*   Bourne   IV

An exciting, rhythmical piece in rapid tempo. Difficult parts for woodwinds. Harmonies dissonant. Skips of a fourth or more in all parts will require work. Time: 3⅔ minutes.

————————   *Pastel for Band*   Mills   III

A publication in contemporary style. Requires fair technique for clarinets. No full score. Contrasting moods follow flowing melodic lines. Time: 4 minutes.

————————   *"Valley Forge" March*   Bo. Hawkes   III

A different 6/8 march, with many chromatic scales. Trio is melodic and full. All parts active, and ranges reasonable. A full and dramatic ending. Printed on march-sized parts, with small printing. Time: 3¾ minutes.

Williams, C.   *Dedicatory Overture*   Marks   IV

Brass fanfare introduction; contemporary sound; no written key signature. Quite chordal and basically homophonic until *allegretto* section, which has considerable counterpoint. Syncopated *maestoso finale*. Full score.

Easy to play; presents only an occasional rhythmic problem. Utilizes shifting triad sounds with many borrowed chords. Some small endurance problems with the brass. Good program material. Time: 4 minutes.

_____ *"The Sinfonians"* Marks IV

Symphonic march. Well scored and of longer duration than most marches. Good color and interesting solo sections for percussion and piccolo, brass choir, low reeds, and timpani. Condensed score only. Time: 5⅓ minutes.

Wood Hawkins *Montmartre March* Robbins IV

Condensed score. Time: approximately 3¾ minutes. Good moving upper winds needed. Every section gets chance at melody. French "Can-Can" march style.

Work, J. *"Driftwood Patterns"* Shawnee IV

Employs many of the less frequently heard combinations of wind sonorities. Ranges, key changes, and rhythmic combinations demanding for grade IV. All players challenged equally. In percussion there are parts for bells, triangle, timpani, vibes, bass drum, snare drum, and cymbals. Full score. Time: 6 minutes.

Zacharias Werle *"Gaucho Carnival"* Mills IV

Adequate scoring with dance rhythms. Difficult for all instruments, but more so for woodwinds and baritones. Excellent light program material. Time: 3 minutes.

Grades V and VI

BAROQUE PERIOD

Bach, J.S. Holst *"Bach's Fugue à la Gigue"* Bo. Hawkes VI

Good arrangement for military band. Rhythmic difficulties for high school bands. Full score.

_____ Frackenpohl *Five Chorales* Shawnee V

Selected numbers from the Christmas Oratorio, Magnificat, and Cantatas. Well edited; excellent woodwind coloring. Full score.

_____ Leidzen *"Jesu, Joy of Man's Desiring"* CF V

Good arrangement. Requires steady first clarinet section but easier material for seconds and thirds. Good woodwind choir.

_____ Leidzen *"Komm, Süsser Tod"* CF V

Excellent for teaching tone quality and expression; emotional maturity needed. No full score.

_____ Moehlmann *Prelude and Fugue in D minor* FitzSimons V

Technically difficult; challenging for high school band. Well edited. Full score.

| | Chiaffarelli | "Sleepers, Awake" | CF | V |

Colorful; style and interpretation of melodic line would need work. Technically not difficult, except the tenuto quarter notes. Be careful of articulations of eighth notes in melody. Full score.

| Frescobaldi | Slocum | *Toccata* | Mills | V |

Well scored for symphonic band. Style becomes repetitious in *Allegro*. Demanding clarinet parts. Well edited. Excellent reading material. Full score.

| Handel | Leidzen | "Care selve" | AMP | V |

Aria from Handel's forgotten opera *Atalanta*. Difficult key of G-flat. Full score.

| | Clark–Maddy | *Handel Suite* | G. Schirmer | V |

Suite of six numbers. Excellent literature contains March, Sarabande, Minuet, Aria, Bourrée, and Gigue. Uses mordents and trills. Six-line score.

| | Beecham | **Gods Go a-Begging** | Chappell | V |

Difficult. Restrict to college level or best high school. Ballet suite from five operas. Full score.

| | Sartorius | **Royal Fireworks** *Music* | Mus. Press | V |

Arranged as a concerto grosso for symphonic band. Arranged so small band may have experience of playing good music. Effective. No full score.

| | Kay | **Water Music** *Suite* | TP | V |

Colorful, interesting, demanding, well-arranged work. Full score.

| Hasse | Moehlmann | *Canzona* | FitzSimons | V |

Treatment of melody is somewhat like an aria. Musically good. Full score.

| Latham | | **Court Festival** | SUM | V |

Written in form and style of sixteenth and seventeenth centuries. Instrumental dances. Thematic material original with one exception. Full score.

| | | *Three Chorale Preludes* | SUM | V |

Originals for band are based on different German choral texts. Rich in color. Well written. First two movements could be played by class IV band. Extreme trumpet work. Be sure of your brass. Full or condensed score.

CLASSICAL PERIOD

| Beethoven | Weiss | *Contra Dance No. 1* | CF | VI |

Arranged for the Goldman Band. A colorful concert piece. Has rhythmic problems. Keeps a good horn player busy. Brass easy, but woodwinds kept very busy.

| Catel | Goldman | *Overture in C* | Mercury | V |

Well-edited overture written for military band in 1792. Elegant piece, with clarity of parts.

Gossec   Goldman   *Classic Overture*   Mercury   V

Bright piece, with some technical difficulties. Care should be exercised to preserve balance and to emphasize contrasts of dynamics and phrasing. Some clarinet passages very high; might present some rhythm problems. Not easy; would require full instrumentation.

_____   Goldman   *Military Symphony in F*   Mercury   V

Good, solid sounding. Band members should know this literature.

Mozart, W. A.   Goldman   **Titus** *Overture*   Mercury   V

Aeolian band and orchestra library. Difficult technical passages; sixteenth-note triplets. Good transcription in characteristic style. Full score.

ROMANTIC PERIOD

Berlioz   Smith   **Damnation of Faust**   Belwin   V
                                            Selections

A work of medium difficulty; demanding of flutes and clarinets. Uses extreme range of trombones. Challenging for high school band.

_____   Heening   *Overture* **Beatrice and**   CF   V
                                            Benedict

Difficult, demanding of all sections, especially woodwinds.

Fauchet   Gillette   *Symphony in B-flat*   WS   V

Interesting, colorful, and challenging.

Gershwin   Bennett   **Porgy and Bess** *Selections*   Gershwin   V

Very difficult arrangement, but excellent in quality. Three-line score.

Grieg   Bain   *First Movement of Piano*   CF   V
                                  Concerto in A minor

Work of medium difficulty, arranged for piano and band. Frequent use of accidentals. Demanding of euphonium.

Mendelssohn   *Overture for Band*   G. Schirmer   V

Difficult, excellent, well-scored, interesting, and colorful work. Would be a great challenge for high school band.

_____   Duthoit   *Trumpet Overture*   Chappell   V

Demanding flute and clarinet parts. Interesting and challenging work. No full score.

Rimsky-Korsakov Harding   *"The Golden Cockerel"*   Kjos   V

Noteworthy strength in lines for low brass and reeds in unison and octaves. Many sudden changes in dynamics and tempo. Builds to tremendous climax; sounds best when performed by full instrumentation. Time: 5⅓ minutes.

Rossini   Cailliet   *italian in Algiers*   Fox   VI
                                            Overture

Full score. Time of performance: approximately 8¾ minutes. Excellent opportunity for rhythm, gracefulness, and contrast. Problems are light tonguing and technique, with

84

sudden dynamic changes, along with demands of technical facility from all sections. Well-transcribed selection for band.

	Meyrelles and Kent	*La gazza ladra* Overture	CF	VI

Some very difficult woodwind passages; G key and style present the greatest problems. Extremely good training literature for developing good band sound and appreciation for music of romantic period.

Saint-Saëns	Laurendeau	*Danse macabre*	CF	V

Challenging to all sections of band, especially to woodwinds. Clarinets have demanding passage, eight measures of 16th notes moving chromatically. No full score.

Sibelius	Cailliet	*Finlandia*	CF	V

Fine arrangement. Full score.

Tchaikovsky	Godfred	*Overture 1812*	Chappell	V

Difficult; requires technical skills of single, double, and triple tonguing of woodwinds and brasses. Frequent use of accidentals. No full score.

	Fletcher	*Two Excerpts from the* **Pathétique** *Symphony*	ECS	VI

1. Andante from first movement

2. March from third movement

Difficult. Gives program notes. Interesting and colorful. No full score.

Wagner	Johnson	*"Album Leaf"*	Ricordi	V

Challenging work. Numerous interesting slurs, ties, and rhythms. No full score.

	Osterling	**Die Meistersinger** *Overture*	Ludwig	V

Gives program and conductor notes. Uses changing time signatures. Interesting and challenging work; well written within tessitura of instrumentation.

	Cailliet	*Elsa's Procession to the Cathedral, from* **Lohengrin**	Remick	V

Difficult key in middle section; some cross-cueing. Full score.

	Cailliet	*Invocation of Alberich*	Fox	VI

Difficult, interesting, colorful, and challenging, demanding technical skills of woodwinds. No full score.

CONTEMPORARY PERIOD

Addinsell, R.		**Warsaw** *Concerto for Band and Solo Piano*	Chappell	VI

Good arrangement of a famous concerto. Challenging to all parts; good for intonation. Balanced blend.

Ashe	Frederic	*Concert Suite*	Volkwein	V

Three movements: (1) *Fanfare and Scherzo*; (2) *Andante religioso*; (3) *Allegro vivace*. Playing time: 10½ minutes. Excellent band music in contemporary vein. Winner of 1963 Ostwald award. Every section of band has excellent part. Full score.

Bax, A.   Duthoit   *"Malta G. C."*   Chappell   V

Typical English-style concert march. Sonorous. Emphasis on balance. Many, many notes in woodwind parts, but easily played. No full score.

Bennett, R. R.   *Suite of Old American*   Chappell   VI
                        Dances

Five movements. Artful use of band sonorities. Rhythmically difficult. Needs complete instrumentation. Three-line score.

Bergsma, W.   *March with Trumpets*   Galaxy   V

Ranges fairly extreme for brass. Interesting dynamic variety and passages of extreme brilliance and color. Beautifully arranged, woodwinds contrasting with brass. Full score. Time: 6 minutes.

Bernstein   Duthoit   **West Side Story** Selection   G. Schirmer   V

Three-line score. Playing time: approximatey 8⅓ minutes. Well arranged for concert bands. Good student appeal because of student familiarity with music; includes most of tunes from original show. Some tricky rhythms and demanding technical sections, but offers good development for high school band.

Cable, H.   *Newfoundland Rhapsody*   Chappell   VI

Technically difficult in all parts. Fine scoring for the idiom. Folk material beautifully treated. Three-line score.

Carter, C.   *"Capitol Hill Concert*   CF   V
                    March"

Three-line score. Time: 2⅔ minutes. A modern concert march which, while basically tonal, contains many fresh harmonic sounds. Rich sounds, interesting modulations, and interior formal design combine to make this an enjoyable march for performers and concert goers alike. Upper woodwinds may experience tuning problems.

_____   *Overture in E-flat*   Bourne   V

Frequent time signature changes. Full score.

Copland   **Emblems**   Bo. Hawkes   V

Commissioned by CBDNA in 1965. The better high school bands could perform this number. Composition a well-worked slow-fast-slow design, with modification of the first section in its return at conclusion. Harmonically the open fourths and fifths melodic lines that mark so much of Copland's music are all characteristic of this piece. Full score. Time: 13 minutes.

_____   Beeler   **Lincoln Portrait**   Bo. Hawkes   V

Well suited to the medium. Needs an excellent group from musical standpoint. Full score.

_____   *Outdoor Overture*   Bo. Hawkes   VI

Not an easy key. Much unison. Requires vigorous rhythmic concept. Range high for woodwinds. Requires a mature group with qualified horns. High musical value. Full score.

Creston, P.   *Prelude and Dance,*   Ricordi   V
                     op. 76

Prelude laced with compelling accent and pulsation as it projects a long legato line above shorter percussive bursts of accompaniment. Dance has cross-rhythms. Articulation must be short and quick. Both full and condensed score. Time: 7 minutes.

Dello Joio, N.	*Variants on a Medieval Tune*	Marks	VI

Consists of introduction, theme, and five variations. Great contrasts in tempo and character, utilizing possibilities of band to highest degree.

Dvorak, R.	**West Point** *Symphony, Third Movement*	Summy-Bir	VI

Movement in 6/8 meter. Difficult for brasses; takes more than average horn section. Contrast of brass and woodwind colors. Musical value average. Three-line score.

Fauchet, P.	*Symphony in B-flat, Nocturne*	Witmark	VI

Second of four movements separately published. Begins with fairly difficult solo for first horn. Difficult in all parts. Interesting solos in most parts. Full score available.

Feller, S.	*"Theme for Tomorrow"*	Bo. Hawkes	VI

A waltz, romantic in quality. Requires competent clarinet section. Good use of the idiom, with wide variety of tonal colors. Full score.

Fletcher, G.	**A Rhapsody of Dances**	Schmitt	V

Contrasting rhythms and tone colors not only make this good educational literature for teaching technical facility but give it appeal for concerts. Some clarinet and flute passages exposed and will need attention for intonation. Band members will enjoy this work.

Ginastera, A.	*"Danza Final"*	Bo. Hawkes	VI

Only word for this one is *excitement*. A driving 6/8 rhythm that has to keep going. Range is no problem. Score calls for piano, harp, and xylo. Must have fine band to perform this work.

Gould	Lang	*"American Salute"*	Mills	V-VI

Three-line score, written in 12/8 time. Rhythm and technical problems. Good high range needed by trumpet and brass players. Requires good brass, woodwind and percussion sections. Several key changes. This demanding but interesting music will challenge most bands.

_____	Bennett	*"Guaracha"*	Mills	V

From the Latin American Symphonette; excellent transcription. Full score.

_____	*"Jericho"*	Mills	V

Descriptive music with alternating 3/4 and 4/4 time signatures and complex rhythms. Condensed score only.

Hanson, H.	*Chorale and Alleluia*	CF	VI

Mature tone needed. Woodwind parts high. Brass must be excellent. Trumpets divided six ways. Tremendous emotional impact. Written well for the idiom. High musical value. Full score.

Hermann, R.   Kiddie Ballet   EMS   VI

Technically difficult in all parts; ranges high. Takes a mature band. Modern idiom; well suited to band. Two-line score.

_____   North Sea Overture   EMS   V

Dynamically, proportions require great endurance. Movie sound track tonality and successions of chordal dissonances provide interest and color. Woodwinds get good technical workout, but not too demanding. G-flat concert will give low brass concern in spots, but technique again is easy. Color and excitement should make for program appeal. Full score.

Hindemith, P.   Symphony in B-flat for   SCH   VI
                                    Band

An extremely difficult work; very dissonant and musically difficult to make sound. Ranges extreme, and all players must be excellent. Mature tone a must. Full score.

Holst, G.   First Suite in E-flat   Bo. Hawkes   V
                                    for Military Band

Full score. Playing time: about 7 minutes, 35 seconds. Three movements: (1) Chaconne; (2) Intermezzo; (3) March. Difficult woodwind passages; several solo passages with solo imitation and answer. Full band instrumentation in every section needed to play parts as written. Intermezzo *vivace*, which demands good technique from woodwinds. Bass trombone, four valve baritones, and four valve tubas needed to do justice to written range.

_____ Smith   **The Planets, "Mars"**   Bo. Hawkes   VI
                                    and "Jupiter"

Good choice of movements for transcription. Full score.

Jacob, G.   **Music for a Festival**   Bo. Hawkes   VI

Contains many different movements; need not play all of them for a program. Fine scoring for the band. Some movements for brass alone. Needs a mature group. Full score.

_____   Original Suite   Bo. Hawkes   VI

Requires good low brass; other parts not difficult. Treats band as new idiom. Last movement has difficult clarinet parts. High musical value. Three-line score.

Jenkins, J.   American Overture for   TP   VI
                                    Band

Requires excellent horn section. Woodwind parts difficult. Difficult ensemble problems. Intense, frantic mood throughout. Four-line score.

_____   "Cumberland Gap"   SHMC   V

1961 Ostwald contest award. Has flavor and rhythm of American folk music without borrowing literally from any known tune. Excellent section writing for various choirs and interesting parts for percussion. Form concise and clear. Full score. Time: 8⅓ minutes.

Johnston, D.   Prelude for Band   SUM   VI
In 7/4 meter. Harmony modern. Main interest is melodic. Long phrases with dynamic changes. Musical value high. Well scored. Full score.

Kechley, G.   *Antiphony for Winds*   CF   V

Thin scoring in important places. Cross-cues provided, but effects of thematic material being tossed from voice to voice will be lost unless intended instruments are used. Brass called on for high register work, but good high school will be able to handle it. Modern sounds and contrapuntal techniques provide interest for all. Full score.

_____   *Suite for Concert Band*   SCH   VI

Difficult work, particularly first and last movements. Middle movement slow and sonorous. Well suited to the idiom. High musical value. Three-line score.

Kenny, G.   *"Julibee"*   SUM   VI

Technically challenging work that requires fine trumpets and horns. Interesting use of march form. High musical value. Two-line score.

Kepner, F.   *"Cuban Fantasy"*   SUM   VI

Need English horn or fine alto sax. Well scored for band. Latin style; excellent work. Four-line score.

Kirk, T.   *Aylesford Variations*   Summy-Bir   VI

Modern idiom. Harmonically fine. Modulation to difficult keys. Well scored for band. Musical value high. Full score.

Klein, J.   *Yellowstone Suite*   Bo. Hawkes   VI

Clarinet parts difficult. Written in modern idiom. Programmatic and obvious. Thickly scored. Melodically interesting. Good musical value. Full score.

Kosma, J.   Werle   *"Baptiste"*   Mills   V

Good contrast in rhythm. All instruments featured in spots. Delicate for tubas and low reeds. Good light program work. Time: 4½ minutes.

LaGassey, H.   *"Sea Portrait"*   Kjos   VI

Rhapsodic style, with much unison and with rhythmic passages; very chromatic style; modulates to some difficult keys. Needs a fine cornet section. Woodwind parts high. Good musical value. Full score.

Lamont, V.   *"Legend of the Canyon"*   Fox   VI

Difficult articulations. Needs adequate horns. Thickly scored. Brass section should have mature tone. Average musical value. Three-line score.

Lang, P.   *Thunderbird Overture*   Morris   VI

Cheap paper. Based on Indian music. Good program notes. Good for intonation development. Some meter changes. Good melody in horn. Condensed and full score, but difficult to read.

Latham, W.   *Three Chorale Preludes*   Summy-Bir   V

1. "Break Forth, O Beauteous Heavenly Light"
2. "O Sacred Head Now Wounded"
3. "Now Thank We All Our God"

Written in modern style and well orchestrated. Will provide interesting challenge to good band. Numbers 1 and 2 can be performed at grade III level. Intricate trumpet work in upper register requires level of V to perform. Full score.

McBeth, F.   *Second Suite for Band*   SMC   V

Rhythm could cause some problems, but difficult only in limited places in last movement. First two movements wide open and will expose sections if weak; otherwise fine composition.

Mennin, P.   *"Canzona"*   CF   V

Full score. Playing time: approximately 5 minutes. Short brisk work, written with broad melodic lines supported by powerful rhythmic figurations. Excellent contemporary band music; a challenge to every section in the band. Commissioned by Edwin Franko Goldman through the League of American Composers.

Morrissey, J.   *"Caribbean Fantasy"*   Marks   VI

Needs good soloists; difficult trumpet solo. Also should have competent percussion section and low brass. Three-line score.

Overgard, G.   *"Fanfare and Fable"*   Fox   VI

In march form, with some difficult key changes. Harmonically interesting; well scored and an extremely effective work. Four-line score.

Persichetti, V.   *Divertimento for Band*   TP   VI

Technically challenging; in the modern idiom, with difficult rhythmic passages. Slow movements require tone control and careful phrasing. Three-line score. Excellent work.

———————————   *"Pageant"*   CF   VI

Full score. Commissioned by American Bandmaster's Association. Slow opening section, followed by lively "parade" section. Good lyrical flute and strong low brass section needed for effective performance. Excellent band music.

———————————   *Psalm for Band*   EV   VI

Beautiful use of sonorities. Harmonically very fine; rhythmically complex. Fine horns and woodwinds needed. High emotional content. Full score.

———————————   *Symphony for Band*   EV   VI

Requires good percussion section. Technically extremely difficult. High musical value. Full score.

Piston, W.   *"Tunbridge Fair"*   Bo. Hawkes   VI

Complex rhythms; difficult woodwind parts. High tessitura. Brass parts not difficult. Full score.

Prokofiev   Goldman   *Athletic Festival March*   Leeds   V

Due to editing and added parts (saxophone, bass clarinet, etc.), lacks interest. Otherwise, a light, interesting original composition. Primarily valuable as change of pace number, although at its extremely fast tempo requires clarity of articulation. Full score.

———————————   Yodor   *Op. 99 March*   Leeds   V

Choice contemporary work. Difficult woodwind parts; otherwise not difficult. High musical value. Three-line score.

Reed, H.   *"La fiesta mexicana"*   Mills   VI

Difficult percussion part. Interesting stage effects; excellent Latin style; choice composition for mature group. Full score.

| | | *Spiritual for Band* | SCH | VI |

Rhythmically complex; appealing modern work. Full score.

| Riegger, W. | | *Dance Rhythms for Band* | AMP | V |

Difficult changing meters and variety of rhythms present challenge. Rapid changes from sixteenth figures to triplets and syncopated figures. Parts pass from section to section within a measure or two.

| Saylor, R. | | *Prisoner of War March* | Kend | VI |

Unusual harmonic idiom. Short and vigorous in style. Very effective. Three-line score.

| Schinstine, W. | | *Tympalero Solo for Tympani* | SUM | VI |

Excellent work to develop a good tympani player. Some rhythm difficulty in all parts. Good for soloist.

| Schuman, W. | | *Chester Overture* | TT | VI |

Only a mature group should attempt this. Rhythmically very complex, with difficult technical problems in most parts. High emotional value. Full score.

| | | *"George Washington Bridge"* | G. Schirmer | VI |

Difficult technically. High emotional content. Full score.

| | | *"When Jesus Wept," Prelude for Band* | TP | VI |

Work opens with baritone and cornet duet. Modern harmonically; slow and sustained. Needs mature tone quality. Full score. Main theme by William Billings.

| Shostakovitch | Paulson | *Allegretto from the Fifth Symphony* | MCA | V |

Needs good horn section; also fine B-flat clarinet player. Full score.

| | Cailliet | *"Burlesque"* | TP | V |

Requires strong piccolo player; other woodwinds relatively easy. Emphasis on melodic fragments tossed from section to section. Good program novelty. No full score.

| | Righter | *Finale from the Fifth Symphony* | Bo. Hawkes | VI |

High emotional quality. Needs fine horn soloist and excellent clarinet section. Excellently scored. Full score.

| Smith, C. | | *"Credence"* | Wingert-Jones | V |

Dynamic and spirited composition, with contrasting legato sustained tonal passages and marked rhythmic patterns. Intriguing melodic lines. Many meter and key changes. One of the best band compositions.

| | | *Incidental Suite* | Wingert-Jones | V |

This composition's demanding qualities, not only of harmony and rhythm but of intonation, are well worth the musical message of this outstanding suite.

| Stravinsky | Goldman | *Berceuse and Finale from the **Firebird** Suite* | Sta | VI |

Well scored. Needs competent brass and complete instrumentation. High emotional value. Four-line score.

| Surinach, C. | | *Sinfonietta Flamenca* | AMP | VI |

Challenging and colorful composition that should be played by only the better bands. Exciting rhythms and ranges make this a tremendous program selection.

| Tansman, A. | | *Carnival Suite* | Leeds | V |

Colorful program music. Woodwinds' range occasionally high, but playable. Technique and rhythm challenging to all. Entire suite too much the same for programming, but any one movement suitable. No full score.

| Tuthill, B. | | *Prelude and Rondo for Band* | SUM | VI |

Unusual melodic style. Clear writing; well scored for band. Difficult clarinet parts; good balance between difficulty and musical worth. Four-line score.

| Vaughan Williams | | *Folk Song Suite* | Bo. Hawkes | V |

Full score. Three-movement suite. March, Intermezzo, and March based on English folk songs. Articulation and light style needed with demanding woodwind passages. Cornet solos throughout. Cornet and oboe unison solo in intermezzo movement. Strong low brass needed for third movement, "March from Somerset." Range is well within that of the average high school brass player. Playing time: about 5 minutes.

| —————————— | | *"Toccata Marziale"* | Bo. Hawkes | VI |

Contrapuntal work of great substance. Need fine low brass. Excellent work. Full score.

| Velke, F. | | *Fanfare and Rondo* | Shawnee | V |

Wide use of dissonance and unresolved dissonant chords, bitonality, shifting of tonal centers, and alternating meter changes. Difficult for players inexperienced in this medium.

| Wagner, J. | | *Concerto Grosso* | MCA | VI |

Two trumpets and baritone form the concertino. Ensemble problems make this work difficult. Full score.

| Washburn, R. | | *Overture, "Elkhart 1960"* | Shawnee | V |

Vigor, intensity, and excitement essential for effective performance. ABA form; contemporary. Two *allegro* sections offset by brief *adagio*. Playable without large instrumentation or special soloists. Full score. Time: 4⅔ minutes.

| Williams, C. | | *Fanfare and Allegro* | SUM | VI |

Requires fine brass section. Advanced rhythmically, with high tessitura for woodwinds. Fine scoring for band. A frantic work. Only for mature groups. Effective number. Full score.

| —————————— | | *Symphonic Suite* | SUM | V-VI |

Intrada full and brassy. Chorale easy. March rhythmically complex. Thickly scored for this level. Antique dance easy and charming. Needs good brasses in last movement. Full score.

Williams, E. *Symphony in C minor* Colin VI

Work well scored for the idiom. Style not extreme. Takes mature band tonally. Solos for many of the instruments. Average musical value. Full score.

Young Wright *Music for **Around the World in Eighty Days*** Chappell V

Variety for all instruments. Good for intonation, rhythm, and slurring techniques in upper brass. No full score.

Zdechlik, J. *Chorale and Shaker Dance* Kjos VI

Dramatic and appealing composition of two musical ideas, the simple melody found in the chorale and the melody from the well-known Shaker hymn "The Gift to be Simple." Demanding on woodwinds, with changing meters and tonal colorings.

ADDENDUM

4

Chamber Music

Chamber music is the heart of the instrumental music program. Here the student develops the ability and capacity to express musical ideas with his instrument. There should be many types and sizes of ensembles in the school program. Therefore, this section of the guidebook lists the compositions by instrumentation of ensemble and by composer or arranger. All students should have the experience of performing chamber music, not only for their musical development, but for their acquaintance with the literature and for future performance opportunities after graduation. Each music educator is encouraged to add compositions on the addendum page as he feels so motivated.

BRASS

Brass Duets

Anon.　　　　　King　　　　　*The Celebrated Arban Duets* WJ　　　　II-IV

Good duets for the intermediate level—melodious. Volume contains 70 duets.

Anon.　　　　　Burgstahler, E.　*37 Trumpet Duets*　　　Pro-Art　　　I-II

All are familiar melodies in easy range. Good to motivate beginners. Students should enjoy them all. Many varied articulations used.

Anon.　　　　　Voxman, H.　　　*Selected Duets*　　　Ru　　　II-V

In two volumes, 48 duets in all. A very good album, and can be used on most levels. Notes and staff large enough for easy reading. Recommended—more for the money.

| Amsden, A. | | *Amsden's Celebrated Practice Duets* | Bar | II-V |

Volume includes daily embouchure exercises. Not many easy duets—most of them approximately grade IV. Excellent work in reading and listening to another part. Good physical construction; plastic-ring binding. Seventy duets.

| _____ | | *Amsden's Celebrated Practice Duets for Trombone or Baritone; also for Cornet, Clarinet, Baritone, Saxophone, French Horn, Bassoon, etc.* | Bar | I-VI |

Books for bass clef and for treble clef. Fine practice duets—start out very easy and progress to very difficult in rhythm and key. Some not too interesting as far as style is concerned but very good for developing sight reading and technique.

| Blazhevich, V. | Raichman, J., ed. | *Concert Duets* | Leeds | V-VI |

Outstanding concert duets in bass, tenor, and alto clefs. Difficult, but a must for trombone players.

| Blume, O. | | *12 Melodious Duets for 2 Trombones, 2 Baritones, 2 Bassoons* | CF | IV-VI |

| Gatti, D. | | *Thirty-Three Celebrated Duets for Trumpets* | CF | III-IV |

Both parts interesting. Can be used for any treble clef instrument. Fits trumpet range and idiom better. Contains high C's. Good reading exercises for dynamics and articulation.

| Handel | Swaysee | *"The Trumpet Shall Sound"* | Boston | III |

Transcription from the *Messiah,* scored for trumpet and baritone with piano accompaniment. Effective brass writing. Suitable for many occasions.

| Heiring, S. | | *More Miniature Classics for Two Trumpets* | CF | III |

Works by many of the masters (Bach, Handel, Purcell, Telemann, Mozart, etc.). Uses low range in 2nd part; a good study in style.

| Mozart, W.A. | Marx | *Twelve Duos for Two French Horns* | McG | IV-V |

Requires flexibility in both high and low registers. Scholarly twelve-page introduction by Josef Marx on the history and controversy of the duets. Good horn literature for serious students.

| Nicolai, O. | | *Duet No. 1 for 2 Horns* | TP | V |

Good contemporary writing. No accompaniment. Both parts interesting and difficult. First of Nicolai's *Six Duets for Two Horns.* Requires much flexibility and agility in both parts. Range not particularly difficult.

From many of the masters. Typical horn writing. Good work for two ambitious horn players. Utilizes low register more than high. Written in two volumes.

| Williams, C. | | *Twenty-Four Duo Studies for Horn* | Summy-Bir | II-IV |

Technical and tonal studies for two French horns that range in difficulty from grade II to IV. Studies for muting, stopping, and transposing are included.

Brass Trios

| Anon. | King | *Two Motets* | Robt King | III-IV |

Good register for each instrument—linear writing. Excellent brass music.

| Anderson, L. | | *"A Trumpeter's Lullaby"* | Mills | III-IV |

An interesting trio, familiar to everyone. Some double tonguing necessary. A good trio for entertainment purposes.

| Bach, C. P. E. | Simon | *March (Fanfare)* | Morris | I-II |

3 trumpets; 3 French horns; 2 trumpets and 1 trombone; or trumpet, French horn, and arrangement.

| Beethoven | | *Trio, op, 87* | Robt King | IV |

Very good composition for three conscientious students. Originally written for 2 oboes and English horn—in four movements.

| Berdell | Ostrander | *"Sound the Trumpets"* | EM | III-IV |

4 trumpets. Student appeal high. Good trumpet scoring.

| Buchtel | | *"Coquette"* | Kjos | II |

Trio for 3 cornets, 3 flutes, 3 clarinets, or 3 alto saxes. Written with conservative ranges and elementary rhythms. No counterpoint used.

| Cherubini Carissimi Willaert | Ostrander | *Suite for Three Brass Instruments* | EM | III-IV |

3 trumpets; 3 French horns; 2 trumpets and 1 trombone; or trumpet, French horn, and trombone. A suite of three movements, each by a representative composer of a particular period: Cherubini (classical), from *Requiem Aeternam*; Carissimi (baroque), from Motet; Willaert (renaissance), from "Hosanna."

| Handel | Goldman | *Air and Variations in B-flat* | CF | II-IV |

3 trumpets and piano. Air and four variations. The first trumpets go to high C. Good transcription.

| _____ | Ostrander | *Suite for Three Trombones* | EM | V-VI |

A six-movement suite using variety of texture. Independent writing in places. Recommended.

Jacobson, I.   *"Three Temperaments for*   Mil   III
                                          Tubas"

A suite of three movements: *Moderato, Andante, Chorale*. All parts interesting, although third can be omitted, making a duet. Requires different styles of playing. Parts often have different dynamic markings.

Martini   Maganini   *Motet—In Three Parts*   EM   III-IV

Melodic one-movement work that divides into three parts with different tempos. Texture mostly linear. Good training material, with interest in each part.

McKay, G.   *"Anita"*   Bar   II

Trumpet trio (also available for 3 saxes) with piano accompaniment in tango style. Except for brief sections, style is chordal, with unison rhythms among parts. Ranges medium to low.

Mozart, W.A.   King   *Divertimento No. 1*   Robt King   V-VI

Originally written for two clarinets and bassoon. Excellent transcription, which demands endurance and musical maturity. Five movements.

_____   Ostrander   *Suite for Three Trombones* EM   I-II

3 trombones. Short suite selected from *Don Juan* [*Don Giovanni*] (Minuet), "Let Us Extend Our Hands in Friendship," and "Ave verum corpus." Fine training material; good work to stress blend, tone, and group phrasing.

Osborne   *Four Fanfares*   Robt King   III-IV

3 trumpets and timpani. Based on 18th-century French hunting calls. Third trumpet contains difficult octave slurs. Part four possibly more suited for Grade V. Very rapid work, both staccato and legato.

Poulenc   *Sonata*   Che   V

Delightful composition. Requires three good players—especially the horn. Many meter changes—typical Poulenc style. Revised by the composer in 1945.

Purcell   Gardner   *"Trumpet Voluntary"*   G. Schirmer   III-IV

3 trumpets and piano accompaniment. Endurance necessary for first part. Fine, effective music.

_____   Maganini   *Chaconne*   EM   III-IV

3 French horns. Single movement; chaconne stated 13 times and appears in all parts. Good transcription for intermediate ensemble desiring something unique but musically sound.

_____   Ostrander   *"Sound the Trumpet"*   EM   I-II

3 trumpets and piano accompaniment. Brief work that suits brass idiom perfectly. First part has a few high A's. Rhythmically easy.

Sanders, R.   *Trio for Brass Instruments* Robt King   V

Written in three movements. Interesting chord changes and many chromatics make a good reading exercise.

Tchaikovsky	Harris	*Toy Soldiers March*	Ludwig	II

Cornet trio with piano accompaniment that stresses correct interpretation of the dotted eighth-sixteenth figure. All three parts move in similar motion, with very little counterpoint.

Vivaldi		*Sonata da camera*	EMT-Pr	III

Good composition in typical baroque instrumental idiom. Four movements: *Prelude, Courant, Air,* and *Gigue.* Educational. Continuo adapted to part 3. (Can be used as four-part arrangement.) Part 1 the most interesting.

Walker		*"Babillage"*	Bar	II-III

Cornet trio written primarily with melody, two harmony parts, and piano accompaniment. First cornet handles most of the technical work; other two parts less challenging.

Horn Trio

Pottag		*Horn Trio Album*	Belwin	III-VI

Two volumes of trios by Pottag, sixteen selections in each volume. Many excerpts from symphonies. Good for developing symphonic style and learning excerpts from the symphonies.

Cornet Trio

Pleyel	Ostling	*"Rondo militaire"*	Belwin	II

Good arrangement. Good use of dynamics, articulations, and ranges for grade I. All parts require a certain amount of technical facility and musical understanding. Good for practice and performance.

Brass Quartet

LIKE INSTRUMENTATION

Bach, J.S.	King	*Sixteen Chorales*	Robt King	I-II

4 trombones. Dignified, expressive music; good for tone control.

Bassett, L.		*Quartet*	Morris	V-VI

Fourth trombone should be a bass. Technically, would require good college students, because of modern harmony and treatment. Tessitura very high in first part.

Beethoven	King	*"Three Equali"*	Robt King	V-VI

4 trombones. The "Three Equali" composed for trombones as music for All Souls' Day. One of the few original brass works from the 19th century. Excellent music for trombones.

Bergsma, W.		*Suite*	CF	V-VI

Excellent piece, written for 1st and 2nd trumpet, baritone, and trombone. Many fast meter changes, covering wide range of dynamic levels. Three parts: *Scherzo, Song,* and *Showpiece.* Last section the most difficult for the trumpets. Utilizes rhythmic imitation that is passed back and forth between the two trumpets. Could be performed only by advanced students.

Berlioz   Lotzenhiser   *Rakoczy March*   Belwin   V-VI

Very good selection. First trombone goes up to A-flat and has most demanding of the three parts.

Bozza, E.   *Suite*   LD   III-IV

4 French horns—no score. Difficult to rehearse, but worth the effort—intervals difficult to read at sight. Delightful piece for these instruments.

Clapp, P.   *Chorale*   Bo. Hawkes   I-II

4 trombones. Excellent training material in good idiom.

Colby, C.   *Allegro con brio*   MPH   III-IV

4 trombones. In moderate range and easy key for trombones. Work has unusual harmony and holds interest.

Dewit   Tallmadge   *"Diane"*   C-Bettony   V-VI

Adapted from "The Maiden and the Huntsman." Good literature, but somewhat demanding.

Franck   Stube   *"Panis angelicus"*   Belwin   I-II

4 trumpets. Slow, sustained work—good for developing breath support and control. In one movement; lasts for 3½ minutes. First part goes to high A.

Graas, J.   *Three Quartets for*   Mills   IV-V
                                 French Horns

All four parts interesting and difficult. Offers many rhythmic changes and problems. Provides real challenge to good horn section.

Hervig, B.   *"Alla marcia"*   Ru   III

Unaccompanied quartet for four trumpets, with nice independent interest in each part. Style crisp and staccato, with brief interlude for contrast. Careful accenting and strict attention to marked dynamics could make for interesting performance.

Johnson, W.   *"A Viking Song"*   Belwin   IV-V

Fairly high range on 1st trombone, and quite demanding on endurance. Good selection; some interesting dynamics and excellent climax and changes.

Koepke, P.   *"Elégie Héroïque"*   Ru   III

Unaccompanied trombone quartet in legato expressive style. Parts equal in difficulty. First trombone has several high notes. Fourth trombone stays in bottom octave of instrument.

Langley   *Quartet for Four Horns* CFP   IV-V

Good horn writing. All parts demanding; requires players with good ear for pitch and accuracy. Good for work in intonation. Three movements: *La Chasse, Cortège, Rondino.*

Leduc, A.   *"Quatuor de horne*   EM   VI
                                 liturgigue"

Very difficult rhythm. Highly contemporary literature, but rewarding if performed well. Bar lines only for keeping track of music. An outstanding selection, but extremely demanding.

Lesur, D.   *Five Interludes*   Interntl   V

Written well for horns. First horn high in spots, but generally moderate. Consistent in difficulty among sections of suite.

Maas   Tallmadge   *Two Grand Quartets*   C-Bettony   V-VI

4 trumpets. Written in classical quartet form, with extensive range. Rewarding to those who meet demands of technique and musical maturity..

McKay, G.   *Suite for Four Horns*   Bar   III-IV

4 French horns and score. No great rhythm problems, but harmony interesting. Needs good low register on 4th horn.

Mozart, W.A.   Ostrander   *"Alleluja"*   EM   III-IV

4 trumpets. Strict four-voice canon in one movement. Equal interest in each voice—obviously. Duration: 1½ minutes.

Pfleger   Tallmadge   *"Hertzengesang"*   C-Bettony   V-VI

Excellent material for tone production and choral style. Ten short selections—unaccompanied but can do wonders for developing nice legato brass tone. Fourth part can be played by tuba.

Scheidt   King   *"Canzon from Collection"*   Robt King   IV

Fun piece for four trumpets or four horns. Contrapuntal and clever in its interweaving of voices. All four parts have equal requirements.

Schmutz, A.   *Divertimento*   Belwin   V-VI

Utilizes meter changes and extreme dynamic contrasts. Requires triple tonguing in all parts and much contrast in articulation. Imitation in all parts, which demands precision playing. Excellent piece for practice and for performance. Instrumentation: 4 French horns.

Tcherepnin, N.   *Six Pieces for Four*   EM   III-V
                             French Horns

Wide range of styles and difficulty. Chorale has easy ranges, but difficult for horn to sustain.

Verdi   Stube   *Triumphal March from* Belwin   II-III
                             Aida

4 trombones and cornet. Good selection—some triple tonguing, but not too difficult. Arranged for good sound and development of ensemble playing.

Wagner   Pottag   *Quartet for Horns*   Belwin   IV-V

On motives by Wagner. Requires very expressive playing. Low 4th part. Typical Wagnerian horn style employed in arrangement.

MIXED INSTRUMENTATION

Bach, J. S.   Corley   *Sarabande and Minuet* Robt King   III-IV

2 cornets, trombone, and baritone. Originally for clavichord. Provides excellent material. Duration: 3½ minutes.

| | Siebart | "Bach" Series of Fugues No. 2 | Mills | III |

2 cornets, tenor horn, and baritone. Fugue starts in baritone and moves up to 1st cornet in order. Interest in all parts.

| Couperin | King | Fugue on the Kyrie | Robt King | III-IV |

One-movement transcription of an organ work. Rhythmically and musically interesting on all parts.

| | King | "Sarabande" and "Carillon" | Robt King | III-IV |

2 cornets, trombone, and baritone. Originally for organ. "Sarabande" is in canon; "Carillon" imitates bell sounds. Mostly middle register used for each instrument. Good brass writing for four voices.

| Des Prés | King | Motet and Royal Fanfare | Robt King | III-IV |

From the motet *Absolom, fili mi.* Linear writing. Fanfare is in canon.

| Gabrieli, G. | King | Canzona per sonare Nos. 1, 2, 3, and 4 | Robt King | III-IV |

Excellent material in every respect. A "must" for brass ensemble.

| Handel | King | Two Pieces | Robt King | III-IV |

2 cornets, trombone, and baritone. Two pieces are March and Gavotte, taken from the operas *Julius Caesar* and *Ottone.* Big, full brass quality.

| Law Hewitt Billings | King | Three New England Hymns | Robt King | I-II |

2 cornets, trombone, and baritone. Music from American Revolutionary period. Easy, but musically sound.

| McKay McVey | | Ten for Brass | Boston | I-II |

Songs are well composed and have some very good musical technical problems, and rhythmic difficulties and styles.

| Mozart, W. A. | King | Fugue | Robt King | III-IV |

One movement. Source: a collection of Mozart's four-hand piano music. Independence of parts stressed, along with endurance on upper three parts.

| Palestrina | King | Ricercari del primo tuono | Robt King | III-IV |

One of the few instrumental works by Palestrina—well suited to brass idiom. Single movement in transposed Dorian mode.

| | King | Three Hymns | Robt King | I-II |

Hymns—slow tempo; sustained quality desired. Excellent material for building endurance and tone quality in young group.

| Purcell | King | Allegro and Air from **King Arthur** | Robt King | I-II |

Originally for orchestra. Contrapuntal writing and excellent material in this piece.

| | King | *Music for Queen Mary* | Robt King | I-II |

Excellent material for beginning brass.

| | Corley | *Two Trumpet Tunes and Ayre* | Robt King | III-IV |

2 cornets, trombone, and baritone. In three movements, Ayre in the middle; transparent style, with ideal range for all instruments. Few technical problems.

| Ramsoe | King | *Menuetto from Quartet No. 2* | Robt King | V-VI |

2 cornets, French horn, and baritone. A good example of Ramsoe's vigorous and melodic style. This Danish composer almost stands alone as a composer of brass chamber music in the 19th century. Strong Beethoven influence.

| | King | *Quartets Nos. 3, 4, and 5* | Robt King | V-VI |

2 cornets, French horn, and baritone. Brilliant brass quartet writing. A "must" for all brass libraries.

| Saint-Saëns | Ostling | *"Alleluia"* | Belwin | I-II |

All parts equally demanding; good contrasts in dynamics. Good use of high range in first cornet and trombone; good low range in second cornet and trombone. Horn part in a lower range.

| Sanders, R. | | *Suite for Brass Quartet* | Robt King | V |

2 cornets and 2 trombones. The movements are Sonatina, Folksong, and March. Second section *con sord*, smooth and melodic. March *senza sord*. Brilliant tonguing, difficult in first cornet.

| Siebert | King | *"Bees-Buzzin'"* | Robt King | IV |

2 trumpets, trombone, and baritone. A brass quartet that exploits technical dexterity of players in rapid and constantly flowing novelty. Good for encore or showpiece.

| Stravinsky | | *Octet* | Robt King | VI |

Very difficult and challenging selection for 2 trumpets, 2 trombones (1 bass trombone), flute, clarinet, and 2 bassoons. Requires a director to perform. Second trombone part has to be played by bass trombone because of low D.

| Wagner | Stube | *Wagner Melodies* | Mills | III |

A collection of tunes: March from *Tannhäuser*, Introduction to third act of *Lohengrin*, and "Pilgrims' Chorus" from *Tannhäuser*. Good exercise for playing triplets together.

Brass Quintet

| Anon. | King | *Sonata* | Robt King | III-IV |

2 cornets, French horn, baritone, and tuba. One-movement work originally for clarinet, cornet, and three trombones. Editor retained characteristics of period in this transcription.

| Anon. | King | Sonata from **Die Bankelsängerlieder** | Robt King | IV |

2 trumpets, horn, and 2 trombones. Requires good tonguing. Several modulations. The piece is well edited. Historical notes included in score.

| Adson | King | Two Ayres for Cornets and Sackbuts | Robt King | I-II |

From Adson's *Courtly Masquing Ayres*. English style of early 17th century. Refreshing sound.

| Bach, J. S. | King | Contrapunctus No. 1 | Robt King | III |

2 cornets, French horn, baritone, and tuba. "Sharagan" slow and melodic, with largely sustained chord work under solo. "Fugue" opens with excellent cantus firmus and develops well. No extreme ranges for this grade.

| _____ | King | Contrapunctus III | Robt King | III-IV |

2 cornets, French horn, trombone, and baritone or tuba. Also from the *Art of the Fugue*. Excellent transcription—good brass music.

| _____ | Gordon | Five Pieces for Brass Choir | MPH | III-IV |

2 trumpets, 2 horns, and trombone or tuba. Movements are March, Chorale, Chorale, Chorale, Minuet. Very interesting piece; students should enjoy it. Much work with dynamics, intonation, and phrasing.

| _____ | Christensen | Three Bach Chorales | Kend | I-II |

2 cornets, trombone, baritone, and tuba. "Awake, My Heart, and Sing," "It Is Certainly Time," and "In Sweet Jubilation" are the chorales. Setting very good, with few technical problems.

| _____ | Uber | Two Chorales | EM | I-III |

2 trumpets, French horn, trombone, and tuba. Outstanding brass arranging.

| _____ | Uber | Two Chorales | EM | III-IV |

2 trumpets, horn, trombone, and tuba. Chorales are "A Mighty Fortress Is Our God" and "O Sacred Head Now Wounded." Very good arrangement. All parts interesting.

| Brade | King | Two Pieces | Robt King | I-II |

2 cornets, French horn, trombone, and tuba. Two pieces are "Allamand" and "Gaillarde." Some phrases end with syncopated figures that bear watching.

| Coleman | Baines | Four Pieces for Sackbuts and Cornets | Oxford | III-IV |

2 trumpets and 3 trombones. Excellent literature and not too difficult. Movements are Allemande, Courante, Short Allemande, and Sarabande. Short pieces are in good baroque style.

| Converse, F. | | Two Lyric Pieces, op. 106, nos. 1 and 2 | Ru | III |

2 trumpets, horn, trombone, and tuba. Requires good reading; phrasing and counting not easy. Two movements: Folk Song, Serenade.

| Corelli | Taylor | *"Serenata"* | Mills | III | 103 |

Two cornets start in parallel thirds with sustained chords underneath. All parts have chance at melody. Parts easily read. Range not too difficult for any part.

| Dahl, I. | | *Music for Brass Instruments* | Witmark | V | |

2 trumpets, French horn, 2 trombones, and optional tuba. Three movements: (1) Choral fantasy on "Christ Lay in the Bonds of Death," (2) Intermezzo, and (3) Fugue.

| Ewald | Voxman | *Quintet in B minor, op. 5, 3rd movement* | Ru | III-IV | |

2 cornets, horn, baritone or trombone, and tuba. Delightful composition—should be met with much enthusiasm from students. Moderately difficult articulation and dynamics.

| Franck | King | *Two Pavans* | Robt King | III-IV | |

2 cornets, French horn, baritone, and tuba. Uses smooth vocal style of writing for instruments. Each part independent and weaves own pattern. Rhythmically and technically easy—ideal brass music. **Duration: 5½ minutes.**

| Grep | King | *"Paduana"* | Robt King | III-IV | |

2 cornets, French horn, trombone, and baritone or tuba. Piece provides excellent material for keeping group alert on intonation and group balance. Middle and lower register. Also usable for sextet.

| Haussmann | Rein | *"Drei Tanze"* | AMP | III-IV | |

2 trumpets and 3 trombones. Polyphonic in texture, with many repeated phrases. Uses upper range very much for 1st instruments.

| Holborne, A. | | *Suite for an Ensemble of Brass* | Oxford | III-IV | |

2 trumpets and 3 trombones. In five movements: Galliard, "The Choice," "As It Fell," "On a Holy Eve" and "The Fruit of Love." Good range for most instruments. First and second trombones in tenor clef.

| Johnson, C. | | *"Mood Militant"* | Ru | II | |

2 cornets, horn, trombone, and tuba. All parts interesting, with contemporary chord changes. Beginners would enjoy playing this number.

| Pezel | King | *Six Pieces* | Robt King | III-IV | |

2 cornets, French horn, trombone, and tuba. Source: Funff-Stimmigte Blasende Music. Original brass music for Stadtpfeifer. Pieces are two Sarabandes, Intrada, Bal Courente, and Gigue. High tessitura in first trumpet.

| _____ | King | *Sonata Nos. 1 and 3* | Robt King | I-II | |

2 cornets, trombone, baritone, and tuba. Two of the Tower Sonatas from Pezel's *Hora Decima* (Leipzig, 1670). Outstanding music for training young brass players.

| _____ | King | *Sonata No. 2* | Robt King | III-IV | |

2 cornets, French horn, trombone, and baritone or tuba. Mostly middle register and emphasis on block sonority. Written in two sections.

| | Brown | Sonata No. 27 from *Hora Decima* | Ru | III-IV |

2 trumpets, horn, trombone, and tuba. Good for public school use; interesting and well edited. Provides good number to use on junior high school level.

| | King | *Three Pieces* | Robt King | III-IV |

2 cornets, French horn, trombone, and baritone or tuba. Lighter music than the Tower Sonatas. The three pieces: Intrada, Bal, and Sarabande. Also usable as sextet. Endurance biggest problem. Few rests. Duration: 4½ minutes.

| | Rein | *Turm-Sonate Nr. 27* | Bo. Hawkes | III-IV |

2 trumpets and 3 trombones. Strong contrapuntal work; phrasing and sonority emphasized.

| Schein | King | *Two Pieces* | Robt King | III-IV |

2 cornets, French horn, trombone, and baritone. Two 17th-century dances from collection of suites *Banchetto Musicale*; dates to 1617. "Paduana" linear; "Gaillarde" harmonic.

| Schmidt, W. | | *Variations on a Negro Folk Song* | Av | V |

2 trumpets, horn, trombone, and tuba. Theme and five variations; a good reading exercise. Tricky rhythms and chromatics and good work in articulation and dynamics.

| Sousa, John | Menken and Baron | *"Semper Fidelis"* | Bo. Hawkes | III-IV |

2 trumpets, horn, trombone, and tuba. Good arrangement. Horn has only rhythmic accompaniment. Other instruments have interesting parts. Easy ranges.

| Stoltzer | King | *"Fantasia"* | Robt King | IV-V |

4 trombones, or 2 French horns and 2 trombones, and 1 tuba; or 3 trombones and tuba. Fine selection based on Hypodorian key. Good selection, somewhat contrapuntal in form but not too difficult. Range medium. Good training literature.

| Tufilli | | *"A Prayer"* | Pro-Art | II |

2 cornets, horn, baritone, and trombone. Easy range; many chromatic alterations and dynamic variations. Good for beginning ensemble.

| Uber, D. | | *"A Day at the Camptown Races"* | EM | III-IV |

2 trumpets, horn, trombone, or baritone and tuba. Novelty number, a portion in jazz idiom. All parts interesting; students would enjoy it.

Brass Sextet

| Beethoven | Lotzenhiser | *Chorale and March* | Ru | III |

Good intonation study in the Chorale. Easy range (A in 1st trumpet) for the instruments. Most parts interesting.

Bohme, O.   *Sextet*   MPH   V-VI

3 trumpets, horn, trombone, baritone, and tuba. Very long piece; would be acceptable at grade IV. Provides excellent work within sections.

Brahms   Niven   "Es ist ein Ros'   Robt King   III
                                 entsprungen"

First cornet needs good range up to G above staff. No exceptional technical problems.

Clapp, P.   "Moonlight Dance"   Bo. Hawkes   IV

From *Suite in E-flat*. Tempo moderato. All parts interesting, with many chromatic. Would take much work in dynamics for it to sound well. Begins with horn solo.

(Compiled)   *Concert Repertoire for*   Ru   II-IV
                                 Brass Sextet

Good and interesting arrangements, 17 in all, by Franck, Johnson, Purcell, Verdi, etc. Parts not difficult; most are interesting. Good scoring used here. Horn parts in F and E-flat; baritone in b.c. or t.c.

Dietz, N.   "Modern Moods"   AMP   III

Employs jazz rhythms and very interesting chord changes. Students would enjoy doing this. A high B-flat in trombone part. All parts interesting.

Frangkiser, C.   "Entry of the Heralds"   Bo. Hawkes   III

Brassy; all parts play most all the time. An enjoyable composition.

Gounod   Ostling   "Marche romaine"   Belwin   II

A good arrangement. All parts interesting; dynamic ranges good; many dotted eighth-sixteenth rhythms. Ranges normal for grade II.

————————————   *Soldiers' Chorus from*   MPH   IV
                                 Faust

Good arrangement of an exciting number. All parts interesting, with good range.

Hanna, J.   "Song of the Redwood   Robt King   III-IV
                                 Tree"

(With timpani.) Adapted from Walt Whitman's *Leaves of Grass*. A narrator speaks the poem at certain places during the piece. No difficult technical problems.

Long, N.   *Brass Sextet Album*   Kjos   II-IV

Includes variety of music. Contains works by many of the masters—Bach, Wagner, Mendelssohn, Liszt, Handel, Mozart, Sullivan, etc. All good arrangements. Also contains novelties, Christmas music, an arrangement of Liszt's *Les Préludes*. A cornet can be substituted for the horn part.

Lully   King   *Overture to* **Cadmus at**   Robt King   III-IV
                                 Mermione

Originally written for string orchestra. Slow first section followed by light contrapuntal final section.

MacDowell   Johnson   **Woodland Sketches**, op. 51, Ru   III
                                 Nos. 1, 3, 6, and 8

2 trumpets, horn, trombone, baritone, and tuba. Pieces are "To a Wild Rose," "At an

Old Trysting Place," "To a Water Lily," and "A Deserted Farm." Very good arranging. Good articulation, dynamics, and chromatics.

| Malotte | Beeler | "The Lord's Prayer" | G. Schirmer | III |

Could be made very exciting. Good arrangement, with conventional accompaniment and harmony.

| Mascagni, P. | | Cathedral Scene and Intermezzo from **Cavalleria Rusticana** | Belwin | III |

Fair arranging of interesting number. Good work in logical dynamics.

| Meyers, C. | | *Rhapsody for Brass* | Meyers | V |

For clarity, best used without multiple instruments. Phrasing difficult; clean tonguing and long phrasing needed.

| Phillips, B. | | *Piece for Six Trombones* | Robt King | IV |

Full command of alternate positions needed. The first brass trombone part could be played on tenor trombone.

| Prokofiev | Ford | *Gavotte* | G. Schirmer | IV |

Good contrapuntal rhythms in interesting contemporary number. Range not very demanding.

| _____ | Porter | *Triumphal March* | Concord | V |

Adapted from *Peter and the Wolf*. Overedited but acceptable.

| Purcell | Brown | *Trumpet Tune and Air* | Ru | III |

2 cornets, horn, baritone, tuba, and trombone. Another good arrangement. All parts fairly interesting; best is 1st trumpet.

| _____ | Corley | *Voluntary on 100th Psalm* | Robt King | V-VI |

Transcribed from organ work based on the Doxology. Well suited to brass idiom.

| Schmutz, A. | | "Fantasy Sketch" | Cf | III-IV |

Good number with interesting rhythm. Somewhat on the contemporary side; a few changes in meter.

| Tchaikovsky | Tallmadge | **Capriccio italien, op. 45** | Belwin | V |

With marimba. Requires good musicians to make up for light scoring. Good arrangement, which could be an exciting composition.

| _____ | Tallmadge | **Lake of the Swan** | Belwin | V-VI |

With marimba. Introduction and Finale from well-known work. The ballet itself was at first seldom performed because of rhythmic difficulty for the dancers. Technically, rhythmically, and dynamically difficult in all parts. For virtuoso players only.

| Verrall, J. | | *Suite for Brass* | MM | III |

All parts essential and not doubled in five contrasting movements. Ranges and technical problems for the various instruments handled with good taste. Enough variety to please all the players.

Wagner, R.   *King's Prayer and Finale,*   AMP   IV
 from **Lohengrin,** *Act 1*

Good arrangement, with important parts covered by cues. Requires full sound with much control. Many accents and dynamic contrasts; a high C in 1st trumpet.

Eight Trombones

Massaino   King   *Music for Brass*   Robt King   IV
 No. 140

6 trombones, horn, and tuba; or 8 trombones. In fugal style. Rhythm fairly complicated; range not too demanding. Interesting selection for large brass group.

Brass Choir

Adler, S.   *"Praeludium"*   Robt King   IV-V

2 cornets, 2 horns, 2 trombones, baritone, and tuba, with timpani. Scored thin for the most part, but excellent full voicing for dynamic change. Frequent change from triple to double rhythm. Good for high school or better.

Arnell, R.   *Ceremonial and Flourish*   AMP   IV

4 trumpets, 4 horns, and 3 trombones. Written for C trumpet, but B-flat parts are also supplied. Does not demand extreme range.

Cobine, A.   *Vermont Suite*   Robt King   IV-V

4 trumpets, 3 horns, 4 trombones, baritone, and tuba. Won the Thor Johnson brass composition award in 1953. Avoids overscoring and unnecessary doubling. Uses horns effectively within moderate range.

Ewald   King   *Symphony for Brass Choir*   Robt King   IV-VI

2 cornets, horn, trombone, baritone, and tuba. Recorded by brass players of the New York Philharmonic Orchestra. If performed in its entirety, would require grade VI. Duration over 13 minutes. Movements could be used separately at grade IV-V.

Findley   *The Junior Brass Choir*   C-Bettony   I-III

Collection contains compositions of all eras by many composers and of many different styles. Works of varying difficulty. Instrumentation: many combinations possible, using basic SATB parts, from quartets to larger brass choirs.

Frackenpohl   *"Shepherds, Rejoice"*   Robt King   IV

Male chorus, 3 horns, baritone, and tuba. Words from a shaped-note book, *The Social Harp*, Philadelphia, 1868. Only the legato style in the trombone parts prevents this from being used in grade III, if desired. Musically suitable for grade V.

Gabrieli, G.   King   *Canzon duodecimi toni*   Robt King   III-IV

1st choir: 2 cornets, horn, trombone, baritone, and tuba; 2nd choir: same as first, organ optional. Brilliant work, well suited to festive occasions.

_____   King   *Canzon quarti toni*   Robt King   V-VI

1st choir: cornet, 2 horns, trombone, and tuba; 2nd choir: 4 trombones and tuba; 3rd choir: same as 1st choir. This triple-choir ceremonial music is one of Gabrieli's finest creations. A rousing brass composition.

	King	*Sonata pian'e forte*	Robt King	I-II

1st choir: 2 cornets, horn, and baritone; 2nd choir: 3 trombones, baritone, and tuba. The earliest known work that prescribes specific instrumentation and dynamic contrast.

Handel	King	*Three Pieces from Water Music*	Robt King	V-VI

2 cornets, 2 horns, baritone, and tuba. Ideal brass music. Outdoor music—lively, but also dignified.

Hogg, M.		*Concerto for Brass*	Robt King	V-VI

3 trumpets, 3 horns, 3 trombones, baritone, tuba, and timpani. Twelve-tone in conception and strongly dissonant. Covers extreme ranges.

	King	*Two Medieval Motets*	Robt King	II

Three-part brass choir. Easy technically, yet challenges listening, tuning, and general musicianship. Written in 13th-century harmonic idiom and contrapuntal style.

Lassus	King	*Canzon septimi toni No. 2*	Robt King	III-IV

1st choir and 2nd choir: 2 cornets, horn, and baritone. Exceptional brass choir writing. Brilliant effect.

	King	*"Providebam Dominum"*	Robt King	III-IV

1st choir: 2 cornets; 2nd choir: cornet, horn, trombone, baritone, and tuba. Originally vocal but there is evidence that Lassus once conducted a brass performance of this. Superior brass material.

Nelhybel, V.		*Three Intradas*	F. Colombo	V-VI

3 trumpets, 2 horns, 3 trombones, and 1 tuba. Excellent modern piece. Technically not too difficult, but very difficult to play in tune, and French horn and trombone parts very demanding in 3rd Intrada. Keeping rhythmic ensemble together is difficult. Requires every variety of articulation.

Obrecht	King	*"Tsat een meskin"*	Robt King	III

Four-part brass choir of trumpet, trombone, I, II, and III, with optional parts for horns and baritone. Fine opportunities for educational training, as well as performance values.

Osborne, W.		*Two Ricercari*	Robt King	V

2 trumpets, 2 horns, trombone, baritone, and tuba. Frequent meter change between 2/4, 4/4, 3/2, 5/4, and 2/4—the only major item to put it in class V. Barring these problems, could be class IV.

Pachelbel	King	*"All Glory Be to God on High"*	Robt King	II

4-part brass choir with organ: 2 cornets, trombone, and baritone or trombone. First of two sections features technique of organ against sustained long tones in brass choir. Second section, Chorale, uses brass alone and is slightly more challenging.

Purcell	Brown	*Trumpet Voluntary*	Summy-Bir	III

Trumpet, 3 cornets, 2 horns, 3 trombones, baritone, and tuba. All parts written sensibly and in good taste. Good contest or concert material.

Schütz, H.		*Antiphony No. 1*	TP	II	109

Based on eight-part vocal motet and transcribed for double brass choir. Each choir consists of two trumpets and two trombones for a total of eight players. Music technically easy.

Scott, W.		*Rondo Giocoso*	Robt King	IV-V

3 trumpets, 4 horns, 4 trombones, baritone, tuba, timpani, snare drum, and cymbal. Requires pedal timpani. Delicate phrasing. A Thor Johnson brass composition award winner in 1953.

Storl	King	*Sonata No. 1*	Robt. King	III

Cornet, horn, trombone, and baritone. Excellent music for study of tonal blend and controlled balance in dynamics. Technically easy, except for endurance problem. Ranges medium high. Two brief movements offer contrast.

WOODWIND

Woodwind Trio

LIKE INSTRUMENTATION

Bach	Cafarelli	*Sinfonia in C minor*	MPH	III-IV

Outstanding baroque material at intermediate level.

Beethoven	Hernvied	*Allegro from op. 87*	Remick	III-IV

Taken from Beethoven's Wind Trio for 2 oboes and French horn. Excellent transcription. Phrasing well marked and sometimes quite long. Good material for breath control and abrupt dynamic change so characteristic in traditional sections of his instrumental works.

———————————		*Grand Trio for Three Flutes, op. 87*	Andraud	V-VI

In three sections: *Allegro, Adagio cantabile, Presto*. Requires good technique and musicianship.

———————————	Fetherston	*Theme and Variations, op. 25*	Belwin	III-IV

Theme and two variations with coda. Use of sixteenth notes in the 4/8 section. Good training material.

Buchtell, F.		*"Dancing Nymphs"*	Kjos	I-II

3 flutes. Adequate for training piece. Easy range in 3/4 and 6/8 meter. Piano accompaniment.

———————————		*"Elfin Dance"*	Kjos	II

3 flutes. Acceptable training piece. Parts lie well for this grade material.

Cox		*Prelude*	EV	III

Melodic piece in interesting canonic style for three B-flat clarinets, unaccompanied. Fine independence in the parts and of moderate technical difficulty. Careful attention to balance will assist in bringing out proper contrapuntal voices and should make for interesting performance. Time: 4 minutes.

| Donato, A. | | *Three Pieces* | TP | III |

3 clarinets, "Autumn Mood" (slow 6/8), "Overcase" (quick 2/4), and "The Twister" (fast 3/4). Solo parts divided among all instruments. Good training material.

| Faber, J. | | *Six Melodies in Ancient Style* | C-Bettony | II-III |

3 clarinets. Overture, Bourrée, Air, Marche, Minuet No. 1, and Minuet No. 2. All movements short except overture. Could delete any movement if desired.

| Grundman, C. | | *Flute Trio, "Flutation"* | Bo. Hawkes | III-IV |

A good degree of melodic interest in all three parts. Accompaniment not too difficult; typical grade III flute trio will find this a number to hold interest.

| Handel | | *Bourrée* | CF | I-II |

3 clarinets. Easy music that "sounds" well.

| Haydn | Taylor | *Rondo scherzando* | Bo. Hawkes | III |

3 flutes. Some long phrases and occasional articulation problems, but musical content excellent.

| Hindemith, P. | | *Trio* | SCH | IV |

3 flutes. Written for soprano, alto, and tenor recorders. Excellent modern material for these instruments.

| Hood | Voxman | *Six Trios for Three Flutes* | Ru | III |

3 flutes. Six charming trios by English composer who lived from 1746 to 1827. Ornamentation indicated, with rhythm to be used noted above embellishment. Not many markings, and range is not extreme. Tessitura from first space F to high C.

| _____ | | *Sonata for Three Flutes* | Bo. Hawkes | IV-V |

3 flutes. In two movements, second movement broken into four sections. In strict classic style with some antiphonal writing—good for training or programming.

| Koepke, P. | | *"Harlequinade"* | Ru | II |

3 flutes. Musically refreshing at an easy level. Count on this capable composer.

| Kummer, G. | | *Trio Brilliant, op. 58* | C-Bettony | IV |

Trio for three B-flat clarinets in three movements marked *Allegro non tanto, Adagio,* and *Allegretto con moto.* Parts require equal technical ability and flexibility. Exceptionally fine contest material and valuable training music. Time: 8 minutes.

| _____ | | *Trio in A, op. 59*
Trio in G, op. 24
Trio in C, op. 53 | C-Bettony | IV-VI |

3 flutes. Advanced work for flute written by outstanding performer and teacher. Rhythm and range difficult. Middle section changes key and goes to adagio-andante style.

Leidzen   *Bourne Trio Album*   Bourne   I

Instrumentation can be any three like instruments, but three clarinets preferable. Simple, well-known tunes in easy arrangements. Large printing.

Liadov   Weston   *"Mosquito Dance"*   Concord   V-VI

3 flutes. Frequent rhythm changes; third flute demands facility in low register. Parts challenging.

Marks   Rosenthal   *Russian Trios*   Marks   III

3 clarinets. Level of difficulty average, and ranges easy. All numbers relatively good and interesting.

McKay, G.   **Four Seasons**   Bo. Hawkes   III-IV

3 flutes. Suite in four different moods. Sections could be used separately. Third flutist must play middle C well.

Mozart, W. A.   Taylor   *March from* **Titus**   Mills   I-II

3 flutes. Valuable work for beginning trio.

Ostransky   *Pastorale and Scherzo*   Ru   II

3 clarinets. Piece for clarinet trio with piano accompaniment that offers few difficulties other than careful working out of contrapuntal style. Music functional if not profound, and ranges of all three parts stay within reasonable, good register. Duration: 4¼ minutes.

Petz, W.   *"Three of a Kind"*   Belwin   I

3 flutes. Provides for independent playing in semicontrapuntal form. All parts have solo at times.

Rosenthal   *Clarinet Trios from Corelli to Beethoven*   Morris   III-V

3 clarinets. Not too much editing; rhythmically interesting and musical content high. Good for training or programming.

Rosenthal   *Clarinet Trios: Russian Composers*   Morris   III-V

3 clarinets. Music from Moussorgsky, Glière, Liadov, Rimsky-Korsakov, Shostakovich, etc. Overedited but quite well arranged. Some pieces rather easy, others quite difficult.

Taylor   *Suite classique in D*   K-K   III-IV

3 flutes. Suite of heterogenous extraction: Prelude—Bach; Courante—Croft; Minuet—Boccherini; Rondo—Steibelt. Fine flute material. A bit demanding to be performed in entirety.

Tchaikovsky   Hummel   *"Danse des mirlitons"*   Ru   V-VI

3 flutes with piano. The Nutcracker Dance is still a good old chestnut for student development. Excellent material for technical advancement.

Tcherepnin, A.   *Trio for Three Clarinets*   Marks   II

3 clarinets. Moderate tessitura. Second part often difficult because of frequent register changes.

	Voxman	*Chamber Music for Three Clarinets, Vol. I*	Ru	I-II
	Voxman	*Chamber Music for Three Flutes*	Ru	III-IV

3 flutes. Equal interest on each part, but first part does contain most of the high notes. Material carefully selected.

	Voxman	*Chamber Music for Three Woodwinds*	Ru	II-III

Flute, clarinet, bassoon. All parts interesting. Pieces by Corelli through Beethoven. Musical content high.

Walker, R.		*"Capriccio"*	Bar	IV

3 flutes. Treats three parts with almost equal importance. Uses variety of styles.

_____		*"Cortège"*	Bar	IV

3 flutes and piano. Rapidly moving and technically active in all parts; first flute part the most demanding. Good study in accurate rhythms and staccato.

MIXED INSTRUMENTATION

Ostransky, L.		*Trio in G minor*	Ru	V-VI

Flute, oboe, and B-flat clarinet. Three selections for trio, unaccompanied. Wide range in dynamics and tempo. Good utilization of the ranges of the three instruments. Good for practice and performance. Rhythmic work would need to be very precise. Many advanced high school students could perform this number.

Woodwind Quartet

LIKE INSTRUMENTATION

Bach, J. S.	Brandenburg	*Bourrée*	CF	III-IV

4 clarinets. Quartet arrangement excellent because of distribution of interesting parts. Markings rather romantic.

Beethoven	Geiger	*Andante cantabile*	Remick	III-IV

4 clarinets.

_____	Toll	*Rondo*	C-Bettony	III-IV

4 clarinets. Taken from Sonata No. 8, op. 13. Many musical problems for good group to solve; a competent transcription; ornaments properly written.

Boccherini	Eck	*Eck Quartet Album for Flutes*	Belwin	II-III

4 flutes. Selections not too long. Each part interesting; range and tessitura not extreme.

Brown, T.		*Piece for Four Clarinets*	G. Schirmer	III

4 clarinets. Appealing to age level of III. Written to avoid difficult register changes in rapidly moving parts.

Carter, E.   *Canonic Suite*   AMP   IV-V

4 clarinets. Difficult work because of key and intricate rhythm problems; requires good staccato. Three movements could be used separately; holds students' interest. One movement could be used alone at level III.

Corelli   Maganini   *Allemande*   EM   I-II

4 flutes. Well written for beginning flutists.

—————————   Maganini   *Allemande*   EM   III-IV

4 clarinets. Very good, well-edited piece.

—————————   Maganini   *Gavotte and Gigue*   EM   III-IV

4 clarinets. Excellent transcription, even though markings are sparse. Provides excellent rhythmic material in Gigue.

Erickson, F.   *Scherzino*   Belwin   I

Flute, clarinet, oboe, and bassoon; or 2 clarinets, flute, and bass clarinet. Good for ensemble practice. Only small amount of melody; emphasis on rhythmic accuracy.

Glazunov   Bettony   *"In modo religioso"*   C-Bettony   III

4 clarinets. More difficult in style than in technique. Well distributed solo parts.

Gluck   Liegl   *"Dance of the Happy*   CF   I-II
                                     Spirits"

4 clarinets. Two upper parts carry melody; good material for this level.

Grundman, C.   *"Bagatelle"*   Bo. Hawkes   III

4 clarinets. Showy for this grade level. No extreme ranges; in an easy key. Enjoyable for junior high students as a reading piece.

Handel   Liegl   *Sarabande*   CF   I-II

4 clarinets. Melody appears in each part. Piece excellent for developing stylistic playing; tone quality stressed.

Handel-Ostling   *Petite Fugue*   Belwin   I-II

Flute, oboe, clarinet, and bassoon; or flute, 2 clarinets, and bass clarinet. Good melody in all parts. Clarinet part requires use of alternate fingerings. Good piece for introducing fugal style. Useful for practice or performance.

                     Holmes   *Clarinet Symphony*   Ru   II-III

4 clarinets. Collection of works, sources of which are given. Ranges not extreme; few markings.

Keith, G.   *Interlude*   Bo. Hawkes   II-III

4 clarinets. Good training material, written in florid style. Parts interesting and require good upper range.

Kohler, E.   *Grand Quartet*   Andraud   V-VI

4 flutes. Technically difficult, but well written.

MacDowell   McKay   *Two Tone Poems*   Bar   II-III

4 clarinets. Capably transcribed. Good use of lower range of clarinet. Includes "Cradle Song" and "March of the Gnomes."

McKay, G.   *Three Nautical Characters*   Bar   II

Flute, oboe, clarinet, bassoon, and optional horn. Three short movements, two of which are "Sailor Jack" and "Barnacle Bill." Good program material. Duration: 3 minutes.

McPeck   *Album of Classical Pieces*   EV   III

Unusual offering to woodwind ensemble, in form of seven classical pieces playable by almost any four woodwinds. Duration: 12 minutes.

Miller, B.   *Prelude and Scherzo*   Belwin   III

4 clarinets. Harmonically interesting. Accidentals used freely, and all parts equally difficult.

Mozart, W. A.   Liegl   *Minuet from **Don Juan** [**Don Giovanni**]*   CF   I-II

4 clarinets. Excellent work for elementary players, using clear, transparent writing.

_____   **Maganini**   *Alleluja*   EM   III-IV

4 clarinets. Beginning a strict four-part canon. First clarinet goes to high F; rhythmically simple.

_____   Toll   *Rondo from Piano Sonata No. 4*   C-Bettony   V-VI

4 clarinets. Excellent material, musically and educationally. Well suited for clarinet.

Rathaus, K.   *Country Serenade*   Bo. Hawkes   III-V

4 clarinets.

Roden, R.   ***Sounds of the Sea***   Bar   III

4 clarinets. Suite in three movements for four B-flat clarinets. Harmonies tastefully modern, and rhythm of each part often independent. Fun to play, and will appeal to student performers. Duration: 4¼ minutes.

Rosenthal   *Clarinet Quartets— 18th Century*   NOR   III

4 clarinets. Nine works from major composers of 18th century. Excellent material; range is not extreme—from a 10th to an octave and a 5th.

Schmutz, A.   *Scherzoso*   FitzSimons   IV-V

4 clarinets. Rapid tempo and difficult interval work, but good voicing.

Schumann   Simon   *Seven Miniatures*   Bo. Hawkes   II

4 clarinets. Seven pieces arranged from *Album for the Young*. Good variety. Considerate range for age level of music. Excellent for any school library for upper elementary or junior high school.

4 clarinets. Transcribed from Telemann's Concerto for Four Violins. First clarinet part difficult to read because of all the cues.

Vivaldi   Maganini   *Sonata da camera*   EM   III-IV

4 clarinets. Usually scored for brass, but clarinet scoring seems to fit. Also arranged for three clarinets.

MIXED INSTRUMENTATION

Bach, J. S.   Cox   *Gavotte*   Bo. Hawkes   I-II

Flute, oboe, clarinet, and bassoon. Fine ensemble material for young students. Rhythm simple and range not excessive.

_____   McKay   *Fugue No. IV*   Bar   V-VI

2 clarinets, alto clarinet, and bass clarinet. Good transcription, but demanding in every respect.

_____   Maganini   *Prelude from No. 12,*   EM   V-VI
                               Well-Tempered Clavichord

2 clarinets, alto clarinet, and bass clarinet. Provides excellent training material; rhythmically demanding. Also scored for 3 clarinets and bass clarinet.

Beethoven   Moehlmann   *Quartet from op. 18,*   Bo. Hawkes   III-IV
                                     no. 4

2 clarinets, alto clarinet, and bass clarinet. *Andante* movement technically and musically demanding, but worth is more than any effort expended.

Bennett, D.   *"Argentine"*   CF   V

2 clarinets, alto clarinet, and bass clarinet. Uses full range of instruments. Showy and interesting; effective dynamic change.

Handel   Barr   *Bourrée from the **Water*** *   Belwin   III
                          Music *Suite*

2 clarinets, alto clarinet, and bass clarinet. Rhythmically easy, but some stylistic problems with ornamentation and dynamic contrasts.

_____   Stang   *Sinfonia*   C-Bettony   I-II

Flute, oboe, clarinet, and bassoon. From the *Messiah*. Flute in very high register; otherwise good transcription.

Hovhaness   *Divertimento*   CFP   IV-V

Oboe, clarinet, horn, and bassoon; or 4 clarinets. Written in seven parts, in style of baroque suite. Excellent musically.

Kraehenbuehl, D.   *Variations on a Pavane*   AMP   IV
                                by Hermann Schein

3 clarinets and bass clarinet.

Liadov–Haydn   Voxman   *Sarabande and Finale*   Ru   V-VI

2 clarinets, alto clarinet, and bass clarinet. Sarabande from *Les Vendrebis* by Liadov and Finale from Haydn's Quartet No. 43, op. 42. Great music and highly refined; musical maturity required to play this work.

Lully   Taylor   *Courante*   Mills   I-II

Flute, oboe, clarinet, and bassoon. Good beginning quartet music. Only a few trills; ranges and tessitura all medium to low—flute has one high E.

Manson, E.   *Fugue for Woodwinds*   AMP   IV-V

Flute, oboe, clarinet, and bassoon. Rhythmically and harmonically difficult for amateur performers. Requires full range of instruments and good phrasing.

McKay, F.   *"Chromatic Caprice"*   Bar   III-IV

2 clarinets, alto clarinet, and bass clarinet. Harmonically interesting; free use of chromatics. Usually appeals to students.

Mozart, W. A.   Bellison   *Suite No. 2*   Ricordi   V-VI

2 clarinets, alto clarinet, and bass clarinet. Superior material for developing musical interpretation.

_____   Cafarella   *Finale from Sonata No. 5*   Witmark   IV

Flute, oboe, clarinet, and bassoon. Good transcription of excellent and interesting music to perform. Good tone and facile technique requisites to performing.

Praetorius   Schmutz   *"Preludial Fantasia"*   FitzSimons   III-IV

2 clarinets, alto clarinet, bass clarinet. Range and tessitura good; musically interesting piece in all parts.

Regner, H.   *"Serenade"*   CFP   IV-V

Oboe, clarinet, horn, and bassoon. Problems in ensemble playing would require experienced ensemble with above average technical facility. Better high school group would find it challenging and rewarding.

Sanders, R.   *"The Imp"*   CF   IV-V

2 clarinets, alto clarinet, and bass clarinet. A cheerful piece, with interesting harmony. Appeals to students who enjoy modern harmony.

Schumann   *Allegro from Sonata No. 1, op. 105*   C-Bettony   V-VI

2 clarinets, alto clarinet, and bass clarinet. Well transcribed; delicate phrasing required.

Singelee, J.   *Allegro de concert*   CF   V-VI

Soprano sax (optional), I alto sax, II alto sax, tenor sax, and baritone sax. Excellent selection for saxophone quartet. Varied range in dynamics and tempo. Good practice piece for slurring and tonguing. Also good piece for performance. B-flat soprano saxophone and first alto saxophone parts interchangeable. Utilizes more than one meter during piece.

2 clarinets, alto clarinet, and bass clarinet. Composers representative from Lully to Schumann. Collection of excellent material in dance form, arranged with taste and discretion.

Woodwind Quintet

FLUTE, OBOE, CLARINET, HORN, AND BASSOON

Bach, J. S.   Sarlit   *Sarabande et Courante*   Baron   III-IV

Although not too difficult, smooth technique and control of tone necessary.

_____ Gordon   *Sarabande and Gavotte*   C-Bettony   III

Arrangement for standard woodwind quintet, both musically interesting and not too difficult. Horn and oboe parts easier than those for clarinet, flute, and bassoon. Contrasting styles of articulations, and fine opportunities for tight ensemble playing. Duration: 3 minutes, 10 seconds.

_____ Henschel   *Sarabande in D minor*   Bo. Hawkes   II-III

Tessitura good and phrases well defined. Ornamentation indicated but not written out.

_____ Sariet   *Sonata*   Baron   III

Not very difficult for high school. Requires good control of instrument and tonal quality.

Bargiel   Harris   *"Mediation"*   C-Bettony   III-IV

Good musical value, not especially hard. Students should find it of interest.

Barthe, A.   *Passacaille*   Baron   III-IV

Very well written and not too difficult.

Bauere   *Juilliard Series of Music*   G. Schirmer   V-VI
                    for Wind Instruments—Bk. 1

Two selections call for A clarinet. The Bach rather overmarked. Excellent training material at high school level.

Bauere   *Juilliard Series of Music*   G. Schirmer   V-VI
                    for Wind Instruments—Bk. 2

Works of Mozart, Beethoven, Grieg, Stravinsky, and others. Rhythmically quite difficult; ranges and tessitura wide.

Beethoven   *Rondo in F*   C-Bettony   V

Not excessive range; requires good staccato.

Bozza, E.   *Scherzo, op. 48*   Baron   VI

Very difficult, but has musical interest. For advanced college or professionals.

_____   *"Variations sur un*   Baron   VI
                    thème libre"*

Difficult, but good musical style.

Clapp, P.		Prelude and Finale	Bo. Hawkes	V-VI

Difficult in all instruments; needs experienced ensemble.

Cohen, S.		Suite in Three Parts	CF	III

Good musical material.

Colomer, B.		Bourrée	C-Bettony	IV

Good musical value. Good clean technique necessary.

Corelli	Trinkhaus	Sarabande and Courante	K-K	I-II

Good arrangement; valuable addition to elementary library.

Cowell, H.		Suite	Mercury	V

Danzi, F.		Blaserquintett B dur, op. 56, no. 1	AMP	V-VI

Debussy, C.		"The Little 'Nigar'"	Baron	III-IV

Excellent composition. Most interesting for students; has audience appeal.

Desporte, Y.		Prelude, Variations, and Finale on a Gregorian Chant	Baron	V

Quite difficult; requires good command of instrument.

Fernandez, O.		Suite	Baron	V

Demands good technique from instrumentalists.

Gayfer, J.		Suite	Bo. Hawkes	V

First section demanding for flute. Other sections playable at grade III or IV. Scored well in respective parts.

Gluck		Gavotte	CF	III-IV

High student interest. Musician will enjoy playing this.

Gould, M.	Taylor	Pavane from American Symphonette No. 2	Mills	III

Adapts well to this ensemble.

Haydn	Geiger	Adagio	C-Bettony	V-VI

Major interest in flute and oboe. Some long phrases present, along with rhythmical interest in all parts.

_____	Perry	Divertimento	Bo. Hawkes	V-VI

Excellent music in a good arrangement.

_____	Meek	Largo	Ditson	III-IV

Quiet, sustained work. Arrangement done with taste and restraint.

Hindemith, P.		Quintet, op. 24, no. 2	Baron	V

Excellent number, very difficult and requires good command of instrument. For advanced high school or college.

Hugues-Cavally		*Allegro scherzoso*	Wil	V-VI

Very difficult number; contains strong, driving rhythms that are good for pupil's practice, and chromatic drills and imitation in fugal manner, making students count and listen to their own particular parts. All parts equally demanding, and ranges exploited.

Ibert, J.		*"Trois pièces breves"*	Baron	V

Difficult number of musical interest for college and advanced high school. Good tonal quality a necessity.

Milhaud, D.		**La cheminée du roi** **Réné** *Suite*	Baron	V

A number of some difficulty for advanced high school and college. Good control of technique necessary; musically very good.

STRING ORCHESTRA

Grade I

	Barnes	*The Very Easy String Folio*	Spr	I
Clark, I.		*String Players Very First Ensemble*	Boston	I
Isaac, M.		*Achievement Orchestra Folio*	CF	I
————————		*Activity Orchestra Folio*	CF	I
Whistler–Hummel		*String Time*	Ru	I

Grade II

Carse, A.		*Peasant's Song and Dance*	Broude	II
	Fyffe	*Fourteen Familiar Christian Carols*	Ditson	II
Handel	Weaver	*From the* **Water Music**	Mills	II
————————	Clark	*Handel Suite (Master Series)*	G. Schirmer	II
————————	Wilson	*Little Fugue and Sarabande*	Gam. Hinged	II
————————	Woodhouse	*Melodies from the* **Messiah**	Bo. Hawkes	II
Hansen		*Little Norwegian Suite*	Bo. Hawkes	II
Haydn	Woodhouse	*Melodies by Joseph Haydn*	Bo. Hawkes	II
Isaac, M.		*"Buttons"—Pizzicato Novelty*		II
	Kuhn	*16th and 17th Century Dance Tunes and Airs*	Belwin	II

McKay, G.		Accent on Strings, Vols. 1, 2, and 3	Witmark	II
Muller, F.		String Orchestra Classics	EMS	II
Offenbach	Woodhouse	Barcarolle from **Tales of Hoffman**	Bo. Hawkes	II
Schumann	Urban	"The Merry Peasant"	Mills	II
	Whistler	Solo for Strings for Individual Playing or Class (Unison)	Ru	II
Whistler-Hummel		Ensemble for Strings	Ru	II
_____		Intermediate Scales and Bowings	Ru	II
Woodhouse		"A Little Romance"	Bo. Hawkes	II
_____		"A Morning Song"	Bo. Hawkes	II
_____		"Spring Tide" (Miniature Overture)	Bo. Hawkes	II

Grade III

Bach, J. S.	Clark	Bach for Strings	G. Schirmer	III
_____		Two Gavottes in D Major	Witmark	III
Bacich, A.		Tone Poem for Strings	Wil	III
Bizet	Woodhouse	March from **Carmen**	Bo. Hawkes	III
Boyce, W.		Sonatas I and II	Galaxy	III
	Church-Glass	Masterworks of Bach, Avison, Purcell, LeClair, and Corelli	Leeds	III
	Church-Glass	Masterworks of Bach, Corelli, and Others	Leeds	III
	Clark	String Music of the Baroque Era—by Corelli, Rameau, Handel, J. S. Bach, Purcell, and Telemann	Boston	III
Corelli, A.	Maganini	Gavotte and Gigue	EM	III
Cowell, H.		Hymn and Fuguing Tune No. 2 for String Orchestra	AMP	III
de Prosse	Isaac	Petite Bourrée	CF	III

Dittersdorf, K.		Andante from String Quartet	Witmark	III
Gillet, E.		Academic String Orchestra Series, "In the Mill"	CF	III
Glazunov	Ponchon	"Interludium in modo antico"	CF	III
	Goehring	String Masters, Book I	Ludwig	III
	Goehring	String Masters, Book II	Ludwig	III
	Gordon	Walt Disney Classics	Bourne	III
Handel	Freudenthal	Suite from **Julius Caesar**	Marks	III
Haydn	Stoissel	"Emperor" Variations from String Quartet, op. 76	CF	III
_____	Clark	Haydn Suite (Master Series)	G. Schirmer	III
Herbert, V.	Watson	String Americana, Bk. I	Witmark	III
_____	Watson	String Americana, Bk. II	Witmark	III
Holesovsky, J.		Variations on a French Folk Tune	H. Elkan	III
Kuhn, W.		25 16th and 17th Century Dance Tunes and Airs	Belwin	III
McBride, R.		"Pumpkin Eater's Little Fugue"	AMP	III
McKay, G.		**Halyard & Capstan** (Sea Shanty Suite)	Birchard	III
_____		Port Royal Suite, 1861	Birchard	III
_____		"Sky Blue and Meadow Green"	Birchard	III
	McKay	Two Folk Songs	TP	III
	McLin	Chorales for Strings	Pro-Art	III
Mendelssohn	Woodhouse	"On Wings of Song"	Bo. Hawkes	III
Monteverdi	Freudenthal	Suite from **Orfeo**	Robbins	III
Morand		"Trepak"	Bo. Hawkes	III
Mozart, W. A.	Woodhouse	"Ave verum corpus"	Bo. Hawkes	III
_____	Szokolay	Divertimento	Bo. Hawkes	III
	Preston	String Ensemble Favorites	Belwin	III
Purcell	Reigger	Cannon on a Ground Bass	AMP	III

	Jacques	*Three Dances from the Fairy Queen*	Oxford	III
	Brown	***King Arthur** Suite*	Galaxy	III
Sabor, N.		*Popular Songs for String Orchestra*	Morris	III
Schumann	Urban	*"The Merry Peasant"*	Mills	III
Somers, H.		*Little Suite for String Orchestra*	AMP	III
	Sopkins	*String Americana, Bk. I*	Harms	III
	Sopkins	*String Americana, Bk. II*	Harms	III
	Stoessel	*University String Album*	CF	III
Valerius	Kindler	*Three 17th Century Dutch Tunes*	CF	III

Grade IV

Bach	Clark	*Bach Suite (Master Series)*	G. Schirmer	IV
Beethoven	Clark	*Beethoven Suite (Master Series)*	G.Schirmer	IV
Bizet	Dasch	*Adagietto from L'Arabesque Suite*	FitzSimons	IV
Corelli	Brown	*Sonata da camera VII and VIII*	Galaxy	IV
	Glass	*Sonata da chiesa, op. 1, no. 2*	BMI	IV
Crowther		*"Gweedore Brae"*	CF	IV
Grieg		*"Heart Wounds" and "Last Spring"*	CF	IV
Lully	Brown	*Six Pieces*	Galaxy	IV
Mozart, W. A.	Clark	*Mozart Suite (Master Series)*	G. Schirmer	IV
	Brown	*Sinfonietta in D Major*	Galaxy	IV
Purcell	Akon	*Five Selected Pieces*	BMI	IV
Sammartini, G.		*Concerto Grosso, op. 14, no. 4*	Mus. Press	IV
Schubert	Perry	*Five Waltzes*	Bo. Hawkes	IV
Walthew, R.		*"Table Music"*	Galaxy	IV

Anderson, L.		"Fiddle Faddle"	Mills	V-VI
Bach	Franko	Arioso	G. Schirmer	V-VI
Copland, A.		Hoe-Down from **Rodeo**	Bo. Hawkes	V-VI
Couperin	Brown	Four Pieces in Form of Suite	Galaxy	V-VI
	Gould	"Go Down, Moses"	Mills	V-VI
Mozart, W. A.	Stoessel	Eine kleine Nachtmusik	CF	V-VI
Prokofiev		Andante for Strings	Bo. Hawkes	V-VI
Purcell	Akon	Five Selected Pieces	BMI	V-VI
Schumann		Fantasiestücke	Galaxy	V-VI
Tchaikovsky	Stoessel	Andante Cantabile from Quartet, op. 11	CF	V-VI
Vivaldi	Kneisel-Damrosch	Concerto in D for Four Solo Violins	CF	V-VI
———————	Brown	Sonata da camera	Galaxy	V-VI

STRING QUARTET

Clarke, I.		Introduction to String Quartets	Boston	I-II

Fifteen short pieces from classical period, containing such technical problems as slurs, staccato, and basic syncopation.

	Clarke	Twelve Short String Quartets from the Masters	G. Schirmer	IV

Shortened version of original pieces by Mozart, Beethoven, Lully, Rameau, Gluck, Schubert, Bach, Dittersdorf, and Boccherini.

Cole, H.		Miniature Quartet No. 2 in A Major	Nov	III

Fairly interesting program number, employing violins in first position, interesting secondary parts, and wide dynamic range.

Corelli	Maganini	Gavotte and Gigue	EM	III
de Lamarter, E.		Quartet No. 2 in F	Mills	III

One of several pieces written especially for school groups. Contains simple harmonies and relatively easy secondary parts.

	Gruenberg	String Quartet Album	G. Schirmer	VI

Contains selections of original quartet music by major composers in two volumes. Numbers range in difficulty from about intermediate to quite difficult.

Hambourg, C.   *Introduction to*   Mills   I-II
                                        Chamber Music:
                                        String Quartet No. 1 in
                                        String Quartet No. 2 in

Two easy string quartet pieces, employing almost contrapuntal texture, in which most voices have interesting parts. Inner voices allowed short solos. Sustained notes and repeated eighths the main technical problems.

Haydn   *A String Quartet in D*   Boston   V
                                        minor, op. 42, no. 4 —
                                        Finale

Representative work of Haydn, not arranged, edited, or abridged. Technical problems are positions in violins and cellos and sixteenth-note runs.

_____ Finney   *Presto from Quartet No. 9* Witmark   V

Rousing fast movement—quite difficult but exciting to play.

_____ Moffat   *"Le Triomphe"*   Mills   III

Simple Haydn number, tuneful and interesting. Employs simple harmonies and basic positions.

_____ Moffat   *Lemberg Minuet and Trio*   Mills   III

Contains cleanly simple melodic line, backed by simple but full harmonies. Technical problems consist of chromatic alterations in violins and eighth-note runs in cello. Optional piano part.

Hoffman   *Fugues of Old Masters*   Moseler   V

Polyphonic fugues by Bach, Harismann, Pachelbel, Walther, and Azchow. All parts quite challenging.

Kreutzer, C.-   *"Prayer" and "Andante*   ABC Stan   III
Mendelssohn   *Religioso"*

Two numbers suitable for use in devotional assembly or church meeting. Sustained notes and long phrases present technical difficulties in otherwise simple texture. Numbers printed back to back on double music sheet.

Liepmann   *Popular Dances from the*   Boston   III
                                        17th Century

Selection of dance tunes, rhythmic and light, conveying mood of fun and enjoyment.

Rossi, S.   *Sinfonie, Galliarde,*   Mercury   III
                                        Canzone, Vol. I

Set of three short pieces, offering change of mood and tempo and employing contrapuntal texture with clear melodic lines in all parts.

Russell   *Eight Pieces for String*   Oxford   I-II
                                        Orchestra or Quartet

Easy string quartet piece, containing full and simple harmonies, interesting melodic lines, and few technical difficulties beyond range of student in latter part of first year of study.

| Samford | *Twelve Easy Pieces* | G. Schirmer | I-III | 125 |

Twelve short pieces, including chorales and dance tunes from early masters. Range in difficulty from very easy to about medium.

| Stoessel | *String Quartet Album (Two Volumes)* | Boston | IV |

Shortened version of original pieces, which range in difficulty from quite easy to difficult. Vol. I: Bach, Boccherini, Delibes, Grieg, Lalo, Schubert, Glazunov, and Tchaikovsky. Vol. II: Albéniz, Beethoven, Bizet, Chaminade, Grieg, and Mozart.

| Wickens, D. | *Miniature Quartet* | Nov | III |

Opens with viola solo; cello solo in second movement. Sustained notes and wide dynamic variation provide the most basic difficulties.

| Yost | *Original Pieces and Transcriptions* | Volkwein | III |

Contains selections from nearly all periods of music. Not all are originally quartets, and some are better than others for use with school children.

ADDENDUM

5

Solos,
Methods,
and Studies

Many instrumental music educators find it difficult to know adequate methods, studies, and solos for all the band and orchestral instruments. This is particularly a problem when no studio musicians are available to assist with this information. The following selected courses of study for each instrument start with grade I for beginning students and develop through grades XI and XII, equivalent to graduate student performance standards.

Literature was chosen from each of the main music history periods. Even though this presentation is minimal, it could provide more than adequate literature for the instrumental musician.

FLUTE

Grade I

Studies   Eck, *Method for Flute, Book 1*—Belwin
           Peterson, *Elementary Flute Method*—Ru
           Wagner, *Foundation to Flute Playing*—CF

Solos   Gossec, *Gavotte*—CF
           Lewallen, *"Poème petite"*—Belwin
           Mendelssohn, *"On Wings of Song"*—G. Schirmer
           Taylor, *"Lament of Pan"*—Consolidtd
           Weber, *"Autumn Leaves"*—Belwin

Grade II

Studies   Eck, *Method for Flute, Books 1 and 2*—Belwin
Endressen, *Supplementary Studies for Flute*—Ru
Wagner, *Foundation to Flute Playing*—CF

Duets   Garibaldi, *Six Little Duos*—C-Bettony

Solos   Bach, *Arioso*—G. Schirmer
Kuhlau, *Minuet*—C-Bettony
Lewallen, *"Poème petite"*—Belwin
Mozart, *Minuet in D*—Pres
Weinberger, *Sonatine*—CF

Grade III

Studies   Cavally, *Melodious and Progressive Studies, Book 1*—SMC
Voxman, *Advanced Method for Flute*—Ru
Wagner, *Foundation to Flute Playing*—CF

Duets   Garibaldi, *Six Melodic Duets, op. 145c*—C-Bettony

Solos   Brun, *"Romance"*—Ru
Donjon, *"Pan"*—CF
Gluck, *Scene from* **Orpheus**—Ru
Lewallen, *"Country Dance"*—Belwin
_____, *"Valse Romantique"*—Belwin
Mozart-Lentz, *Andante*—Belwin

Grade IV

Studies   Cavally, *Melodious and Progressive Studies, Books 1 and 2*—SMC
Koehler, *35 Exercises for Flute, op. 33 (Books 2 and 3)*—CF

Duets   Koehler, *Forty Progressive Duets, op. 55 (Books 1 and 2)*—CF

Solos   Bach, *Polonaise and Badinage*—CF
Brun, *"Romance"*—Ru
Godard, *Suite for Flute*—CF
Lewallen, *"Fantasie"*—Belwin
Molique, *Andante*—SMC
Platti-Waln, *Adagio and Allegro from G Major Sonata*—SCH

Grades V and VI

Studies   Anderson-Varrere, *Etudes for Flute, op. 21 and 33*—CF
Cavally, *Melodious and Progressive Studies, Book 3*—SMC
Hughes, *Forty New Studies for Flute*—Ricordi
Pares, C., *Daily Exercises and Scales for Flute or Piccolo*—Ru

Duets   Kuhlau, *Duos Concertants, op. 39, 57, and 90*—C. Bettony
Taylor, *The Flutist's Classic Duet Repertoire*—Witmark
Telemann, *Sechs Duette*—Kall

Solos   Ganne, *Andante and Scherzo*—SMC
Handel, *Seven Sonatas for Flute and Piano*—CFP

Quantz, *Sonata No. 1*—CFP
Saint-Saëns, *"Romance"*—Dur
Telemann, *Sechs Sonaten in Kanon*—G. Schirmer

Grades VII and VIII

Studies   Bandman, *Studio for Flute, Vols. 1 and 2*—CF
Fuerstenau, *Flute Studies*—Fillmore

Duets   Bach, Wilhelm Friedemann, *Sechs Duetto für 2 Flöten*—BRH
Cavally, *Famous Flute Studies and Duets*—SMC
Kuhlau, *Three Grand Duets, op. 39*—C-Bettony

Solos   Anderson, *24 Instructive Studies*—SMC
Cavally, *Fifteen Concert Pieces for Flute*—SMC
Debussy, *Second Arabesque*—Dur

Grades IX and X

Studies   Altes, *Célèbre méthode complète de flûte, Book 2*—LD
Andraud, *The Modern Flutist*—SMC
Moyse, Macel, *Exercises journaliers pour la flûte*—LD
Reichert, *Daily Exercises, op. 5*—AMP

Duets   *Concert Duos, op. 10 and 11*—CF

Solos   Blavet, *Sonata No. 3*—Bo. Hawkes
Doppler-Eck, *"Fantasie," op. 10*—Belwin
Haydn, *Sonata in G*—CFP
Ibert, *"Piece for Flute Alone"*—LD
Twelve-four Etudes Artistiques—SMC
Vivaldi, *Sonata in G minor*—TP

Grades XI and XII

Studies   Altes, *Célèbre méthode complète de flûte, Book 2*—LD
Brooke, Arthur, *Orchestral Studies*—C-Bettony
Moyse, Marcel, *Exercises journaliers pour la flûte*—LD
Zimmerman, *School of Virtuosity for Flute, op. 60*

Solos   Anderson, *24 Etudes Techniques, op. 63*—SMC
_____, *24 Virtuoso Studies, op. 60*—SMC
Chaminade, *Concertino*—Bo. Hawkes
Enesco, *Cantabile and Presto*—Bo. Hawkes
Mozart, *Concerto in D Major*—C-Bettony
Perilhou, *Ballade*—SMC

OBOE

Grade I

Studies   Andraud, *Progressive Method*—SMC
Gekeler, *Elementary Method*—Belwin
Hovey, *Elementary Method*—Ru
Niemann, *Method for the Oboe*—CF

Solos   Handel, *Air and Rondo*—Che
Labate, *Minuetto*—CF
_____, *"Pomposos"*—CF
_____, *"Strolling"*—CF
Naverd, *"Serenade"*—Alf
Weber, *First Solo Album*—TP

Grade II

Studies   Bleuzet, *Techniques of the Oboe, Parts 1 and 2*—LD
Gekeler, *Elementary Method for Oboe, Book 2*—Belwin
Niemann, *Method for the Oboe*—CF

Solos   Bakaleinikoff, *"Pastorale"*—Belwin
Labate, *Oboist's Repertoire Album*—CF
_____, *Seguidilla*—CF
Pierné, *Piece in G minor*—C-Bettony
Weinberger, *Sonatine*—CF
Willner (arr.), *Classical Album*—Bo. Hawkes

Grade III

Studies   Andraud, *Practical and Progressive Oboe Method*—SMC
Gekeler, *First Book of Practical Studies*—Belwin
Niemann, *Method for the Oboe*—CF

Solos   Bakaleinikoff, *"Elegy, a Danse"*—Belwin
Bizet, *Aragonaise from* **Carmen**—CF
Cohen, *Arioso*—CF
Corelli, *Air and Dance*—EM
Labate, *Oboist's Repertoire Album*—CF
Purcell, *Two Pieces*—Bo. Hawkes
Templeton, *Siciliana*—LD

Grade IV

Studies   Andraud, *First Book of Studies for Oboe*—SMC
_____, *Practical and Progressive Oboe Method*—SMC
Pares, *Book of Scales*—Ru
Voxman, *Selected Studies for the Oboe*—Ru

Solos   Bassi, *Lamento*—Ru
Corelli-Barbirolli, *Concerto*—Oxford
Jeanjean, *"Remembrances"*—Alf
Labate, *Villanella*—CF
Latham, *Sonata*—Spr
Niverd, *"Elegy"*—Alf
Reger, *Romance in G*—BRH
Schuman, *Three Romances*—G. Schirmer
Telemann, *Sonata in G minor*—SMC

Grades V and VI

Studies   Andraud, *Practical and Progressive Oboe Method*—SMC
Ferling, *Forty-Eight Etudes for Oboe*—SMC

Solos   Albinoni, *Concerto No. 3*—Bo. Hawkes
Bach, *Sonata in G minor*—Ricordi
Barbirolli, *Concerto on Themes of Pergolesi*—Oxford
Handel, *Concerto No. 1 in B-flat Major*—Bo. Hawkes
Labate, *Miniature Concert Repertoire*—CF
_____, *Tarantella*—CF
Pierné, *Piece in G minor*—C-Bettony
Weinberger, *Sonatine*—CF

Grades VII and VIII

Studies   Andraud, *Practical and Progressive Oboe Method*—SMC
Labate *16 Daily Exercises for Oboe*—CF

Solos   Godard, "*Légende pastorale*"—Belwin
Guilhaud, *First Concertino*—Ru
Handel, *Concerto Grosso No. 8*—SMC
_____, *Sonatas 1 and 2*—SMC
Krenek, *Two Themes by Handel*—SCH
Lees, *Concerto*—Bo. Hawkes
Loeillet, *Sonatas in E and G*—Lemoine
Marcello, *Concerto in C minor*—Interntl
Telemann, *Sonata in A minor*—SMC
Vivaldi, *Sonata in C minor*—SCH

Grades IX and X

Studies   Andraud, *Practical and Progressive Oboe Method*—SMC
_____, *VadeMecum of the Oboist*—SMC
Mayer, *Oboe Passages Extracted from Symphonic Works*—Belwin

Solos   Dunhill, *Three Pieces*—Bo. Hawkes
Handel, *Concerto in G minor*—SMC
Haydn, *Concerto in C*—BRH
Ibert, *Escales No. 2*—LD
Mozart, *Concerto in C Major*—Bo. Hawkes
Piston, *Suite*—G. Schirmer
Poulenc, *Sonata*—Che
Still, *Incantation and Dances*—CF
Tchaikovsky-Porsch, "*Chant sans paroles*"—AMSCO
Verroust, *Fourth Solo de Concert*—SMC
_____, *Souvenir of Old Quebec*—SMC

Grades XI and XII

Studies   Andraud, *VadeMecum of the Oboist*—SMC
Bas, *Orchestra Studies* (Solo passages from orchestra works)—LD

Solos   Andraud, *Fifteen Grand Solos*—SMC
Bozza, "*Fantasie pastorale*"—LD
Cimarosa, *Concerto for Oboe and String Orchestra*—Bo. Hawkes
Dittersdorf, *Concerto in G*—BRH
Grovelez, *Sarabande and Allegro*—Cost
Handel, *Sonata No. 3*—SMC

Hindemith, *Sonata*—AMP
Mozart, *Quartet for Oboe and Strings*—Bärenrtr
Mozart-Desportes, *Concertino*—SMC
Reizenstein, *Sonatina*—Bo. Hawkes
Saint-Saëns, *Sonata*—Dur
Strauss, R., *Concerto*—Bo. Hawkes
Vaughan Williams, R., *Concerto*—Oxford

CLARINET

Grade I

Studies   Hovey, *Elementary Clarinet Method*—Belwin
Langenus, *Clarinet Method, Book 1* (First three parts)—CF
Whistler, *Lazarus-Klosé*—CF

Duets   Saro, H., *Studies in Canon Form for Wind Instruments*—C-Bettony
Wiedemann, L., *30 Duets* (First 15)—CF

Solos   Hovey and Leonard, "Valse Grazioso," "Aria Cantando," "Solo Semplique"—Belwin
Langenus, "Scale Waltz," "In the Forest," "Mt. Vernon Minuet"—CF

Grade II

Studies   Hovey, *Elementary Clarinet Method, Book 2*—Belwin
Langenus, *Clarinet Method* (Parts 4 and 5)—CF
Whistler, *Lazarus-Klosé*—CF

Duets   Wiedemann, L., *30 Duets, Book 1* (Last 15)—CF
_____, *30 Duets, Book 2*—CF

Solos   Hovey and Leonard, *Encore Folio for Clarinet, Gypsy Moods*—Belwin
Langenus, *Clarinet Repertoire*—CF
Voxman, "Fanfare of the Poppies"—Ru

Grade III

Studies   Cavallini, *30 Caprices for the Clarinet*—Ricordi
Klosé, *Daily Exercises for the Clarinet*—CF
Rose, *32 Studies*—CF
Whistler, *Modern Pares Foundation Studies for Clarinet*—Ru

Duets   Voxman, *Selected Duets for Clarinet, Vol. 1*—Ru

Solos   Beethoven, *Adagio Cantabile*—SMC
Howland, *Concert and Contest Collection*—Ru
_____, *Valse teniral*—Ru
Morrissey, *Interlude*—MPH
Mozart-Waln, *Waltz Fantasy*—Kjos

Grade IV

Studies   Klosé, *Celebrated Method for the Clarinet*—LD
Kroepsch, *Book I*—Internatl

Langenus, *Clarinet Method, Book 3*—CF

Voxman, *Selected Studies for Clarinet*—Ru

Duets   Voxman, *Selected Duets for Clarinet, Vols. 1 and 2*—Ru

Solos   Avon, *"Fantasie de concert"*—EMT

Delmas, *"Promenade"*—Ru

Gilhaud, *Concertino*—CF

Mozart, *Adagio religioso*—Ande

Pierné, *Canzonetta*—Ru

Weber, *Concertino*—CF

_____, *First Concerto*—BRH

Grades V and VI

Studies   Baermann, *Book 3*—CF

Gornston, David, *Clarinet Velocity*—Leeds

Klosé, *Celebrated Method for Clarinet*—LD

Langenus, *Clarinet Method, Book 3*—CF

Kroepsch, *Books 1 and 2*—Interntl

Duets   Magnani, A., *Duets for the Clarinet*—C-Bettony

Voxman, *Selected Duets for Clarinet, Vol. 2*—Ru

Solos   Dere, *Andante and Scherzo*—SMC

Jeanjean, *Arabesques*—Alf

Marty, *"Premiere Fantasy"*—C-Bettony

Mozart, *Concerto, op. 107*—BRH

Weber, *Concerto 2*—BRH

Grades VII and VIII

Studies   Klosé, *Celebrated Method for the Clarinet*—LD

Kroepsch, *Book 2*—Interntl

Langenus, *Clarinet Method Book 3*—CF

Solos   Meister-Langenus, *"Erwin Fantasie"*—C-Bettony

Saint-Saëns, *Sonata in E-flat*—Dur

Sobeck-Langenus, *Concert Piece*—CF

Stubbins, *Recital Literature for the Clarinet*—George Wahr

Weber, *Romance and Polacca*—SMC

Grades IX and X

Studies   Baermann, *Book IV*—CF

Klosé, *Celebrated Method for the Clarinet*—LD

Kroepsch, *Book 3*—Interntl

Langenus, *Clarinet Cadenzas and How to Phrase Them*—CF

Solos   Lefebvre, *Fantasie caprice*—C-Bettony

Mazellier, *Fantasie de ballet*—LD

Schubert, *Introduction, Theme, and Variations from Schnuchts-Waltzer*—
CF

Spohr, Mozart, and Weber, *Clarinet Classics, Vol. 1*—C-Bettony

Stubbins, *Recital Literature for the Clarinet, Vols. 2 and 3*—George Wahr

Studies   Bonade, *Orchestral Studies for Clarinet*—Leblanc
           Kroepsch, *Books 2-4*—Interntl
           Stark, *24 Grand Virtuoso Studies, op. 51*—C-Bettony
           _____, *24 Studies in all Keys, op. 49*—C-Bettony

Solos   Bernstein, *Sonata for Clarinet and Piano*—Witmark
           Bonade, *Fifteen Grand Solos de Concert for Clarinet and Piano*—SMC
           Brahms, *Quintet, op. 115*—CFP
           _____, *Sonatas, op. 120, nos. 1 and 2*—CFP
           Haydn (arr. DeCaprio), *Concerto for Clarinet*—Ru
           Mozart, *Quintet, K. 581*—BRH
           Weber, *Quintet, op. 34*—CFP
           Weber-Langenus, *Fantasia and Rondo, op. 34*—CF

SAXOPHONE

Grade I

Studies   Calliet, *Saxophone Method, Book 1*—Belwin
           Hovey, *Elementary Method for Saxophone*—Ru
           Vereecken, *Foundation to Saxophone Playing*—CF

Solos   Bach-Rasher, *Minuet*—Belwin
           Cui, *Cantabile*—C-Bettony
           Lehar-Weber, *"Vilia"*—Belwin
           Scarlatti-Barnes, *Aria*—Spr
           Tchaikovsky, *Melodie*—Robbins
           Voxman, *Lament and Tarantella*—Summy-Bir
           Weber, *"Evening Shadows"*—Belwin

Grade II

Studies   Calliet, *Saxophone Method, Books 1 and 2*—Belwin
           Hovey, *Elementary Method for Saxophone*—Ru
           Vereecken, *Foundation to Saxophone Playing*—CF

Solos   Gluck-Rascher, *Tambourin*—Belwin
           Gurewich, *Sequidilla*—CF
           Handel-Mule, *Largo*—SMC
           Haydn, *Serenade*—C-Bettony
           Klughart-Muller, *Romanze*—Spr
           Purcell-Maganini, *Suite in F Major*—EM
           Tomasi, *"Chant Corse"*—Alf
           Warner, *"Valse Caprice"*—Remick

Grade III

Studies   Calliet, *Saxophone Method, Book 2*—Belwin
           DeVille, *Universal Method for Saxophone*—CF
           Skornicka, *Intermediate Method for Saxophone*—Ru
           Vereecken, *Foundation to Saxophone Playing*—CF

Solos   Beethoven-Lefebvre, *Romance*—CF
Bozza, *Aria*—LD
Busch, *Valse Elegiae*—Alf
Durand, *First Valse in E-flat*—CF
Guilleu, *Sonatine*—LD
Kreisler-Leeson, *Rondino*—Foley
Mana-Zucca, *Walla-Kye*—Leeds
Mozart-Webb, *Sonatina*—Belwin
Pergolesi-Barnes, *Canzona*—Spr
Perrin, *Poème*—SMC

Grade IV

Studies   DeVille, *Universal Method for Saxophone*—CF
Hovey, *Daily Exercises for Saxophone*—Ru
Voxman-Gower, *Advanced Method for Saxophone*—Ru
Whistler, *Modern Pares Foundation Studies for Saxophone*—Ru

Solos   Anderson, *Sonata*—SMC
Andrieu, *Premier solo de concours*—Alf
Bach-Leeson, *Air from Suite in D*—Baron
Corelli-Felix, *Sonata in F Major*—EM
Glazunow-Leeson, *Serenade espagnol*—Baron
Gurewich, *Fantasy in F minor*—Ricordi
Handel-Mule, *Sonata No. 1*—SMC
Paul, *Estilian Caprice*—Ru
Shostakovich, *Satirical Danse*—EM

Grades V and VI

Studies   DeVille, *Universal Method for Saxophone*—CF
Gillete, Mickey, *Saxophone Method, Book 3*—Belwin
Pares, *Daily Technical Exercises*—Ru
Voxman-Gower, *Advanced Method for Saxophone*—Ru

Solos   Andrien, *First Contest Solo*—Alf
Bennett, *"Moderne"*—CF
Gurewich, *"Capriccioso"*—Ricordi
————, *Concerto in E minor*—Ru
Handel-Rascher, *Sonata No. 3*—Chappell
Jeanjean, *Capriccioso*—Alf
Leclair, *Gigue*—LD
Pares, *Premier solos de concours*—Alf
Tcherepnin, *Sonatine sportive*—LD

Grades VII and VIII

Studies   DeVille, *Universal Method for Saxophone*—CF
Gillete, Mickey, *Saxophone Method, Book 3*—Belwin
Traxler, *Grand Virtuoso Sax Studies*—Belwin

Solos   Barat, *Danse espagnole*—Sel
Dubois, *Sonata*—LD

Fiocco-Rascher, *Allegro*—Bourne
Gurewich, *Fantasy in F minor*—Ricordi
Ibert, *Concertino de camera*—SMC
Lacome, *Rigaudon*—SMC
Lapham, *Concerto in A-flat*—Leeds
Moritz, *Sonata*—W-Levant
Pascal, *Sonatine*—LD

Grades IX and X

Studies   Ferling, *48 Famous Studies for Two Oboes or Saxophone*—LD
Karg-Elert, *25 Capriccios*—Ru
Rascher, *156 Exercises*—CF

Solos   Bach-Mule, *Sonatas Nos. 4 and 6*—LD
Bilotti, *Sonata*—W-Levant
Bozza, *"Pulcinella"*—LD
Creston, *Sonata*—Shawnee
Eccles-Rascher, *Sonata*—H. Elkan
Glazunow, *Concerto*—LD
Heiden, *Sonata*—SCH
Lecail, *Fantasie concertante*—Ru
Tomasi, *Introduction and Dance*—SMC
Vivaldi-Rascher, *Sonata No. 6 in G minor*—McG

Grades XI and XII

Studies   Mayeur, *20 Studies for Saxophone*—CF
Rascher, *Top Tones*—CF
Runyon, *Dynamic Etudes*

Solos   Bozza, *"Scaramouche"*—LD
Camarata, *Rhapsody for Saxophone*—Mills
Combelle, *1st Solos de concours*—Alf
Debussy, *Rhapsodie*—Dur
Guillou, *Sonatine*—LD
Karg-Elert, *Sonata (with 25 Caprices)*—Zim
Krol, *Sonata*—CFP
Leinert, *Sonata*—BRH
Singelee, *Concerto No. 1*—SMC
Tcherepnin, *Sonatine sportive*—LD

BASSOON

Grade I

Studies   Fields, Dall, *Method for Bassoon, Book 1*—Cole
Lentz, *Beginning Method for Bassoon, Book 1*—Belwin
Skornicka, *Elementary Method*—Ru

Solos   Buchtel, *"Jolly Sailors"*—Mills
Classical Album for Bassoon—Bo. Hawkes
Handel, *Aria from* **Scipio**—Witmark

Haydn, *Theme*—Bo. Hawkes
Isaac, *"The Jolly Dutchman"*—Belwin
Pergolesi, *Aria*—Witmark

Grade II

Studies   Lentz, *Beginning Method for Bassoon, Books 1 and 2*—Belwin
Weissenborn, *Practical Bassoon Method*—CF

Solos   Boyd, *Famous Melodies for Bassoon*—Witmark
Glazunov, *Serenade espagnol*—CF
Ibert, *"The Little White Mule"*—LD
Klughart, *Romanza*—C-Bettony
Maganini, *"Rastus Ryan"*—CF
Massenet, *Elegy*—MPH
Petrie, *"Asleep in the Deep"*—Witmark

Grade III

Studies   Lentz, *Beginning Method for Bassoon, Book 2*—Belwin
Weissenborn, *Etudes, Book I*—CF
_____, *Practical Bassoon Method*—CF

Solos   Bakaleinikoff, *Ballad, Humoresque, and March Eccentric*—Belwin
Boyd, *Famous Melodies for Bassoon*—Witmark
Mozart-Pezzi, *Adagio*—SMC
Ratey, *Impromptu*—Alf
Ropartz, *"Petit pièce in A minor"*—Baron
Schmutz, *"Melodie lyrique"*—Belwin
Smith, *Caprice*—CF
Weinberger, *Sonatina*—CF
Weissenborn, *Capriccioso*—C-Bettony

Grade IV

Studies   Jancourt-Collins, *Bassoon Studies*—Bo. Hawkes
Pares, *Book of Scales*—Ru
Weissenborn, *Practical Bassoon Method*—CF

Solos   Bossi, *"Improviso"*—Bongiovanni
Galliard, *Six Sonatas, Vol. 1*—McG
Jancourt, *"Rêverie"*—C-Bettony
Milde, *Andante-Rondo in F*—LN
Rathaus, *"Polichinelle"*—Belwin
Stamitz, *Concerto in F*—SMC
Stravinsky, *"Pallid Moonlight"*—EM

Grades V and VI

Studies   Bozza, *15 Daily Drills*—LD
Kessler, *Bassoon Passages, Book 1*—CF
Pares, *Book of Scales*—Ru
Weissenborn, *Practical Bassoon Method*—CF

Solos   Galliard, *Six Sonatas, Vol. 2*—CF
Pierné, *Concert Piece*—Interntl
Telemann, *Sonata No. 3 in F minor*—Interntl
Vivaldi, *Sonata in A minor*—Interntl
Weber, *Hungarian Fantasy*—Ru
Weissenborn, *Rondo from Capriccio, op. 14*—C-Bettony
Wolf-Ferrari, *Concertino Suite*—Ricordi

Grades VII and VIII

Studies   Kessler, *Bassoon Passages, Book 2*—CF
Milde, *Concert Studies, Book 1*—C-Bettony
Orefici, *Studi melodie*—LD
Weissenborn, *Practical Bassoon Method*—CF

Solos   Beethoven, *Sonata, op. 17*—C-Bettony
Bordeau, *Premier Solo*—Ru
Grafe, *Grand Concerto*—C-Bettony
Hoffman, *Serenade Basque*—Bo. Hawkes
Jeanjean, *Capriccioso*—LD
Pierné, *Solo de concert*—Ru
Senaille, *Allegro spiritoso*—SMC

Grades IX and X

Studies   Milde, *Concert Studies, Book 2*—C-Bettony
Piard, *90 Etudes*—Cost
Weissenborn, *Etudes, Book 2*—CF
————————, *Practical Bassoon Method*—CF

Solos   Bloch, "*Fantaisie Varié*"—C-Bettony
Gottwald, "*Fantaisie Héroïque*"—C-Bettony
Handel, *Concerto in C minor*—SMC
Jacob, *Concerto for Bassoon*—Mills
Jeanjean, *Prelude et Scherzo*—SMC
Kortchmaroff, *Sketch on a Theme of Kirgiz*—Russian State
Mazellier, *Prelude and Dance*—LD
Mozart, *Concerto in B-flat*—Spr
Vivaldi, *Concerti in C, F, and G*—Ricordi
Weber, *Concerto in F*—LD

Grades XI and XII

Studies   Flament, *Technical Exercises*—LD
Mazas, *24 Studies*—CF
Piard, *90 Etudes*—Cost
Weissenborn, *Practical Bassoon Method*—CF

Solos   Blazevitsch, *Concerto No. 5*—Interntl
Boismortier, *Concerto*—LD
Bruns, *Concerto No. 5*—Leeds
Busser, *Portugesa*—LD
Hindemith, *Sonata*—SCH

Jancourt, *Cantilene*—Richault

Saint-Saëns, *Sonata, op. 168*—Dur

Schreck, *Sonata in E, op. 9*—Hof

Wolf-Ferrari, *Concertino Suite, op. 16*—Ricordi

CORNET OR TRUMPET

Grade I

Studies   Beeler, *Method for Cornet, Book 1*—Remick

Edwards-Hovey, *Cornet Method Book 1*—Belwin

Getchell, *Practical Studies, Vol. 1*—Belwin

Vincent-Weber, *The Cornet Student* (With supplements)—Belwin

Solos   Arnold, *32 Elementary Trumpet Solos*—AMSCO

Dearnley, *Eight Easy Pieces by Classical Composers*—Che

Lawton, *The Young Trumpet Player, 3 vols.*—Oxford

Grade II

Studies   Arban, *Complete Method*—CF

Beeler, *Method for Cornet, Book 2*—Remick

Edwards-Hovey, *Cornet Method, Book 2*—Belwin

Endresen, *Supplementary Studies*—Ru

Getchell, *Practical Studies, Vol. 2*—Belwin

Hering, *Forty Progressive Etudes*—CF

Little, *Embouchure Builder*—ProArt

Solos   Arnold, *32 Elementary Trumpet Solos*—AMSCO

Lawton, *The Young Trumpet Player, 3 vols.*—Oxford

Price, *"Let Us Have Music"*—CF

Schneider, *Little Pieces by Old Masters*—SCH

Grade III

Studies   Arban, *Complete Method*—CF

Clarke, H., *Technical Studies*—CF

Hering, *32 Etudes*—CF

Klosé, *209 Tone and Finger Exercises*—Gornston

Laurent, *Etudes pratiques, Vol. 1*—LD

Smith, W., *Lip Flexibility*—CF

Solos   Arnold, *42 Selected Trumpet Solos*—AMSCO

Hering, *Classic Pieces for the Advancing Trumpeter*—CF

Johnson, *Sacred Solos*—Ru

Voxman, *Concert and Contest Collection*—Ru

Grade IV

Studies   Arban, *Complete Method*—CF

Clarke, H., *Characteristic Studies*—CF

————, *Technical Studies*—CF

Reinhardt, *Selection of Concone Studies*—Elkan-Vogel, Inc.

Schlossberg, *Daily Drills and Technical Studies*—Baron
Voxman, *Selected Studies for Cornet*—Ru

Solos   Balay, *Prelude and Ballade*—Baron
Beeler, *Solos for the Trumpet Player*—Schirmer
Cords, *Romanze*—C-Bettony
Corelli-Fitzgerald, *Sonata 8*—Ricordi
Fitzgerald, *Rondo Capriccio*—CF
Handel-Voisin, *Sonata No. 3*—IMC
Jeanjean, *Capriccioso*—IMC
Purcell-Voisin, *Sonata in D*—IMC
Voxman, *Concert and Contest Collection*—Ru

Grades V and VI

Studies   Bordogni, *24 Vocalises*—LD
Huffnagle, *Trumpet Velocity*—Gornston
Laurent, *Etudes pratiques, Vol. 2*—LD
Schlossberg, *Daily Drills*—Baron
St. Jacombe, *Grand Method*—CF
Voxman, *Selected Studies*—Ru

Solos   Barat, *Andante et Scherzo*—Elkan-Vogel
Bozza, *Badinage*—LD
DeBoeck, *Allegro de concours*—CF
Handel-Fitzgerald, *Aria con variazione*—Ricordi
Mager, *Nine Grand Solos de Concert*—SMC
Porret, *Six Esquisses*—Baron
Simon, "*Willow Echoes*"—Fillmore

Grades VII and VIII

Studies   Brandt, *Orchestra Etudes*—Leeds
Dufresne-Voisin, *Develop Sight Reading*—Colin
Gates *Odd Meter Etudes*—Gornston
Nagel, *Speed Studies*—Mentor
Sachse, *100 Etudes*—IMC
St. Jacome, *Grand Method*—CF

Solos   Clarke, "*Southern Cross*"—CF
Goedicke, *Concert Etude*—IMC
Haydn, *Concerto*—King
Mager, *Nine Grand Solos de Concert*—SMC
Telemann-Voisin, *Concerto*—IMC
Thome, *Fantasia*—IMC

Grades IX and X

Studies   Charlier, *Etudes transcendantes*—LD
Colin, *Advanced Lip Flexibilities*—Colin
Hall, *Orchestra Passages*—Bo. Hawkes
Sabarich, *Dix études*—Selmer
St. Jacome, *Grand Method*—CF
Williams, *Transposition Studies*—Colin

Solos	Chaplaevsky, *Valse caprice*—Leeds
	Enesco, *Legend*—IMC
	Goedicke-Nagel, *Concerto, op. 41*—IMC
	Hindemith, *Sonate*—SCH
	Hummel-Ghitalla, *Concerto*—King
	Savard, *"Morceau de concours"*—C-Bettony
	Torelli-Thilde, *Concerto in D Major*—Bill
	Veracini-Thilde, *Concerto in E minor*—Bill

Grades XI and XII

Studies	Bozza, *Etudes*—Elkan-Vogel
	Brandt, *24 Last Etudes*—MCA
	Foveau, *Traits Difficiles for Trumpet*—LD
	Geier, *11 Studies*—IMC
	Gisondi, *Bach for the Trumpet*—McGinnis
	Glantz, *Advanced Daily Studies*—Colin
	Harris, A., *Advanced Studies*—Colin
Solos	Bornstedt, *Sonata*—MPH
	Bozza, *Caprice*—Baron
	Giannini, *Concerto*—MPH
	Kennan, *Sonata*—Remick
	Pilss, *Concerto*—AMP
	Stevens, *Sonata*—AMP

FRENCH HORN

Grade I

Studies	Hauser, *Foundation to French Horn Playing*—CF
	Horner, *Primary Studies*—EV
	Maxima-Alphonse, *Etudes, Vol. 1*—LD
	Pottag-Hovey, *Method for Horn*—Belwin
	Sansone, *Modern Method*—SMC
Solos	Arnold, J., *Everybody's Favorite French Horn Solos*— AMSCO
	Dearnley, *Eight Easy Pieces by Classical Composers*—Che
	Jones, *First Solos for the Horn Player*—G. Schirmer

Grade II

Studies	Endresen, *Supplementary Studies*—Ru
	Horner, *Primary Studies*—EV
	Kopprasch-Gumbert, *Studies, Book 1*—CF
	Maxime-Alphonse, *Etudes, Vol. 1*—LD
	Sansone, *Modern Method*—SMC
	Schantl, *Etudes*—Wind
Solos	Bakaleinikoff, *Cavatine*—Belwin
	Langrish, *Eight Easy Pieces*—Oxford
	Phillips, I., *Classical and Romantic Album*—Oxford

Grade III

Studies   Franz, *Method for Horn*—C-Bettony
Kopprasch-Gumbert, *Studies, Book 1*—CF
Maxime-Alphonse, *Etudes, Vol. 2*—LD
Pottag-Hovey, *Method for Horn*—Belwin
Sansone, *Modern Method*—SMC
Schantl, *Etudes*—Wind

Solos   Beethoven, *Adagio cantabile*—SMC
Hauser, *Modern Repertoire Album*—CF
Ranger, *Solos for Contest and Recital*—SMC
Wiedmann, *Nocturne*—Belwin

Grade IV

Studies   Franz, *Duets, Book 1*—SMC
Kopprasch, *Etudes, Book 2*—CF
Krol, *Cadenzas to Mozart Horn Concertos Nos. 3 and 4*—SIM
Maxime-Alphonse, *Etudes, Vol. 2*—LD
Pottag, *French Horn Passages, Book 1*—Belwin
Sansone, *Modern Method*—SMC

Solos   Beethoven, *Sonata for Horn*—G. Schirmer
Gottwald, *Fantaisie Héroïque*—C-Bettony
Mozart-Chambers, *Concerto No. 3 in E-flat*—IMC
Mozart-Kling, *Concert Rondo*—Bo. Hawkes
Schumann, *Adagio and Allegro*—IMC
Telemann-Leloir, *Concerto in D Major*—Peg

Grade V

Studies   Franz, *Duets, Book 2*—SMC
Kopprasch, *Etudes, Book 2*—CF
Maxime-Alphonse, *Etudes, Vol. 3*—LD
Mueller, *Etudes*—SMC
Pottag, *French Horn Passages*—Belwin
Strauss-Chambers, *Orchestral Excerpts*—IMC

Solos   Cherubini-Chambers, *Sonatas Nos. 1 and 2*—IMC
Corelli, *Sonata in G minor and F Major*—EM
Handel-Eger, *Sonata in G minor*—AMP
Heiden, *Sonata for Horn*—AMP
Mozart-Chambers, *Concertos Nos. 1 and 2*—IMC
Saint-Saëns, *Romance*—IMC

Grade VI

Studies   Farkas, *Orchestral Passages*—Dur
Kopprasch, *Etudes, Book 2*—CF
Maxime-Alphonse, *Etudes, Vol. 4*—LD
Pottag-Andraud, *Selected Studies, Book 1*—SMC
Thevet, *Traits difficiles, Book 1*—LD
Wagner-Chambers, *Orchestral Excerpts*—IMC

Goedicke-Chambers, *Concerto for Horn*—IMC
Haydn-Steves, *Concerto No. 2*—Bo. Hawkes
Sansone, *Concertino*—SMC
Tomasi, *Concerto for Horn*—LD

Grades VII and VIII

Studies   Bozza, *18 études en forme d'improvisation*—Chappell
Gallay-Thevet, *Unmeasured Preludes*—LD
Maxime-Alphonse, *Etudes, Vol. 5*—LD
Strauss, R., *Concert Studies*—C-Bettony
Thevet, *Fifty Transposing Exercises*—LD
——————, *Traits difficiles, Book 2*—LD

Grades IX and X

Studies   Bach-Faulx, *20 études de virtuosité*—Brog
Gallay, *Etudes brillantes, op. 43*—LD
Jones, *20th Century Orchestral Studies*—G. Schirmer
Maxime-Alphonse, *Etudes, Vol. 6*—LD
Thevet, *50 Transposing Exercises*—LD

Solos   Hindemith, *Concerto*—SCH
Kudelski-Sansone, *Concertino*—SMC
Lamy, *Cantabila et Scherzo*—LD
Strauss, R., *Concerto No. 1, op. 11*—G. Schirmer
Vivaldi-Sabatini, *Concerto*—Cor

Grades XI and XII

Studies   Gallay, *Caprices, op. 32*—LD
——————, *Etudes brillantes, op. 43*—LD
Maxima-Alphonse, *Etudes, Vol. 6*—LD
Schuller, *Studies for Unaccompanied Horn*—Oxford

Solos   Hindemith, *Sonata*—SCH
Hovhaness, *Concerto No. 3*—Robt King
Strauss, R., *Concerto No. 2*—Bo. Hawkes
Weber-Kling, *Concertino*—Bo. Hawkes

TROMBONE

Grade I

Studies   Arban-Randall-Mantia, *Method for Trombone*—CF
Beeler, *Method for Trombone*—War
Cornette-Procter, *Method for Trombone*—C-Bettony

Solos   Arnold, J., *78 Easy Trombone Solos*—AMSCO
Dearnley, *Eight Easy Pieces by Classical Composers*—Che
Lawton, *The Young Trombonist*—Oxford

Grade II

Studies   Arban-Randall-Mantia, *Method for Trombone*—CF
Cornette-Procter, *Method for Trombone*—C-Bettony
Endresen, *Etudes and Solo Studies*—MMC
Mueller-Brown, *Studies, Book 1*—IMC

Solos   Handel-Lethbridge, *Solo Album*—Oxford
Lawton, *The Young Trombonist*—Oxford
Smith, H. C., *First Solos for the Trombone Player*—G. Schirmer

Grade III

Studies   Arban-Randall-Mantia, *Method for Trombone*—CF
Blume, *12 Melodious Duets*—CF
Bordogni-Rochut, *Melodious Studies, Book 1*—CF
Mantia, *Technical Studies*—CF
Mueller-Brown, *Studies, Book 2*—IMC

Solos   Handel-Lethbridge, *Solo Album*—Oxford
Klughart, *Romanze*—Spr
Phillips, I., *A Classical and Romantic Album*—Oxford
Pryor, "La Petite Suzanne"—CF
_____, "Starlight"—CF

Grade IV

Studies   Arban, *Method for Trombone*—CF
Blume, *12 Melodious Duets*—CF
Bordogni-Rochut, *Melodious Etudes, Book 1*—CF
Kopprasch, *Etudes, Book 1*—CF
Mantia, *Technical Studies*—CF
Mueller-Brown, *Studies, Book 2*—IMC

Solos   Cords, *Romance*—C-Bettony
Handel-Brown, *Sonata No. 3*—IMC
Pryor, "The Tip Topper"—CF
Telemann-Brown, *Sonata in A minor*—IMC
Voxman, *Concert and Contest Collection*—Ru

Grade V

Studies   Amsden, *Duets*—Bar
Blazhevich, *Clef Studies*—MCA
Blume, *12 Melodious Duets*—CF
Bordogni-Rochut, *Melodious Etudes, Books 1-2*—CF
Kopprasch, *Etudes, Book 1*—CF
Mueller, *Studies, Book 3*—IMC

Solos   Croce-Spinelli, *Solo de concours*—Belwin
Grafe-Laube, *Grand Concerto*—C-Bettony
Ostrander, *Four Solo Suites*—E
Romsseau, *Pièce concertante*—C-Bettony
Tuthill, *Phantasy Piece*—CF

Vivaldi-Brown, *Sonata No. 2*—IMC
Weber, *Romanza appassionata*—LD

Grade VI

Studies   Amsden, *Celebrated Duets*—Bar
Blazhevich, *Clef Studies*—MCA
Bordogni-Rochut, *Melodious Etudes, Book 2*—CF
Ferrari, *Orchestral Studies, Book 1*—Ricordi
Kopprasch, *Etudes, Books 1-2*—CF
Seidel, *Studies*—C-Bettony

Solos   Galliard, *Sonatas*—McG

Studies   Amsden, *Celebrated Duets*—Bar
Blazhevich, *Clef Studies*—MCA
Ferrari, *Orchestral Studies, Book 2*—Ricordi
Kopprasch, *Studies, Book 2*—CF
Tyrrell, *40 Progressive Studies*—Bo. Hawkes

Solos   Blazhevich, *Concert Piece No. 5*—Belwin
Cimera, *Concerto for Trombone*—Remick
David-Gibson, *Concertino*—IMC
Gaubert, *Morceau symphonique*—SMC
Marcello-Brown, *Sonata in C, D, and G*—IMC
Salzedo, *Pièce concertante*—IMC

Grades IX and X

Studies   Bordogni-Rochut, *Etudes*—CF
_____, *Melodious Etudies, Book 3*—CF
Ferrari, *Orchestral Studies, Book 3*—Ricordi
Kopprasch, *Etudes, Book 2*—CF
Kreutzer-Schaefer, *Ten Famous Etudes*—Fillmore
Vobaron, *Etudes*—C-Bettony

Solos   Blazhevich-LaFosse, *Concerto No. 2*—IMC
Buesser, *Variations in D-flat*—LD
Hindemith, *Sonata*—SCH
Ropartz, *Andante and Allegro*—C-Bettony

Grades XI and XII

Studies   Blazhevich, *Duets*—IMC
_____, *Twenty-six Sequences*—IMC
Couillaud, *Vocalises*—LD
Kopprasch, *Etudes, Book 2*—CF

Bach-LaFosse, *Unaccompanied Cello Suites*—LD
Bachelet, *Concert Piece*—IMC
Barat, *Andante et Allegro*—SMC
Lebedev-Ostrander, *Concerto*—EM
Mazellier, *Solo de concours*—IMC
Salzedo, *Pièce concertante*—IMC

VIOLIN

Grade I

Studies   Hofmann, *Op. 25, Book 1*—G. Schirmer
Lamoureux, *Practical Method for Violin, Part 1*—G. Schirmer
Sevčik, *Op. 1, Part 1* (Use op. 6 in school for beginners)—G. Schirmer
Waller, *Violin Method*—Kjos
Whistler-Hummel, *First Etude Album*—Ru
Wohlfahrt, *Op. 45, Book 1*—G. Schirmer

Solos   To be chosen from literature comparable to *Music* by Herfurth—Wil
Band, G., *Scale-tune Book*—G. Schirmer
Doflein, *Series*—SCH
Isaac, *Album of Favorite Violin Solos*—Cole
Sontag, *Folk and Master Melodies*—G. Schirmer
Suzuki, *Series*—S&B
Whistler, *Solos for Strings*—Ru

Grade II

Studies   Lamoureux, *Practical Method for Violin, Part 2, and Its Supplement*—G. Schirmer
Sevčik, *Op. 2, Book 2*—BRH
Whistler, *Introducing the Positions, Book 1*—Ru
Wohlfahrt-Blay, *Op. 74, Book 2*—G. Schirmer

Solos   Greenwood, *Violinist's Introduction to Bach*—Wil
Herfurth, *Music the Whole World Loves*—Wil
Perlman, *Violinist's Program Builder*—CF
Reiding, *Concerto, op. 5, in D Major*—Bo. Hawkes
Seitz, *Violin Concerto No. 2*—G. Schirmer
Stone, D., *6 Second Position Etudes*—Bo. Hawkes

Grade III

Studies   Accolay-Perlman, *Concerto No. 1 in A minor*—G. Schirmer
Hofmann, *Melodious Double Stops*—Boston
Kayser-Anzoletti, *Studies, Book 1*—Ricordi
Sevčik, *Op. 2, Book 2*—BRH
Whistler, *Introducing the Positions, Book 2*—Ru

Solos   Corelli, *Sonata in A*—Leeds
Dittersdorf, *Sonata in G*—Hof
Huber, *Concertino No. 4, op. 8*—G. Schirmer
Portnoff, *Concertino in D, op. 92*—CFP

Studies	Dont, *30 Progressive Exercises, op. 38*—G. Schirmer
	Hofmann, *Melodious Double Stops*—Boston
	Kayser-Ansoletti, *Book II*—Ricordi
	Sevčik, *Op. 8*—G. Schirmer
	Whitler, *Introducing the Positions, Book 2*—Ru
	_____, *Preparatory to Kreutzer, Book 2*—Ru
Solos	Corelli-Moffat, *Introduction and Jiga*—CF
	DeBeriot, *Concerti Nos. 7, 8, and 9*—CFP
	Gingold, J., *Music for the Violin Player*—G. Schirmer
	Handel, *Six Sonatas*—CFP
	Kreutzer, *Concerto No. 14*—CF

	Kreutzer-Flesch, *Etudes*—Hug
Solos	Corelli-Jensen, *12 Sonatas*—SCH
	Fioco, *Allegro*—SCH
	Handel, *Six Sonatas*—CFP
	Mozart-Flesch-Schnabel, *Sonatas*—CFP
	Nardini-Nachez, *Concerto in A minor*—SCH
	Vivaldi-Nachez, *Concerto in A minor*—SCH

Grade VI

Studies	Dont, *24 Preparatory Exercises, op. 37*—CFP
	Fiorillo, *36 Etudes or Caprices*—BRH
	Kreutzer-Flesch, *42 Studies*—Hug
	Mazas-Davisson, *Brilliant Studies, op. 36, Book 2*—CFP
Solos	Handel, *Six Sonatas*—CFP
	Haydn, *Concerti 1, 2, and 3*—CFP
	Kreutzer, *Concerto No. 13*—CF
	Rode, *Concerti 4 and 7*—CFP
	Viotti-Abbado, *Concerto No. 18*—Ricordi

Grade VII

Studies	Casorti-Mitell, *The Technique of the Bow, op. 50*—G. Schirmer
	Fiorillo, *36 Etudes or Caprices*—BRH
	Mazas-Davisson, *Brilliant Studies, op. 36, Book 2*—CFP
Solos	Corelli-Leonard, *La folia*—G. Schirmer
	De Bériot, *Scène de ballet*—CFP
	Grieg-Lichtenberg, *Sonatas 1, 2, and 3*—G. Schirmer
	Kreutzer, *Concerti Nos. 18 and 19*—CFP
	Mozart-Flesch, *Concerto in G Major*—CFP
	Viotti, *Concerti No. 28 and 29*—Ricordi

Grade VIII

Studies   De Bériot-Berkley, *30 Concert Studies, op. 123*—G. Schirmer
Fiorillo, *36 Etudes or Caprices*—BRH
Mozart-Hermann, *Artist's Studies, op. 36, Book 3*—CF
Rode-Galamian, *24 Caprices*—Interntl
Tartini-Lichtenberg, *The Art of Bowing*—G. Schirmer

Solos   LeClair, *Sonata in A, No. 15*—ESC
Rode, *Concerto No. 8*—CFP
Spohr-Svecenski, *Concerto II*—G. Schirmer
Tartini-Bonelli, *Six Sonatas*—CFP
Veracini, *12 Sonatas*—CFP
Viotti-Lichtenberg, *Concerto No. 22*—G. Schirmer

Grade IX

Studies   Fiorillo, *36 Etudes or Caprices*—BRH
Gaviniès, *24 Studies*—G. Schirmer
Rode-Galamian, *Caprices*—Interntl
Vieuxtemps, *Concert Etudes*—CFP
Wieniawski-Sitt, *Caprices, op. 18*—Interntl

Solos   Bazzini-Auer, *Allegro de concert, op. 15*—G. Schirmer
Burleigh, *Concerto No. 2*—CF
Mozart, *20 Sonatas*—BRH
Vivaldi-Franko, *Concerto in G minor, op. 4, no. 6*—CFP

Grade X

Studies   Gaviniès, *24 Studies*—G. Schirmer
Rode-Galamian, *Caprices*—Interntl
Rovelli-Polo, *Twelve Caprices*—Ricordi
Wieniawski-Sitt, *Caprices, op. 18*—Interntl

Solos   Bach-David, *Six Sonatas*—CFP
Bruch-Francescatti, *Concerto in G minor*—Interntl
Mozart-Joachim, *Concerti in D or A*—Interntl
Wieniawski-Galamian, *Concerto No. 2*—Interntl

Grades XI and XII

Studies   Paganini-Flesch, *Caprices*—Interntl
Wieniawski, *Modern School, op. 10*—Interntl

Solos   Bach-Joachim, *Sonatas and Partitas*—Interntl
Concerti by Mendelssohn, Beethoven, and Barber
Lalo-Menuhin, *Symphonie espagnole*—CFP
Saint-Saëns-Francescatti, *Concerto No. 3 in B minor*—Interntl
Sonatas by Brahms, Beethoven, Franck, Debussy, Prokofiev, Dvořák, Mozart, and Bartók
Vivaldi, **The Seasons,** from *Violin Concertos, op. 8*
Ysaÿe, *Six Sonatas, op. 27*—G. Schirmer

VIOLA

Grade I

Studies   Dancla, *Easy School of Melody*—Interntl
Herman, *Bows and Strings, Book 1*—Belwin
Hofmann, *First Studies, op. 86*—Interntl
Sitt-Ambrosio, *Practical Viola Method*—CF
Waller, *Viola Method*—Kjos

Solos   Bach, *Chorale Prelude, "I Call to Thee"*—CF
Brahms, *"My Inmost Heart Doth Yearn"*—CF
Harvey, *Viola Player's Repertory*—TP

Kreuz, *Progressive Studies, op. 40*—Augener
Sitt-Ambrosio, *Practical Viola Method*—CF
Whistler, *Introducing the Positions, Book 1*—Ru
Wohlfahrt-Isaac-Lewis, *Foundation Studies, Book 1*—CF

Solos   Bakaleinikoff, *Minuetto*—Belwin
Harvey, *Viola Player's Repertory*—TP
Klengel, *Classic Pieces*—CFP
Mozart-Piatigorsky, *Sonatine in C Major*—EV
Watson-Forbes, *First Year Classical Album for Viola*—Oxford

Grade III

Studies   Kreuz, *Progressive Studies, op. 40*—Augener
Whistler, *Introducing the Positions, Book 2*—Ru
Wohlfahrt-Isaac-Lewis, *Foundation Studies, Book 2*—CF

Solos   Bach-Wilhelmj-Pagels, *Air from Suite in D*—CF
Bossi, *Romanza, op. 89*—AMP
Brahms-Primrose, *"Soft Strains of Music Drifting"*—CF
Duke, *Melody in E-flat*—TP
Ibert, *Aria*—LD
Moffatt-Palaschko, *Old Masters for Young Players*—SCH
Mozart, *Adagio*—Oxford
Russetto, *Arioso*—Witmark
Vivaldi-Franko, *Intermezzo*—G. Schirmer

Grade IV

Studies   Dont-Svečenski, *20 Progressive Exercises, op. 38*—G. Schirmer
Hofmann, *15 Studies, op. 87*—Interntl
Mazas, *Special Studies, op. 36, Book 1*—Interntl
Schradieck-Pagels, *School of Viola Technique, Book 1*—Interntl

Solos   Ariosti, *Sonatas 1 and 2*—Santis
    Bach-Shore, *Praeludium*—Bo. Hawkes
    Boetja, *Viola Music for Concert and Church*—Boston
    Corelli-Katims, *Sonata in D minor*—Interntl
    Kodály, *Adagio*—Kul
    Marais-Aldis-Rowe, *5 Old French Dances*—Che
    Marcello-Gibson, *Sonata in G*—SCH
    Mozart-Piatigorsky, *Divertimento in C Major*—EV

Grade V

Studies   Bruni-Schulz, *25 Melodious and Characteristic Studies*—Interntl
    Kayser, *Thirty-Six Studies, op. 43*—Interntl
    Kreutzer-Consolini, *42 Studies*—Ricordi
    Schradieck-Pagels, *School of Viola Technique, Book 2*—Interntl

Solos   Boccherini-Ross, *Concerto No. 3*—G. Schirmer
    Hoffmeister-Doktor, *Concerto in D*—Interntl
    Huë, *"Thème varié"*—SMC
    Klengel, *Album of 24 Classical Pieces*—Interntl
    Nardini-Katims, *Sonata in D Major*—Interntl
    Telemann-Katims, *Concerto in G*—Interntl

Grade VI

Studies   Fiorillo-Spindler, *36 Studies*—Hof
    Kreutzer-Consolini, *42 Studies*—Ricordi
    Mazas, *Op. 36, Book 2*—Interntl
    Primrose, *Art and Practice of Scale Playing on the Viola*—Mil

Solos   Corelli, *"La folia"*—G. Schirmer
    Doktor, *Solos for the Viola Player*—G. Schirmer
    Elgar-Tertis, *Concerto, op. 85*—Nov
    Marcello, *Sonatas in F, G, and C*—Interntl
    Roger, *Irish Sonata, op. 37*—FDH
    Schubert-Katims, *Sonata in A minor*—Interntl
    Stamitz-Laugg, *Concerto in D Major, op. 1*—CFP
    Vivaldi, *Sonatas in A and B-flat*—Interntl

Grade VII

Studies   Dounis, *Specific Technical Exercises for Viola, op. 23*—CF
    Fiorillo-Spindler, *36 Studies*—Hof
    Mazas, *Op. 36, Book 2*—Interntl
    Rode-Pagels, *24 Caprices*—Interntl

Solos   Handel-Casadesus, *Concerto in B minor*—ESC
    Reger, *Suite, op. 131*—BRH
    Stamitz-Primrose, *Sonata in B-flat Major*—Interntl

Grade VIII

Studies   Bach-Forbes, *Three Viola da Gamba Sonatas*—CFP
    Beethoven-Primrose, *Notturno, op. 42*—SCH

Bruch, *Romance, op. 85*—SCH
Enesco, *Concertpiece*—Interntl
Haydn-Piatigorsky, *Divertimento in D*—EV
Schubert-Katims, *Arpeggione Sonata*—Interntl
Weber-Primrose, *Andante and Hungarian Rondo, op. 35*—Interntl

Grade IX

Studies   Campagnoli-Primrose, *Caprices, op. 22*—Interntl
Dounis, *Specific Technical Exercises, op. 23*—CF
Palaschko, *Studies, op. 36*—Interntl

Solos   Bach-Pessl, *Sonata in C minor*—Oxford

Grade X

Studies   Campagnoli-Primrose, *Caprices, op. 22*—Interntl
Hermann, *Six Concert Studies, op. 18*—Interntl
Rode, *24 Caprices*—Interntl
Schloming, *Studies, op. 15, Vol. 1*—SIM

Solos   Bach-Forbes, *Cello Suite for Viola*—CFP
Clarke, *Sonata*—Che
Handel-Barbirolli, *Concerto*—Oxford
Milhaud, *Sonatas 1 and 2*—TP
Rubbra, *Concerto in A*—Len
Shulman, *Theme and Variations*—Chappell
Vaughan Williams, *Suite*—Oxford

Grade XI

Studies   Campagnoli-Primrose, *Op. 22*—Interntl
Rode, *24 Caprices*—Interntl
Schloming, *Studies, op. 15, Vol. 2*—SIM

Solos   Bax, *Sonata*—Chappell
Brahms-Katims, *Sonatas, op. 120*—Interntl
Britten, "*Lachrymae*"—Bo. Hawkes
Harris, *Soliloquy and Dance*—G. Schirmer
Hindemith, *Sonatas*—SCH
Porter, *Concerto*—AMP
Schumann-Schradieck, "*Märchenbilder," op. 112*—BRH
Serly, *Concerto*—Leeds

Grade XII

Studies   Review and continuation of studies in previous grades

Solos   Bartók-Serly, *Concerto*—Bo. Hawkes
Benjamin, *Sonata*—Bo. Hawkes
Bloch, *Suite*—G. Schirmer
Hindemith, *Concerto*—SCH
Honegger, *Sonata*—ESC
Walton, *Concerto*—Oxford

CELLO

Grade I

Studies   Dotzauer-Klingerberg, *Studies, Book 1*—Interntl
Grutzmacher, *Daily Exercises, op. 67*—Augener
Lee, *Method, op. 30*—CF
Schröder, *Cello Method, Book 1*—CFP

Solos   Deák, *Juvenile Suite (No. 1, "Autumn Song"; No. 2, "Norwegian Dance"; No. 3, "Lullaby"; No. 4, "Waltz")*—CF
Moffat-Such, *Old Masters for Young Players*—SCH
Schmidt, *Six Easy Pieces, op. 44*—BMC
Waybright, *Six Miniature Pieces in First Position*—Wil

Grade II

Studies   Deák, *Cello Method, Book 1*—EV
Dotzauer-Klingerberg, *Studies, Book 1*—Interntl
Lee, *40 Melodic Studies, Book 1*—SCH
Schröder, *Cello Method, Book 2*—CFP
Whistler, *Introducing the Positions, Book 1*—Ru

Solos   *Forgotten Melodies*—AMP
Graded Teaching Pieces, First Series—Augener
Moffat-Rapp, *Old Master Melodies for Young Cellists*—SCH
Romberg, *Early Sonata*—Interntl

Grade III

Studies   Deák, *Cello Method, Book 2*—EV
Dotzauer-Klingerberg, *Studies, Book 2*—Interntl
Kummer, *Melodious Studies, op. 57*—Ricordi
Lee, *40 Melodic Studies, Book 2*—SCH
Schröder, *Cello Method, Book 2*—CFP
Whistler, *Introducing Positions, Book 2*—Ru

Solos   Franko-Bach, *Arioso*—G. Schirmer
Graded Teaching Pieces, Second Series—Augener
Lindner-Handel, *Sonata No. 1 in G minor*—Interntl
Marcello-Cassado, *Sonatas No. 1 and No. 4*—Interntl
Vivaldi, *Sonata No. 3*—Internal

Grade IV

Studies   Deák, *Cello Method, Book 2*—EV

Dotzauer-Klingerberg, *Studies, Book 2*—Interntl
Kummer, *Melodious Studies, op. 57*—Ricordi
Lee, *40 Melodic Studies, Book 2*—SCH
Whistler, *Introducing the Positions, Book 2*—Ru

Solos   *Forgotten Melodies*—AMP
Kreisler, *Chanson Louis XIII and Pavane*—Foley
Marcello-Cassado, *Sonata No. 5*—Interntl
Vivaldi, *Sonata No. 5*—Interntl

Grade V

Studies   Deák, *Cello Method, Book 2*—EV

Handel-Lindner, *Sonatas Nos. 1, 2, and 3*—BRH
Popper, *Hungarian Rhapsody*—Interntl
Vivaldi-Rose, *Six Sonatas*—Interntl

Grade VI

Studies   Franchomme-Klengel, *12 Etudes, op. 35*—CFP
Grutzmacher, *Etudes, Book 2*—CFP
Kummer, *Melodious Studies, op. 57*—Ricordi
Schröder, *Cello Method, Book 3*—CFP

Solos   Bach, *Pastorale*—Interntl
Dukelsky, *Concerto*—CF
Goltermann-Rose, *Concerti Nos. 1 and 4*—Interntl
Klengel, *Suite in D minor, op. 22*—Interntl

Grade VII

Studies   Franchomme-Klengel, *12 Etudes, op. 35*—CFP
Grutzmacher, *Etudes, Book 2*—CFP
Kummer, *Melodious Studies, op. 57*—Ricordi
Schröder, *Cello Method, Book 3*—CFP

Solos   Breval-Stutschevsky, *Sonata in C*—SCH
Galeotti-Rogister, *Sonata No. 2 in G*—ESC
Granados-Piatigorsky, *"Orientale"*—Interntl
Marais, *Suite in D minor*—SCH
Mozart-Grutzmacher, *Sonata in B-flat, K. 292*—CFP
Pasqualini, *Sonata in A*—Augener
Piatti, *Studienkonzert in D minor, op. 26*—Hof
Porpora, *Sonata in F*—SCH
Romberg, *Concertino in D minor*—Interntl

Grade VIII

Studies   Cossman, *Technical Studies*—Interntl
Duport-Schulz, *Etudes*—G. Schirmer
Franchomme-Klengel, *12 Etudes, op. 35*—CFP
Schröder, *Cello Method, Book 3*—CFP

Solos   Bach-Piatti-Rapp, *Six Suites*—SCH
Frescobaldi-Cassado, *Toccata*—UE
Goltermann-Schulz, *Concerto No. 3, op. 51*—CF
Grazioli-Salmon, *Sonata in G*—Ricordi
Nardini-Salmon, *Sonata in do*—Ricordi
Sammartini-Moffat, *Sonata in G*—SCH
Vitali-Kurtz, *Chaconne in G minor*—AMP

Grade IX

Studies   Cossman, *Technical Studies*—Interntl
Duport-Schulz, *Etudes*—G. Schirmer
Franchomme-Klengel, *12 Caprices, op. 7*—Interntl
Schröder, *Cello Method, Book 3*—CFP

Solos   Bach-Piatigorsky, *Concerto No. 1 in G*—Interntl
Barber, *Concerto Garbonsova, op. 22*—G. Schirmer
Boccherini-Piatti, *Six Sonatas*—Ricordi
Boccherini-Sammartini, *Sonatas*—Ricordi
Dohnányi, *Sonata in B-flat Major, op. 8*—SCH
Goltermann-Rose, *Concerto No. 1, op. 14*—Interntl
Romberg, *Concerto No. 2*—CFP
Sammartini-Salmon, *Sonata in G minor*—Ricordi
Shulman, *Concerto*—Chappell

Grade X

Studies   Cossman, *Technical Studies*—Interntl
Duport-Schulz, *Etudes*—G. Schirmer
Franchomme-Klengel, *12 Caprices, op. 7*—Interntl

Solos   Boccherini-Haydn, *Sonatas*—Ricordi
Boccherini-Piatti, *Six Sonatas*—Ricordi
Franchomme, *Concerto No. 1*—HL
Haydn-Grutzmacher, *Concerto No. 2 in D Major*—BRH
Haydn-Piatti, *Sonata in C*—Interntl
Romberg, *Concerti Nos. 5, 6, and 7*—Bill

Grade XI

Studies   Duport, *Etudes*—G. Schirmer
Popper, *Studies, op. 73*—Leeds
Servais-Becker, *Six Caprices, op. 11*—SCH

Solos   David, *Concerti Nos. 1, 2, 3, and 4*—Bill
Lalo-Rose, *Concerto in D minor*—Interntl
Popper-Rose, *Hungarian Rhapsody, op. 68*—Interntl

Romberg, *Concerti Nos. 8 and 9*—Bill
Saint-Saëns, *Concerti Nos. 1 and 2*—Dur

155

Grade XII

Studies   Grutzmacher-Klengel, *24 Studies, op. 38, Book 2*—Interntl
Popper, *Studies, op. 73*—Leeds

Solos   Boccherini-Papin, *Concerto No. 3 in G*—LD
d'Albert, *Concerto in C, op. 20*—CFP
Dvořák, *Concerto, op. 104*—SIM
Locatelli-Piatti, *Sonata in D*—Interntl
Mozart-Trowell, *Concerto in A*—Augener

Grade I

Studies   Cruft, *The Eugene Cruft School of Double Bass Playing*—Nov
Marcelli, *Basic Method, Book 1*—CF
Simandl, *New Method for the Double Bass, Book 1*—CF
Zimmerman-Slama, *66 Etudes in all Major and Minor Keys*—Interntl

Solos   Isaac-Lewis, "Country Gardens"—CF
Sterling, *2 Eighteenth Century Pieces*—Augener
Whistler, *Solos for Strings*—Ru

Grade II

Studies   Bottesini-Sterling, *24 Exercises*—Augener
Cruft, *The Eugene Cruft School of Double Bass Playing*—Nov
Marcelli, *Basic Method, Book 2*—CF
Simandl, *New Method for the Double Bass, Book 1*—CF
Slama-Zimmerman, *66 Etudes in All Major and Minor Keys*—Interntl

Solos   Bach-Zimmerman, *Gavotte*—CF
Boccherini-Capon, *Adagio*—LD
Koussevitzky, *Valse Miniature, op. 1, no. 2*—Interntl
Purcell, *Aria*—Interntl

Grade III

Studies   Cruft, *The Eugene Cruft School of Double Bass Playing*—Nov
Kayser-Winsel, *36 Studies, op. 20*—Interntl
Simandl, *New Method for the Double Bass, Book 1*—CF
_____, *Thirty Etudes for Double Bass*—Interntl

Solos   Bach, *Adagio from Organ Toccata in C*—Interntl
Corelli-Sterling, *Prelude from Sonata No. 8*—Augener
Glière, *Prelude*—Interntl

Grade IV

Studies   Bille, *Nuovo metodo per contrabasso, Part 1, No. 2*—Ricordi
Corso Practico—Ricordi
Gamberini, *Scale e arpeggi per contrabasso*—Cu
Simandl, *Thirty Etudes for Double Bass*—Interntl

Solos   Corelli, *Sonata in D minor*—Interntl
Farkas, *Sonatina*—Kul
Fauré, *Sicilienne, op. 78*—Interntl
Handel, *Sonata in G minor*—Interntl
Porter, *"Lyric Piece"*—CFE

Grades V and VI

Studies   Bille, *Nuovo metodo per contrabasso, Part 1, No. 2*—Ricordi
Gouffe, *45 Etudes*—Bill

Solos   Bach-Sankey, *Sonata No. 2 in D*—Interntl
Beethoven-Khomenko, *Sonata, Aria for Piano and Horn*—Leeds
Eccles, *Sonata in G minor*—Interntl
Larsson, *Concertino*—Gehrmans

Grades VII and VIII

Studies   Bille, *Diciotto studii*—Ricordi
_____, *Nuovo metodo per contrabasso, Part 2*—Ricordi

Solos   Boccherini-Sankey, *Sonata in A, No. 6*—Interntl
Eccles, *Sonata in G minor*—Interntl
Galliard, *Sonata in F*—Interntl
Jullien, *Allegro de concert*—LD
Marcello, *Sonata in F*—Interntl

Grades IX and X

Studies   Bille, *Nuovo metodo per contrabasso, Part 2*—Ricordi
Nanny, *Etudes de Kreutzer et de Fiorello*—LD

Solos   Dittersdorf, *Jaeger Concerto in E*—SCH
Dragonetti-Nanny-Sankey, *Concerto in A*—Interntl
Marcello, *Sonata in G minor*—Internl
Mozart-Sankey, *Concerto, K. 191 (Originally for bassoon)*—Interntl
Ratez, *Six pièces charactéristiques*—Bill
Schubert-Sankey, *Sonata in A minor*—Interntl

Grades XI and XII

Studies   Bille, *Nuovo metodo per contrabasso, Part 2*—Ricordi
_____, *Sei studii caratteristici*—Ricordi
Nanny, *Dix études caprices*—LD

Solos   Bach-Nanny, *Six Suites (Originally for violoncello unaccompanied)*—LD
Bottesini-Nanny-Sankey, *Concerto*—Interntl
Bottesini-Zimmerman, *Tarantella*—Interntl
Hindemith, *Sonata*—SCH
Koussevitzky, *Concerto, op. 3*—Interntl

6

Group Methods

Because of time, facilities, personnel, and budget, beginning instrumental students in the public schools are started in large groups. Although group teaching has motivational and instructional advantages, it should be accompanied by a private lesson program. The following methods have been used by successful band and orchestra directors and are recommended for your consideration.

ORCHESTRA

Class Methods for Beginning String Instruments

Gordon–Beckstead	*Visual Method for Strings*	Highland

Piano by Gregory Stone. Excellent visual illustrations. Music adequate for young beginning student.

Herfurth, P.	*A Tune a Day, Books 1, 2, and 3*	Boston

For beginning, intermediate, and advanced. Average—better materials available.

Herman, H.	*Bow and Strings in Three Books*	Belwin

Material suited for young beginners. Book 3 for grade II. Lacks illustrations. Piano accompaniment included with full score. Adequate.

Isaac, M.	*Merle Isaac String Class Method, Books 1 and 2*	Cole

Good illustrations and directions. Exercises and tunes adequate.

Jones–Dasch–Krone	*Strings from the Start*	CF

Excellent illustrations, instructive detail, and exercises. Music good; designed for older students.

Keller–Taylor	*Easy Steps to the Orchestra, Book 1*	Mills

Good illustrations and music material. Full score and directions for teacher.

Waller, G.	*Waller String Class Method, Books 1 and 2*	Kjos

Good illustrations and adequate material. Above average.

Whistler–Nord	*Beginning Strings*	CF

Minimum of illustrations. Good exercises and music material. Excellent.

Class Studies for String Instruments

GRADE I

Whistler–Hummel	*Elementary Scales and Bowings for Strings*	Ru

Good supplementary material.

GRADE II

Waller, G.	*Waller Vibrato Method for Strings*	Kjos

Use as supplement for intermediate level.

Whistler–Hummel	*Intermediate Scales and Bowings for Strings*	Ru

Good supplementary exercises and drills.

GRADE III

Applebaum	*Belwin String Builder* (Three volumes)	Belwin

One of the better current beginning string methods that has been popular with most string teachers.

Bergh, H.	*String Positions*	Summy-Bir

Keys E through A-flat. Exercises and musical selections in each key. Good supplementary material.

Johnson, H.	*The Positions for All Strings*	FitzSimons

For advanced students grade III or above. Excellent musical material.

BAND

Beginning Class Methods

Douglas, W.   Weber, ed.   *Belwin Band Builder,*   Belwin
Book 1

Somewhat simplified approach; musical material rather dry. Piano conductor.

Kinyon, J.   *The MPH Band Method*   Witmark

Contains practice time record for each page, but boxes small to write in. Last page contains progress chart for pages completed—good device to help students take pages in order.

Leidig-Neihaus   *A Visual Band Method*   Highland

Unique approach to developing instrumentalists through harmonic experiences.

Peters, C.   Yoder, ed.   *Master Method for Band*   Kjos

This approach utilizes much literature and many melodies. Would make good supplementary method book. Good ensemble work.

Prescott-   *Preparatory Beginning Band*   H-McCreary
Phillips-Schmidt   *Method*

Good combination of technical and melodic material. Slightly more advanced approach than most methods. Piano conductor score.

Sawhill-Erickson   *Bourne Guide to Band,*   Bourne
Book 1

Emphasis on technique and fundamentals of musicianship. Four-line score. For beginning and intermediate students.

Skornicka-   *Band Method*   Bo. Hawkes
Bergeim

Organizes instruments into groups having similar range. Use of harmony in rhythmic patterns from beginning. Unison playing done by small groups. Unison for entire ensemble comes after ranges have been expanded.

Smith-Yoder-   *Ensemble Band Method,*   Kjos
Bachman   *Book 1*

Progresses more rapidly than average method through unison, harmony, and full band. Material well arranged. Position pictures and fingering charts included. Few directions to instructor. (Special fingering charts available.)

Taylor, M.   *Easy Steps to the Band*   Mills

Very good method book, but will need supplementing. Should be brought up to date. There is a need for more interesting material for students. Contains melodic and technical exercises, very complete basic approach. Designed for full band use, but can be used for private or class instruction.

Weber, F.   *First Division Band Method,* Belwin
                                 Part 1

Material for each area of musical development, written by men of outstanding achievement.

Beginning Class Studies and Exercises

Church–
Dykema   *Modern Band Training*   Summy-Bir

Good supplementary material.

Goldman, E. F.   *Goldman Band System,*   CF
                          Books 1 and 2

For developing tone, intonation, and phrasing. Good suggestions to instructor in conductor's manual.

Weber, F.   *Belwin Progressive Band*   Belwin
                    Studies

Divided into eight units. Five solos for each instrument. Harmonized pieces may be played with various instrumental combinations.

White   *Unisonal Scales, Chords,*   CF
                 and Rhythmic Studies
                 for Band

Very good for unison technical drill. May be used from late beginning through advanced stages of development.

Intermediate Class Methods

Douglas, W.   Weber, ed.   *Belwin Band Builder,*   Belwin
                               Book 2

Somewhat simplified. Piano, conductor.

Rusch, H.   *Hal Leonard Intermediate*   Leo
                    Band Method

Exciting and logical approach to band.

Smith-Yoder-
Bachman   *Intermediate Band Method*   Kjos

Conductor's score condensed to four staves. Covers keys from one sharp to six flats. Emphasis on rhythm and intonation. Fresh musical material.

Taylor, M.   *Intermediate Steps to the*   Mills
                    Band

Good suggestions for teaching in an appealing format. Emphasis on rhythmic problems.

Emphasis on technical development. Uses condensed conductor score. Solos for individual instruments included at end of book.

_____   *First Division Band Method,* Belwin
Parts 2, 3, and 4

Material for each area of musical development, written by men of outstanding achievement. Suggested supplementary material—such as ensembles, solos, concert pieces, and supplementary technique—included.

Exercises for Ensemble Drill Schmitt

Excellent technical studies and rhythm drills, intermediate and advanced. (May also be used for orchestra.)

Rusch, H.   *Twenty-four Arban-Klosé-*   Belwin
Concone Studies

Unison with A band part, or unison with A and B band parts. Study material good. May be used for intermediate band.

Yaus, G.   *101 Rhythmic Rest Patterns*   Belwin

Emphasis entirely on rhythmic patterns. Little melodic interest. Valuable if supplemented with other material to assure transfer. Intermediate grades upward.

Intermediate and Advanced Class Studies and Exercises

Laas, B.   *50 Chorales for Band*   Belwin

Good musical material for general musicianship, intonation, etc.

Rusch   *25 Lazarus-Concone Studies* Belwin

This study book is a follow-up of the 24 Arban-Klosé-Concone. Studies may be used either unison or with full band parts.

Smith-Yoder-   *S.Y.B. Technic*   Kjos
Bachman

Scales, arpeggios, and rhythm studies through various keys, major and minor (two sharps-seven flats). Good selection.

Yaus, G.   *20 Rhythmical Studies*   Belwin

Styled and designed to make division of measure interesting. For development of individual player, ensemble, or complete band.

ADDENDUM

7

Instrumental
Music Bibliography

The following texts and pamphlets are presented as a reference for the instrumental music educator. The more a performer/teacher knows about the instruments, the better he/she is able to motivate and inspire students. Much has been written about the instruments. Consequently, much is expected from this reservoir of important bibliography. Most higher learning libraries should have these reference materials, and all public schools should have a good sampling. Students deserve the opportunity to make these rich resources a part of their performing lives.

The following titles are so specific that in most cases an annotation seemed needless. Each music educator is encouraged to strengthen this list as other references become available.

TEXTS

Adkins, *Treatise on the Military Band.* 2nd ed. rev. London: Boosey and Hawkes, 1958.

Altmann, Wilhelm. *Chamber Music Literature.* Leipzig: F. Hofmeister, 1945. Literature since 1841. For a later edition of this material, see Richter, Johannes Friedrich, below.

Andrews, Frances M., and Joseph A. Leeder. *Guiding Junior High School Pupils in Music Experiences.* Englewood Cliffs, N.J.: Prentice-Hall, Inc., 1953.

Andrews and Cockerille. *Your School Music Program.* Englewood Cliffs, N.J.: Prentice-Hall, Inc., 1958.

Applebaum, Samuel, and Sada Applebaum. *With Artists.* New York: John Market and Co., 1960.

164   Baines, Anthony. *Woodwind Instruments and Their History.* New York: W. W. Norton, 1947. 3rd ed. London: Faber, 1967.

Band and Orchestra Handbook, The. Elkhart, Inc., Pan-American Band Instruments Division of C. G. Conn, Ltd., 1956.

Bartlett, Harry R. *Guide to Teaching Percussion.* Dubuque, Iowa: W. C. Brown, 1964.

Basic Concepts in Music Education. The Fifty-Seventh Yearbook of the National Society for the Study of Education. Part I. Chicago: The University of Chicago Press, 1958.

Boehm, Theobald. *The Flute and Flute Playing.* New York: McGinnis and Marx, 1960.

Bostelmann, Louis. *An Analysis of Violin Practice.* Philadelphia: Oliver Ditson, 1947.

Bradley, Vincent. *Playing at Sight for Violinists and Other Instrumentalists.* London: Oxford University Press, 1949.

Brand, Erick D. *Selmer Band Instrument Repairing Manual.* 2nd ed. Elkhart, Ind.: H.&A. Selmer, Inc., 1942.

Camden, Archie. *Bassoon Technique.* London: Oxford University Press, 1962.

Carse, Adam. *The Orchestra from Beethoven to Berlioz.* Cambridge: W. Heffer and Sons, Ltd., 1948.

Collins, Myron D., and John E. Green. *Playing and Teaching Percussion Instruments.* Englewood Cliffs, N.J.: Prentice-Hall, Inc., 1962.

Colwell, Richard. *The Teaching of Instrumental Music.* New York: Appleton-Century-Crofts, 1969.

Cook, Clifford. *String Teaching and Some Related Topics.* Urbana, Ill.: American String Teachers, 1957.

Duvall, W. Clyde. *The High School Band Director's Handbook.* Englewood Cliffs, N.J.: Prentice-Hall, Inc., 1960.

Dykema, Peter, and Hannah Cundiff. *School Music Handbook.* Boston: C. C. Birchard & Co., 1955.

Dykema, Peter W., and Karl W. Gehrkens. *The Teaching and Administration of High School Music.* Boston: C. C. Birchard & Co., 1941.

Eisenberg, Maurice, in collaboration with M. B. Stanfield. *Cello Playing of Today.* London: The Strad, 1957.

Farish, Margaret K. *String Music in Print.* New York: R. R. Bowker Co., 1965.

Farkas, Phillip. *The Art of French Horn Playing.* Evanston: Summy-Birchard Publishing Co., 1956.

Galamian, Ivan. *Principles of Violin Playing and Teaching.* Englewood Cliffs, N.J.: Prentice-Hall, Inc., 1962.

Geiringer, Karl. *Musical Instruments.* New York: Oxford University Press, 1945.

Goldman, Richard F. *The Band's Music.* New York: Pitman Publishing Corporation, 1938.

_____. *The Concert Band.* New York: Rinehard & Co., Inc., 1946.

_____. *The Wind Band.* Boston: Allyn and Bacon, Inc., 1961.

Green, Elizabeth H. *Orchestral Bowings and Routines.* Ann Arbor, Mich.: Ann Arbor Publisher, 1947. 2nd ed. 1957.

_____. *The Modern Conductor.* Englewood Cliffs, N.J.: Prentice-Hall, Inc., 1961. 2nd ed. 1969.

Havas, Kató. *A New Approach to Violin Playing.* London: Bosworth, 1961.

Hendrickson, Clarence V. *Fingering Charts for Instrumentalists: Handy Manual for Teachers, Directors, and Students.* New York: Carl Fischer, Inc., 1957. Often referred to as *Instrumentalist's Handy Reference Manual.*

Hindsley, Mark H. *School Band and Orchestra Administration.* New York: Boosey & Hawkes, Inc., 1940.

Hoffer, *Teaching Music in the Secondary Schools.* Belmont, Calif.: Wadsworth Publishing Co., Inc., 1964.

Holmes, Malcolm. *Conducting an Amateur Orchestra.* Cambridge, Mass.: Harvard University Press, 1951.

Hunt, Norman. *Guide to Teaching Brass.* Dubuque, Iowa: William C. Brown Publishers, 1968.

Jones, Archie D., ed. *Music Education in Action: Basic Principles and Practice Methods.* Boston: Allyn & Bacon, Inc., 1960.

Jones, Llewellyn B. *Building the Instrumental Music Department.* New York: Carl Fisher, Inc., 1949.

Keller, Hermann. *Phrasing and Articulation.* Translated from German by Leigh Gerdine. New York: W. W. Norton and Co., Inc., 1965.

King, A. Hyatt. *Chamber Music.* New York: Chanticleer Press, 1948.

Kleinhammer, Edward. *The Art of Trombone Playing.* Evanston, Ill.: Summy-Birchard Publishing Co., 1963.

Krolick, Edward. *Basic Principles of Double Bass Playing.* Washington: Music Educators National Conference, 1957.

Kuhn, Wolfgang E. *Instrumental Music.* Boston: Allyn & Bacon, Inc., 1962.

_____. *Principles of String Class Teaching.* Rockville Centre, N.Y.: Belwin, Inc., 1957.

Langwill, Lyndesay Graham. *The Bassoon and Double Bassoon.* London: Hinrichsen Edition, 1948.

Leeder, Joseph A., and William S. Haynie. *Music Education in the High School.* Englewood Cliffs, N.J.: Prentice-Hall, Inc., 1958.

Leidig, Vernon. *Contemporary Woodwind Technique.* Hollywood, Calif.: Highland Music, 1960.

Malko, Nicolai. *The Conductor and His Baton.* Copenhagen: Wilhelm Hansen, 1950.

McKay, George F. *Creative Orchestration.* Boston: Allyn & Bacon, Inc., 1963.

Matesky, Ralph, and Ralph Rush. *Playing and Teaching Stringed Instruments.* See Rush, Ralph, and Ralph Matesky, below.

166   Moore, E. C. *The Brass Book.* Kenosha, Wis.: G. Leblanc Co., 1954.

Morgan, Hazel N., ed. *Music Education Source Book.* Washington, D.C.: Music Educators National Conference, 1951.

————. *Music in American Education.* Source Book No. 2. Washington, D.C.: MENC, 1955.

Morley-Pegge, R. *The French Horn.* New York: Philosophical Library, 1960.

Mueller, John H. *The American Symphony Orchestra.* Bloomington, Ind.: Indiana University Press, 1951.

Music Education Materials . . . A Selected Bibliography. Published as Vol. 7 (Spring 1959) of the *Journal of Research in Music Education.* Washington, D.C.: MENC, 1959.

Music in the Senior High School. Washington, D.C.: MENC, 1959.

Neidig, Kenneth L., ed. *The Band Director's Guide.* Englewood Cliffs, N.J.: Prentice-Hall, Inc., 1964.

Normann, Theodore F. *Instrumental Music in the Public Schools.* Bryn Mawr, Pa.: Theodore Presser Co., 1941.

Organ, Robert J. *Bassoon and Oboe.* Denver: Rebo Music Publications (842 South Franklin, Denver, Colo. 80209), 1954.

Palmer, Harold G. *Teaching Techniques of the Woodwind.* New York: Belwin, 1952.

Peterson, O. A. *The Cornet.* New York: W. Jacobs, 1957.

Phillips, Harvey. *Play Now.* Morristown, N.J.: Silver Burdett Co., 1968.

Piston, Walter. *Orchestration.* New York: W. W. Norton & Co., 1955.

Potter, Louis. *The Art of Cello Playing.* Evanston, Ill.: Summy-Birchard Publishing Co., 1964.

Prescott, Gerald R., and Lawrence W. Chidester. *Getting Results with School Bands.* New York: Carl Fischer, Inc.; and Minneapolis: Paul Schmitt Music Company, 1938.

Rendall, F. Geoffrey. *The Clarinet.* New York: Philosophical Library, 1954.

Richter, Johannes Friedrich. *Kammermusik-Katalog: Verzeichnis der von 1944 bis 1958 Veröffentlichen Merke. . . .* Leipzig: F. Hofmeister, 1960.

Righter, Charles B. *Success in Teaching School Orchestras and Bands.* Minneapolis: Paul Schmitt Music Company, 1945.

————. *Teaching Instrumental Music.* New York: Carl Fischer, Inc., 1959.

Rothwell, Evelyn. *Oboe Technique.* London: Oxford University Press, 1953. Rev. ed., 1964.

Rowen, Ruth Halle. *Early Chamber Music.* New York: King's Crown Press, Columbia University, 1949.

Rush, Ralph, and Ralph Matesky. *Playing and Teaching Stringed Instruments.* 2 vols. Englewood Cliffs, N.J.: Prentice-Hall, Inc., 1963.

Saltonstall and Smith. *Catalog of Music for Small Orchestras.* Washington, D.C.: The Music Library Association, 1947.

Sansone, Lorenzo. *French Horn Music Literature with Composers' Biographical Sketches.* New York: Sansone Musical Instruments, 1962.

Sawhill, Clarence, and Bertram McGarrity. *Playing and Teaching Woodwind Instruments.* Englewood Cliffs, N.J.: Prentice-Hall, 1962.

Scherchen, Hermann. *Handbook of Conducting.* London: Oxford University Press, 1933.

Schonberg, Harold C. *Chamber and Solo Instrument Music.* New York: Alfred A. Knopf, 1955.

Schuller, Gunther. *Horn Technique.* London: Oxford University Press, 1962.

Schwartz, H. W. *Bands of America.* Garden City, N.Y.: Doubleday and Co., 1957.

_____. *The Story of Musical Instruments.* Elkhart, Ind.: Pan-American Band Instruments, 1938. Also Garden City, N.Y.: Garden City Publishing Co., Inc., 1943.

Singleton, Ira C., and Simon V. Anderson. *Music in Secondary Schools.* Boston: Allyn & Bacon, Inc. 1963. 2nd ed. 1969.

Sur, William R., and Charles F. Schuller. *Music Education for Teenagers.* New York: Harper and Guthers, 1958. 2nd ed. 1966.

Sweeney, Leslie. *Teaching Techniques for the Brasses.* New York: Belwin, Inc., 1953.

Thompson, Helen M. *The Community Symphony Orchestra.* Charleston, W. Va.: American Symphony Orchestra League, Inc., 1952.

Thorton, James. *Woodwind Handbook.* San Antonio, Tex.: Southern Music Co., 1960.

Thurston, Frederick. *Clarinet Technique.* London: Oxford University Press, 1956.

Timm, Everett L. *The Woodwinds: Performance and Instructional Techniques.* Boston: Allyn & Bacon, Inc., 1964.

Trzcinski, Louis. *Planning the School String Program.* New York: Mills Music Company, 1963.

Ulrich, Homer. *Chamber Music.* New York: Columbia University Press, 1948. 2nd ed. 1966.

Van Bodegraven and Wilson. *The School Music Conductor.* Chicago: Hall and McCreary Co., 1942.

Ward, Sylvan D. *The Instrumental Director's Handbook.* Chicago: Rubank, Inc., 1940.

Weast, Robert D. *Brass Performance.* New York: McGinnis and Marx, 1961.

Willeman, Robert. *The Clarinet and Clarinet Playing.* New York: Carl Fischer, 1954.

Winslow, Robert W., and John E. Green. *Playing and Teaching Brass Instruments.* Englewood Cliffs, N.J.: Prentice-Hall, Inc., 1961.

Winter, James Hamilton. *The Brass Instruments.* Boston: Allyn & Bacon, Inc., 1964.

PAMPHLETS

American String Teachers Association. Published String List. 606 South Mathews Street, Urbana, Illinois.

Artley, Joe. *How to Make Double Reeds.* Elkhart, Ind.: H. & A. Selmer, Inc., 1940. 2nd ed. Old Greenwich, Conn.: J. Spratt, 1953.

Berger, Kenneth. *Band Bibliography.* Evansville, Ind.: Berger Band, 1955. Complete revision in *Band Encyclopedia* (Evansville, Ind.: Band Associates, 1960).

_____. *Band Discography.* Evansville, Ind.: Berger Band, 1956. Complete revision in *Band Encyclopedia (Evansville, Ind.: Band Associates, 1960).*

_____. *Bandmen.* Evansville, Ind.: Beger Band, 1955. Complete revision in *Band Encyclopedia* (Evansville, Ind.: Band Associates, 1960).

_____. *Band Music Guide.* Evansville, Ind.: Berger Band, 1956. Some volumes have been kept up to date by addenda.

Best, Clarence J. *Music Rooms and Equipment.* Washington, D.C.: MENC, 1949.

Chamber Music and Other Music for String and Wind Instruments. New York: C. Peters Co., Music Publishers, 1955.

Chamber Music by Contemporary Composers. New York: American Music Center (250 West 57th St.), 1954.

Chidester, Lawrence W. *International Wind-Band Instrumentation.* San Antonio, Tex.: Southern Music Co., 1946.

Contemporary Music. Washington, D.C.: MENC, 1959. Rev. ed. 1964. A suggested list for high schools and colleges.

Crockett, Frank. *Organizing String Programs.* Chicago: American String Teachers Association, 1957.

Educational Music Bureau Guide. Chicago: Educational Music Bureau, 1959. Often referred to as *EMB Guide.* Music of all publishers available by mail.

Fennell, F. *Time and the Winds.* Kenosha, Wis.: G. LeBlanc Co., 1954.

Helm, Sanford. *Catalog of Chamber Music for Wind Instruments.* Ann Arbor, Mich.: Braun-Brumfield, Inc., 1952.

How to Care for Your Instrument. Elkhart, Ind.: C. G. Conn, 1942.

Kent, Earle L. *The Inside Story of Brass Instruments.* Elkhart, Ind.: C. G. Conn, 1956.

King, Robert D. *Music for Brass.* North Easton, Mass.: Robert King Music Co.

Lanier, Frances B., et al. *Suggested String Syllabus for Annual Achievement Examinations.* Chicago: American String Teachers Association, Commission on Publications, Paul Rolland, Chairman, 1951.

LeBlanc Teaching Aids (catalog). Kenosha, Wis.: G. LeBlanc Corp. Listing of texts and methods for woodwinds and band directors and the Clinical Notes series of pamphlets on many subjects of interest to woodwind players (*The Flute, Oboe, Clarinet, Saxophone, Brass Book, Playing at Sight, The Band Book*).

Leidig, Vernon. *Contemporary Brass Technique.* Hollywood-Highland Music Co., 1960.

Lyons, Howard R. *Recruiting the School Band and Orchestra.* Chicago: Lyons Band & Instruments Co., 1941.

Maddy, Joseph. *The Interlochen List of Recommended Materials for Instrumental Ensembles.* Interlochen, Mich.: National Music Camp, 1953.

MENC. *Contemporary Music: A Suggested List for High Schools and Colleges.* Prepared by Committee on Contemporary Music, George Howerton, Chairman.

_____. *Materials for Miscellaneous Instrumental Ensembles.* Prepared by Commission 169
  Standards of Music Literature and Performance, George Waln, Chairman.

Music Buildings, Rooms, Equipment. Washington, D.C.: MENC, 1955. Rev. ed. 1966.

National Federation Festivals Bulletin. New York: The National Federation of Music
  Clubs, 445 West 23rd Street.

Orchestra Director's Manual. 3rd ed. Cleveland, Ohio: Scherl & Roth, Inc., 1956.

Orchestra Director's Manual No. 4. Cleveland, Ohio: Scherl & Roth, Inc., 1958.

Reed, Alfred. *The Balanced Clarinet Choir.* Kenosha, Wis.: G. LeBlanc Corporation,
  1955.

Selective Music Lists, Band, Orchestra, String Orchestra and Choral ...

... series of ten brochures bound in eight
  pamphlets.

University of Illinois String Publications. Urbana, Ill.: University of Illinois Music Exten-
  sion Division, February 1957 catalog. A list of excellent publications for string
  teachers; also helpful pamphlets in other instrumental teaching areas.

Weber, Fred, et al. *Building Better Bands.* New York: Belwin, Inc., 1957.

You Fix Them. Cleveland, Ohio: Scherl & Roth, Inc., 1955.

ADDENDUM

8

Selected

Composers-Compositions

Many composers do not write music that is within the performance capabilities of the young aspiring instrumental musician. The following selected list includes representative composers and compositions for public school performances. Therefore, many composers are not included, and not all compositions of the composers are listed.

The music educator should have available those composers and publishers that are the very best, yet compose and publish music for public school use. No biographical dictionary seems to fill this need. The educator is encouraged to strengthen this list by adding composers' and publishers' names on the addendum page.

Information for this list was obtained from the following sources: *Baker's Biographical Dictionary of Musicians*, rev. by Nicholas Slonimsky (New York: G. Schirmer, 1971); *Grove's Dictionary of Music and Musicians*, ed. by Eric Blom, vols. I-X (New York: The Macmillan Company, 1966); John Tasker Howard, *Our American Music* (New York: Thomas Y. Crowell Company, 1958); and J. A. Westrup and F. L. Harrison, *The New College Encyclopedia of Music* (New York: W. W. Norton and Company, Inc., 1959). The reader is referred to these excellent works for more complete information.

ALFORD, HARRY L.

Born 1888; died 1933. An American composer. Many bandstrations—mostly novelties and marches.

Works

"Call of the Elk"
"Drumology"
"The Hustler"
"The Imp"
"Law and Order"

"Maria Mari"
"Purple Carnival"
"Spooks"
"Thunder Cloud"
"Yankee Boy"

ALFORD, KENNETH J. (Fred J. Ricketts)

Born 1881; died 1945. Graduate of Kneller Hall; English organist and composer. Wrote under pen name of Kenneth J. Alford. Bandmaster for Royal Marines from 1928 to 1944. He has written for military band.

Works

"Colonel Bogey"
"Army of the Nile"
"By Land and Sea"
"The Vanished Army"
"The Middy"

"Standard of St. George"
"This Red Line" (His first march)
A suite:
  "The Smithy"
  "The Hunt"

ANDERSON, LEROY

Born June 29, 1908, in Cambridge, Massachusetts; died May 18, 1975. Graduated from Cambridge High and Latin School (1925), and Harvard University (A.B. 1929, M.A. 1934). Studied organ with Henry Gideon and bass viol with Gaston Defresne and tutored in music at Radcliffe while working on master's degree. His conducting experiences included four years as director of the Harvard University Band and subsequently several orchestras in Boston.

Works

"Jazz Pizzicato" (1939)
"Jazz Legato" (1944)
"Promenade" (1946)
"Chicken Reel" (Arr. 1946)
"Fiddle Faddle" (1947
"Governor Bradford March" (1948)
"Christmas Day" (1948)
"Sleigh Ride" (1948)

"Serenata" (1949)
"Ticonderoga March" (1950)
Sarabande (1950)
"A Trumpeter's Lullaby" (1950)
"Clarinet Candy Band"
Irish Suite
"Summer Skies" (Band, orchestra)

ASSOCIATED MUSIC PUBLISHERS

Organized in 1927. A New York publisher and sales agent for foreign publishers, including the following:

Hainauer—Breslau
Editions Eschig—Paris
Choudens—Paris
Hansen—Copenhagen
Nagel's Music Archives
B & B—Bote und Bock—Berlin
B & H—Breitkopf and Hartel—Leipzig
BMP—Bomart Music Publications
C1BMI—Canada

OBV—Oesterrichischer
PHL—Philharmonia Scores
Sch—B. Schotts Sohne-Schott & Co., Ltd.—
  Mainz
Sim—N. Simrock, A. Benjamin—Leipzig
SZ—Edizioni Suvini Zerboni
UE—Universal Edition—Vienna
UME—Union Musical Espanola—Leuckart

BAINUM, GLEN CLIFFE

Born in Olney, Illinois, January 6, 1888; died 1974. American college music educator and conductor, professor of music and director of the Band Department at Northwestern University School of Music (1926). Conductor of 75-piece professional Glen Cliffe Bainum Concert Band, which played around Chicago 1935-42. President of American Bandmasters Association 1947-48. He was an excellent arranger.

BARBER, SAMUEL

Eminent American composer, born in West Chester, Pennsylvania, March 9, 1910. He attended the Curtis Institute of Music in Philadelphia. He

Works

Two ballets:
  Media
  Souvenirs
"Essays for Orchestra" Nos. 1 and 2
Symphony in One Movement
Second Symphony
Adagio for Strings
Opera: **Vanessa** (Libretto by Menotti)

Concerto for Violin and Orchestra
Concerto for Cello and Orchestra
Sonata in E-flat minor for Piano
"Knoxville: Summer of 1915" (Voice
  and orchestra)
"Prayers of Kierkegaard" (Chorus,
  soprano, and orchestra)
"Commando March"

BARTÓK, BÉLA

Born March 25, 1881, in Nagy-szent-miklas (Hungarian District of Yugoslavia); died in New York on September 26, 1945. He appeared at ten as a composer and pianist. He was a great student of Hungarian folk music—it permeates his compositions. He is often associated with Kodály. Early in his career there was much opposition in Hungary to his "new" music. On March 3, 1918, his Second String Quartet was performed for the first time, and from then on he was recognized as the leading figure in Hungarian music. The chief characteristic of Bartók's music is intense dynamism and rhythmic strength.

Works

STRING ORCHESTRA

Roumanian Folk Dances (Arr.
  Woodhouse)

ORCHESTRA

Five Pieces for Younger Orchestra
Six Pieces for Younger Orchestras (Arr.
  McKay)
Bartók Suite (Arr. Serly)

Nocturne (Arr. Gardner)
"An Evening in the Village" (Arr. Leidzen)

"Four Sketches" (Arr. Schafer)
"Bear Dance" (Arr. Leidzen)
"Bear Dance" (Arr. Walters)
"Petite Suite" (Arr. Cushing

BEECHAM, SIR THOMAS

British conductor and arranger, born in 1879 near Liverpool, England; died in 1961. Beecham began studying composition at the Rossall School under Dr. Sweeting. He later went to Oxford, where he studied under Dr. V. Roberts. In 1899 he started an amateur orchestra at Huyton but left this in 1902 to become conductor of Truman's Traveling Opera Company. His first bows as a symphony conductor came in 1905, when he conducted the London Queen's Hall Orchestra. In 1906 he became the conductor of the New Symphony Orchestra but left that two years later to start the Beecham Symphony. He turned again to opera in 1910 and became well known for the variety and freshness of his productions. From 1916 to 1919 he was the artistic director of the Royal Philharmonic Society. In 1917 he was appointed president of the Royal College of Music at Manchester, and in 1920 he became the conductor of the Covent Garden Opera in London and the London Symphony. He is known for his arrangement and introduction of the composer Delius's works and for the one-week Delius festival which he arranged and conducted shortly before the composer's death.

Works (Arrangements and Transcriptions)

ORCHESTRA

Mozart, *Symphony No. 38*
Delius, *"The Walk to Paradise Garden"*

BAND

Handel, *"The Gods Go a-Begging"*

BENJAMIN, ARTHUR

Born in Sydney, Australia, in 1893; died in 1960 in London, England. He studied at the Royal College of Music in London. He became professor at the Sydney Conservatory and later returned to England as professor at the Royal College. He conducted the Vancouver Orchestra.

Works

OPERAS

The Devil Take Her
Prima Donna
A Tale of Two Cities (A prize winner at Festival of Britten)

INSTRUMENTAL WORKS

Pastoral Fantasia (Carnegie Award, 1924)
Sonatina for Violin and Piano

Concertino for Piano and Orchestra
Violin Concerto

LIGHT MUSIC FOR ORCHESTRA

Overture to an Italian Comedy
Romantic Fantasy
"Prelude to a Holiday"
"Jamaican Rumba"
Symphony No. 1
Piano Concerto

BENNETT, ROBERT RUSSEL

American composer, arranger, and conductor, born in Kansas City in 1894. He began musical studies with his parents at the age of nine. He was copyist and arranger for G. Schirmer, orchestrator of musical comedies in New York, and studied with Nadia Boulanger in Paris. He has worked in films and radio and was one of the first to introduce the jazz idiom into serious musical form. A serious composer, he is praised for a consummate command of his technique and a fine respect for form, and his approach to aesthetic problems reveals a sound classicist.

Works

Eight etudes   orchestra; includes jazz idiom)

BERGSMA, WILLIAM

Born in Oakland, California, in 1921. Studied at Stanford and then Eastman. In recent years he taught at Juilliard. Honors: Bearnes Prize, 1943; Grant from American Academy of Arts and Letters, 1945; Guggenheim Fellowship, 1946.

Works

Two Ballets:
  Paul Bunyan (1937)
  Gold and the Señor Commandante
    (1941)
  Symphony for Chamber Orchestra
    (1942)

Two string quartets
Suite for Brass Quartet (1940)
One symphony
Many songs and choral works
March for Trumpets (Band)

BOOSEY-HAWKES, INC.

Boosey-Hawkes, Inc., is an international publisher of music of all categories, including vocal, choral, band, orchestra, chamber music, operas, pocket scores, and recordings—now specializing in the contemporary idiom. They are exclusive agents for most of the music of Copland, Britten, Bartók, R. Strauss, and Stravinsky. Boosey and Company was established in 1816 by Thomas Boosey, at first to import foreign music. Later the company imported the works of many composers, especially the operas of Bellini, Donizeti, and Verdi. However, in 1854 a copyright ruling of Parliament destroyed the value of this business. Then the firm turned to the publication of other materials in great variety.

BOYCE, WILLIAM

Born in London, 1711; died in London, February 7, 1779. He was a noted English organist and composer, and compiler of three volumes of the cathedral music which remained in use almost to the end of the 19th century. Because of increasing deafness he retired in 1768 and assumed the task of editing the Cathedral Music Series started by Dr. Maurice Greene, once Boyce's master. Included in the collection are works by Tallis, Morely, Gibbons, Byrd, Blow, and Purcell. The Oxford Companion to Music states that Boyce's music is not always quite satisfactory by modern standards. He was buried in St. Paul's Cathedral.

Works

Twelve overtures
Many masques and odes
*Twelve sonatas for two violins and
    bass*
Many songs

Te Deums
Anthems
Services
Eight symphonies
Suite in A (For orchestra)

BRADSHAW, MERRILL

One of America's respected contemporary composers, writing for choirs, bands, and orchestras; composer of oratorios, sonatas, piano pieces, etc. Born June 18, 1919, at Lyman, Wyoming. He studied composition at Brigham Young University and the University of Illinois, where he received his DMA. At present he is chairman of composition and theory at Brigham Young University.

Most Recent Compositions

ORCHESTRA

"Four Mountain Sketches"
"Peace Memorial"
"Feathers"
Four symphonies

BAND

"Festivities"
"Elegy, Improvisation and Romp"
"Fanfares and Solemnities"
Divertimento for Band

BRITTEN, BENJAMIN

Born in Lowestoft, Suffolk, England, on November 22, 1913; died at Aldeburgh, England, on December 4, 1976. He played piano and composed at a very early age. In 1930, at the Royal College of Music, he studied with Frank Bridge, John Ireland, Arthur Benjamin, and Harold Samuel. While he was in the United States, World War II broke out, and he returned to England in 1942. He was a conscientious objector and was therefore exempt from military duty. Many people have stated that he was the first significant British composer of operas since Henry Purcell. His first opera was *Paul Bunyan*; and it was performed at Columbia University on May 5, 1941. His first successful opera, *Peter Grimes*, was performed in London on June 7, 1945. He edited the *Beggar's Opera* (1948) and has written several other operas. He wrote a substantial amount of ensemble, string, and choral works and songs.

ORCHESTRA

Matinées musicales (Boosey & Hawkes)

Simple Symphony for String Orchestra (Oxford)
"Hot Staccato" (Shapiro-Bernstein)
A Young Person's Guide to the Orchestra

BROUDE BROS. MUSIC COMPANY

Address: 56 West 45th Street, New York, N.Y. 10036. The company's catalogue consists of

He received his Bachelor of Music from Ohio State University and his Master of Music from Eastman School of Music. He has taught at Ohio State University and is now an instructor at Florida State University.

Works

Symphonic Overture
Three Pieces in Antique Style
Miniature Chorale and Fugue
Polyphonic Suite

Metropolis Overture
Overture for Winds
Overture in E-flat

CATEL, CHARLES SIMON

Born 1773; died 1830. French composer, conductor, author, and theorist. Pupil of Gossec and Gobert at Paris Ecole R. du Chant (later Conservatory). He was an accompanist and professeur-adjoint (1787) of the school. From 1790 to 1802 he was an accompanist at the opera. In 1790 he became a conductor, jointly with Gossec, of the Garde Nationale, for which he wrote a vast quantity of military music. In 1795 he was professor of harmony at the Paris Conservatory. He began the harmony text Traité d'harmonie, published in 1802. In 1810 he was one of the inspectors of the conservatory, from which position he resigned in 1814. In 1815 he was elected member of the institute and in 1824 was made a Chevalier of the Legion of Honor. Besides military music, he wrote symphonies for wind only and quintets and quartets for strings and wind.

Works

BAND

"Hymn of Victory" (Band and chorus)
Symphony in C

Symphony in F
Overture in F

Ten operas

CIMAROSA, DOMENICO

Born in Naples in 1749; died in Venice in 1801. Eminent Italian composer. He was the son of a poor mason and orphaned at an early age. His first music teacher was Polanco, organist at the monastery. Cimarosa's talent was so marked that he received a scholarship at the conservatory, where he studied voice under Sacchini, counterpoint under Fenaroli, and composition under Piccini; with his opera *La Finta Pargina*, he was launched on a dramatic career. His works became known far beyond the bounds of Italy, and he accepted a position at St. Petersburg. Comic opera was his forte, and in his happiest moments he rivals Mozart, even in opera seria. His fluidity of melodic vein, his supreme command of form, and his masterly control of orchestral resources still excite astonishment and admiration. He composed 76 operas. Many articles and books are written about him.

Works

Overture to A Secret Marriage (Arr. Winter) (Boosey & Hawkes)

Three Brothers Overture (Arr. Winter) (Boosey & Hawkes)
Concerto for Oboe and Strings

COPLAND, AARON

Born November 14, 1900, in Brooklyn, New York. He studied under Ruben Goldmark, then Paul Vidal at Fontainebleau Conservatory in France. He felt that he found his teacher in Nadia Boulanger, with whom he studied privately. Plagued by lack of funds, he finally found the chance to write with two years of a Guggenheim Fellowship. Koussevitzky was responsible for many of Copland's successes.

Works:

Music for the Theatre (Uses jazz idiom)
Concerto for Piano and Orchestra (Uses jazz idiom)

BALLETS

Billy the Kid
Rodeo

ORCHESTRA

El salón méxico
Appalachian Spring
Symphony #3
The Tender Land (Opera)
The Second Hurricane (Play-opera)

A Lincoln Portrait (Narrator and orchestra)
Quartet for Piano and Strings
Piano Sonata
Piano Fantasy
Concerto for Clarinet and Strings
Orchestra Variations
Nonet
Outdoor Overture
Symphonic Ode
Quiet City (Trumpet, English horn, and strings)

BAND

"Variations on a Shaker Melody"

American composer and pianist, born in 1897 and died in 1965. He did not attend school. He started studying the violin when he was five, but his health became so poor when he was eight that he gave up the violin and devoted his time to the development of "more perfect hearing in his mind." When 14 years old he spent all his time at an old piano he bought, since he did not go to school. He discovered what he called the "tone cluster." He studied at the University of California and was later an assistant in the Music Department. During World War I he conducted an army band. He went on several tours of Europe and America, where he provoked scenes bordering on riots by his extremely experimental pianoforte music. He was active in many modern music organizations and a stimulating influence on young composers, espe-

CRESTON, PAUL (Joseph Guttoveggio)

Born in New York on October 10, 1906, he received a Guggenheim Fellowship in 1938-39. In 1956 he was elected president of the National Association for American Composers and Conductors. His music has a feeling of spontaneity and is noteworthy for its strong melodic lines and full harmony. His instrumental writing offers opportunities for virtuoso performance. He has written five symphonies, many orchestral works, many pieces for solo instrument and orchestras, and several chamber works.

Works

BAND

Celebration Overture (Shawnee)
"Legend" (Leeds)
Prelude and Dance (Franko
   Colombo)
Zanoni, op. 40 (G. Schirmer)

ORCHESTRA

Dance Overture, op. 62 (Shawnee)

STRING ORCHESTRA

Gregorian Chant for String Orchestra
   (Shawnee)

DASCH, GEORGE

American violinist, conductor, and arranger, born in 1877. Dasch played with the Cincinnati Symphony Orchestra from 1895 to 1898, when he joined the Chicago Symphony. He was a member of the Hugo Hermann String Quartet for two years, the Hugo Kortschak String Quartet for three years, and the George Dasch Quartet for twelve years. He became conductor of the Chicago Civic Orchestra and after two years left to conduct the Joliet Illinois Symphony Orchestra. He taught at the Cincinnati College of Music for two years, after which he became a violin teacher at Northwestern University, where he also conducted the University Symphony Orchestra and other smaller groups.

Andante and Gavotte
"Colonial Dance"
Scherzo
"Youth Courageous"

ARRANGEMENTS FOR FULL ORCHESTRA

Beethoven, *Largo from Sonata No. 4*
Glinka, **A Life for the Czar**

ARRANGEMENTS FOR STRING
ORCHESTRA

Volkmann, *Waltz from Serenade Suite*
Bach, *Gavotte and Musette*
Bizet, *Adagietto from **L'Arlésienne**
  Suite*
Bolzoni, *Minuetto*
Dittersdorf, *Allegro*
Grieg, *Allegro quasi andantino*
Handel, *Allegro*
Mozart, *Menuet*
Schubert, *Adagio from Quartet, op. 25,
  no. 1*

DELLO JOIO, NORMAN

Born on January 24, 1913, in New York. Composer, pianist, and soloist with the New York Philharmonic and Cleveland Symphony Orchestras.

Works

"Prelude to a Young Dancer" (Piano)
"Prelude to a Young Musician" (Piano)
Nocturne in E (Piano solo)
Trio (Flute, cello, and piano)
"The Mystic Trumpeter" (Chorus,
  soloist, and horn)
Suite for Piano
"On Stage"—Ballet for T.V.

Sonata No. 2 for Piano
Piano Sonata No. 3
"A Psalm of David" (Chorus and
  orchestra)
"New York Profiles" (Symphony
  orchestra)
The Triumph of Joan (Opera)
"Variants on a Medieval Tune" (Band)

DEMUTH, NORMAN

Born in London in 1898, Demuth was one of the founders of the RAM New Music Society. In 1950 he was nominated officer of L'Académie by the French government. He is a composer in larger forms, mainly self-taught, and his symphonies lie with French composers from France to Roussel. His music is somewhat austere, with few definable tunes, and its complex but subtle harmonic structures show some affinity with d'Indy or Roussel. In matters of form, Demuth is greatly attracted to cyclic methods and is fond of building complete major works from one or two short motifs.

Works

CHORAL

"Pan's Anniversary" (For chorus and
  orchestra)

"Sonnet" (For baritone, chorus, and
  orchestra)

BAND

Concerto for Saxophone and Band (1938)
"The Sea" (1939)
Regimental March for the Royal Pioneer Corps (1943)

MISCELLANEOUS

Violin Concerto (1937)
Concertino for Flute and Strings

Elegiac Rhapsody for Viola and Small Orchestra (1942)
Piano Concerto for the Left Hand (1947)
Sonatina for Flute, Oboe, and Piano (1946)
Trio for Flute, Oboe, and Bass (1949)
Trio for Violin, Viola, and Cello (1950)
Sonata for Flute and Pianoforte (1938)
Six symphonies

recent years.

Works

Twenty-eight operettas from 1767 (Mostly humorous)
Oratorios:
  Isaak (1767)
  Esther (1773)
Many cantatas and masses

One hundred fifteen symphonies
Thirty-five concertos for violin, piano, or other instruments
Twelve string quintets
Six string quartets

DURAND ET CIE.

One of the principal French music publishing houses. It was started in 1869, a partnership of Durand and Schoenwerk, and built on the catalogue and premises acquired from publisher Alexander Flaxland. The firm became a private limited company in 1947 under the direction of Mme Jacques Durand, René Mommange, and Adriene Raveau. It publishes nearly all the works of Saint-Saëns and many by Bizet, Castillon, Debussy, Dukas, Fauré, Franck, d'Indy, Poulenc, and Ravel.

ERICKSON, FRANK

Born in Spokane, Washington, September 1, 1923, he attended the University of Southern California and received his Bachelor of Music in 1950 and his master's degree in 1951. From 1958 through 1961 he served on the faculties of UCLA and San Jose State College, teaching composition and band arranging. He is presently associated with the Belwin Publishing Co. in their band music division as a composer and arranger. His music is mainly for band and ranges from a very good quality to average. The band director must be selective to choose his better compositions, some of which are listed below. (All those listed are published by Bourne.)

Works

BAND

First Symphony for Band
Second Symphony for Band
Toccata for Band
"Balladair"
Irish Folk Song Suite
"Legendary Air"
Norwegian Folk Song Suite
Premiere for Band
"Soliloquy"
Symphonette for Band
"Black Canyon of the Gunnison"
Ceremonial for Band

Chaconne
Deep River Suite
Fantasy for Band
"Golden Gate"
"Legend of the Bells"
Overture to **Billy**
"Summer Holiday"
"Tamerlane"
Chorale and Fugue
Scherzo for Band

ORCHESTRA

Air for Orchestra

FAUCHET, PAUL

Recent French composer, born in 1858 and died November 15, 1936, in Paris. He was chef du chant at the Opéra comique. He was a composer of opera and of works for orchestra, ensemble, and band.

Works

Symphony in B-flat for Band

FILLMORE, HENRY

American bandleader and composer of band music. Born in Cincinnati, Ohio, on December 2, 1881, and died in Miami, Florida, on December 7, 1956. He was educated at the Miami Military Institute and later, in 1916, while in Cincinnati, Ohio, he organized the Henry Fillmore Concert Band. In 1938 he settled in Florida. Under the name of Harold Bennett he published a collection called The Bennett Band Book (4 volumes), and under the names of Al Hayes and Harry Hartley he compiled several military band pieces. Among the many marches is the very popular "Military Escort March."

Works

"Americans We"
"Bones Trombone"
"Dusty Trombone"
"Footlifter"
"His Honor"
"Honor and Glory"
"Lassus Trombone"
"Man of the Hour"

"Men of Florida"
"Men of Ohio"
"One Hundred"–36th U.S. Field Artillery
"Poet, Peasant and Light Cavalryman"
"President's March"
"The Star Spangled Banner" (B-flat)
"Waves" ("Over the Waves")

FISCHER, CARL

Carl Fischer, the founder of the publishing house which bears his name, came to New York from Saxony in 1872. During his lifetime the firm expanded and established branches at Boston and Chicago. Its catalogues cover every branch of music publishing from classic to modern. In addition to its own publications, it also represents several British houses. After the founder's death in 1923, Walter S. Fischer carried on the business. He tried to show encouragement to American composers. In 1935 he opened offices for the educational side of the business in Los Angeles and Chicago.

FOSTER, ARNOLD

WORKS

"The Fairy Isle"
"Autumn Idyll"
Suite on English Folk Airs

Fantasy for Piano Quartet
Sword Dance Suite (Oxford)
Suite of Morris Dances (Oxford)

GIANNINI, VITTORIO

Born October 19, 1903, in Philadelphia, Pennsylvania; died in 1967. He studied at the Royal Academy of Music Giuseppe Verdi, Milan, Italy; the American Academy, Rome; and the Juilliard Graduate School. He studied violin with Albert Spalding, violin and chamber music with Hans Letz, and composition with Rubin Goldmark and Trucco. He received many awards and appeared throughout the world as a violinist and conductor.

Works

OPERA

Lucedia
The Scarlet Letter
Beauty and the Beast
Blennerhasset

BAND

Praeludium and Allegro (Columbo)
Symphony No. 3 (Columbo)
"Fantasia" (Columbo)

ORCHESTRA

Springtime (Chamber cantata)
Theodore Roosevelt Requiem
Requiem
Piano Concerto
Triptych (Voice and strings)
Opera Ballet
Violin Concerto
Concerto Grosso for Strings
Frescobaldiana
Concerto for Trumpet and Orchestra
Symphony in One Movement
Prelude and Fugue for Symphony
   Orchestra (Chappell)
Symphony No. 2
Many other songs and chamber works

GILLETTE, JAMES R.

Born on May 30, 1886. American arranger, composer, and organist. He is a graduate of Syracuse and has toured on recitals. He is a professor of organ and bandmaster at Carleton College in Minnesota and a member of ASCAP. He published *The Organist's Handbook.*

Works

Two cantatas
Three symphonic works
Fifty organ pieces

BAND

Chorale Prelude by Bach
Symphony in B-flat (Movements 1 and 4 by Fauchet)
"Crossroads"

"Cabins" (Rhapsody)
"Cotton Blossoms"
"Fugal Fantasy"
"Legends"
"Phantom Trumpeters" (Tone poem)
"Vistas" (Tone poem)
Sinfonietta (Unpublished)
Symphony for Band (Unpublished)
Short Classics for Band (Arranged)

GILLIS, DON

Born in 1912 in Cameron, Missouri, he was educated at Texas Christian University (A.B., B.M., M.M., and honorary doctorate). He is a composer, conductor, and teacher; director of bands at Texas Christian University; instructor at Southwestern Baptist Theological Seminary; composer for radio station WAP; writer of various broadcast series; reorganizer of the NBC Symphony of the Air; and composer-in-residence at the National Music Camp. He has also been director of the American Opera Workshop.

Works

Twelve symphonies (Two for bands)
Seven symphonic poems
Five string quartets
Four operas

Four concerted works
Many works for band
Various suites

GOLDMAN, EDWIN FRANKO

Born January 1, 1878, in Louisville, Kentucky; died February 21, 1956. He was well known as a cornet soloist and band director as well as composer. He was the founder of the American Bandmasters Association and honorary life president of that organization, and the author of *The Foundation of Trumpet Playing, Band Betterment,* and *Facing the Music* (autobiograhy). He wrote clarinet solos, cornet solos, band pieces, and songs.

Works

"On the Mall"
"Emblem of Freedom"
"On the Air"
"On the Campus"
"On Parade"

"Central Park"
"Sunapee"
"Sagamore"
"Eagle Eyes"
"Indian March"

"Radio City"
"Mother Goose"
"Boy Scouts of America"
"Young America"
"League of Composers"

"On Guard"
"Golden Rule"
"Ever-Ready"
"Kentucky"
"V.F.W."

GOLDMAN, RICHARD FRANKO

Born December 7, 1910, in New York. Son of Edwin Franko Goldman. He has been a member of the faculty at Juilliard School of Music since 1947. He is the author of *The Band's Music, Landmarks of Early American Music, and The Concert Band and*

GOSSEC, FRANÇOIS JOSEPH

Born in Vergnis, Hamault, on January 17, 1734; died in Passay, near Paris, on February 16, 1829. Belgian composer. He was a chorister in the Cathedral of Antwerp until the age of fifteen. After studying violin, he went to Paris and got a job through Rameau to conduct a private band maintained by Fermier—General La Poupelinière—for the purpose of playing the compositions of Rameau. After La Poupelinière's death in 1762, Gossec composed for the House of Prince de Conti. In 1760 he wrote "Tuba mirium" (from his *Messe des morts*) for two orchestras, with wind instruments of one orchestra concealed outside and the strings of the other orchestra in the church, playing pianissimo and tremolando in the upper registers. Gossec was noted for his curious orchestral experiments and was the forerunner of Berlioz. His comic operas were good, but his serious ones were failures. He founded the Concert des Amateurs in 1770; regenerated the Concert Spirituel in 1773; and organized the Ecole Royale de Chant, the predecessor of the Conservatoire de Musique, in 1784. From 1780 to 1785 he was director (not conductor) of the opera and the revolution conductor of the National Guard. This band was formed by Bernard Sarrette and was the first modern wind band. The instrumentation was raised from 45 to 90 in 1790. While he conducted this band he wrote his first real masterpieces of band music. Gossec exerted a great influence on the development of instrumental music in France. He himself was influenced by J. Stamitz, and he presented the first models of the symphony and introduced horns and clarinets into the opera orchestra.

Works

BAND

Classic Overture in C
Military Symphony in F

COMPOSITIONS

"Hymne à l'être suprême"
"Peuple, reveille-toi"
Music for funeral of Mirabeau (Use of gong)
"Exposition des principes de la musique"

GOULD, MORTON

Born in Richmond Hill, New York, on December 10, 1913. American pianist, conductor, and composer. He began music early, piano at four and composition at six. Until age 17 he was attached to the NBC as solo pianist; then WOR Mutual engaged him to conduct and arrange his own programs. His staff was arranged at Radio City Music Hall. In 1942 Toscanini produced his "Lincoln Legend." In 1944 Erich Leinsdorf commissioned him to write a concerto for orchestra for the Cleveland Symphony. His Second Symphony on Marching Tunes was written for the YMCA Centenary in 1944 and performed by the New York Philharmonic. He wrote film music for *Delightfully Dangerous* and performed in the picture with his own orchestra. He also wrote a ballet, *Fall River Legend,* which was commissioned by the Ballet Theatre and produced at the Metropolitan in 1948.

Works

ORCHESTRA

Chorale and Fugue in Jazz (1933)
Swing Sinfonietta (1936)
Spirituals (1941)
"Lincoln Legend" (1942)
"Harvest for Strings" (1945)
Homespun Overture
American Symphonettes Nos. 1-4
"Jingle Bells"
"Corn Cob"
"Hill-Billy"
"Night Song" from **Americana**
"Indian Nocturne"
"Serenade of Carols" (In 4 movements for small orchestra)

SOLO

Pianoforte Concerto with Chamber Orchestra (1937)

Viola Concerto (1944)
American Concertante for Pianoforte
Concertette for Viola

BAND

"Jericho"
St. Lawrence Suite
Ballad for Band
"Santa Fe Saga"
Symphony for Band

TRANSCRIPTIONS

"American Salute"
Pavane
"Cowboy Rhapsody"
"Dixie"
"Jingle Bells"-"Silent Night"

GRAINGER, PERCY ALDRIDGE

Born in Melbourne, Australia, on July 8, 1882; died February 20, 1961. He was a pianist and composer and was taught by his mother until age 10. After further study with Louis Pabst in Melbourne, he went to Germany and studied with James Kwast and Busoni. In London he played the piano solo in Grieg's concerto. Grieg had special esteem for Grainger and perhaps influenced him to continue his work in recovering old English folk songs. In 1912 Grainger received a great deal of recognition at the Balfour Gardiner Concerts in London. He wrote many selections for both accompanied and unaccompanied choral works.

ORCHESTRA

"Suite in a Nutshell"
"Colonial Song" (Two voices and small orchestra)
"Mock Morris" (String orchestra)
Clog Dance—"Handel in the Strand"
"To a Nordic Princess"
"Green Bushes"

"My Robin Is in the Greenwood Gone" (Flute, English horn, and six strings)
"The Three Ravens" (Solo voice, chorus, six clarinets, and organ)
Also some pianoforte selections and Kipling settings from **The Jungle Book**

SELECTIONS FOR MILITARY BAND

"Blithe Bells"
"The Warriors"

CHAMBER MUSIC

Hill Songs No. 1 (Twenty-three solo instruments)
Hill Songs No. 2 (Twenty-four solo instruments)
"Walking Tune" (Wind quintet)
"The Two Corbies" (Baritone and full strings)
"Lisbon" (Flute, oboe, clarinet, horn, and bassoon)

TRANSCRIPTIONS

"Christian Heart"
"Country Gardens"
"Handel in the Strand" (Goldman)
"The Immovable Do"
"Lads of Wamphrey" (Fischer)
"Molly on the Shore"
"Colonial Song"
Hill Song No. 2 (Leeds)
Irish Tune from County Derry
"Shepherds Hey"
"Ye Banks and Braes of Bonnie Doon"

GRUNDMAN, CLARE

Born May 11, 1913, in Cleveland, Ohio. He obtained his B.S. in education at Ohio State University and was a member of the band, orchestra, chorus, Phi Mu Alpha Sinfonia, and the Kappa Kappa Psi. In 1934 he taught instrumental music at University High School, Columbus, Ohio, and in the following year became instrumental teacher in the Lexington, Kentucky, Public Schools. In 1937 he returned to Ohio State as instructor of orchestration, woodwinds, and band, and in 1940 he received his master's degree from that university. He studied composition under Paul Hindemith at Tanglewod before entering the military service. In 1945 he did the orchestration for Lend an Ear and conducted this Broadway show for six months. He has done original scores for RKO-Pathe motion pictures, including the This is America series, and also the following for radio and television: The Clock, Treasury Agent, Holiday Hotel, Candid Microphone, Mr. and Mrs. North, the Ford and General Motors anniversary programs, and Caesar's Hour. He has also been orchestrator and arranger for Broadway musicals, recordings, and various motion picture scores.

American Folk Rhapsody
"Atlantic Seabord"
"The Blue and the Grey"
"Quiet Christmas"
"Cowboy in Cuba"
Fantasy on American Sailing Songs
"An American Scene"
"The Black Knight"
"Blue Tail Fly"
Three Songs for Christmas
"Diversion"
"Grand March"
"The Green Domino"
"Holiday"
"Kentucky 1800"

Little Suite for Band
Music for a Carnival
"The Stage Coach Trail"
"Two Moods"
Westchester Overture
"Pipe Dream"
"Harlequin"
"Interval Town" (Study)
Little March
March Processional
Second American Folk Rhapsody
Two American Songs
"Walking Tune"
"Conversation for Cornet"
Hebrides Suite

HADLEY, HENRY

Born in 1871; died in 1937. American composer and conductor. He made great efforts to have many contemporary works performed. He rose to prominence as a conductor during the 1930s. He founded the National Association for American Composers and Conductors and was considered a very facile and prolific composer. He wrote in all the forms, using every combination, vocal and instrumental.

Works

Four symphonies (The first was **Youth and Life**)
Ten to twelve operas (**Cleopatra's Night** is considered the best)
"Scherzo Diabolique"
Salome (Tone poem)
Concertino for Piano and Orchestra
Three ballet suites
Cello Concerto
Resurgam (Secular oratorio)

BAND

"Festival March"
"Youth Triumphant" (Overture)

ORCHESTRA—GRADE IV

Ballet of the Flowers
Enchanted Castle Overture (Good)
Suite ancienne
Concert Overture

HALVORSEN, JOHAN

Born in Norway in 1864; died in 1935. Norwegian violinist and composer. In 1887 he was leader of the orchestra at Bergen. He was strongly influenced by Grieg, whose niece he married.

Works

Incidental music for plays
Cantata for coronation of King Haakon
Three symphonies
Violin Concerto
Three suites for violin and pianoforte

Arrangement of Passacaglia by Handel for violin and viola
Set of "slatter" (Norwegian peasant dances) transcribed for solo violin
Nine orchestral suites

HANSON, HOWARD

Born in Wahoo, Nebraska, October 28, 1896. American composer and teacher of Swedish descent. In 1921 he won the Prix de Rome, which entitled him to three years' work and study in Rome. After guest conducting the New York Philharmonic in 1924, he returned to Rome and while there was offered the directorship of the Eastman School of Music in Rochester, which he accepted. In Rochester he inaugurated the American Composers concerts. A member of the Royal Swedish Academy of Music, he received the Pulitzer Prize for his Fourth Symphony in 1945.

Works

"Children's Dance" from **Merrymount**
Excerpt from first movement of Symphony No. 2 (**Romantic**) (Eastman Rental)

"March Carillon" (Transcription)
Second movement from Symphony No. 1 (Transcribed by Maddy)

Five symphonies
"Song of Democracy"

HARRIS, ROY

American composer, born in Lincoln County, Oklahoma, February 12, 1898. He studied at the University of California and privately with Farrell, Nadia Boulanger, Moritz Altschuler, and others. His music is rich in qualities Americans regard as reflecting their national life.

Works

ORCHESTRA

Seven symphonies
Andante (1926)
Andantino (1931)
"When Johnny Comes Marching Home" (1934)
"Time Suite" (1936)
"Fanfare" (1942)
"Folk Rhythms of Today" (1942)
"March in Time of War" (1943)
Chorale (1944)
"Memories of a Child's Sunday" (1945)
"Children at Play" (1946)
"Melody" (1946)
"Kentucky Spring" (1949)

"Elegy"
"Evening Piece"
"Ode to Consonance"

BAND

"Cinnamon" (1941)
"Fruit of Gold" (For symphony band) (1949)
"Folk Rhythms of Today" (1942)
"Dark Devotion" (For SB) (1950)

SOLO

Concerto No. 1 (For pianoforte and band, 1941)

Fantasy (For pianoforte and band, 1943)
Chorale (For organ and brass, 1944)
Toccata (For organ and brass, 1946)
Fantasy (For pianoforte and popular dance band, 1951)

Concerto (For clarinet, string quartet, and pianoforte, 1927)
Soliloquy and Dance (For viola and piano, 1938)
"Four Easy Pieces" (For violin and piano, 1942)

HINDEMITH, PAUL

German violist and composer. Born Hanau, Germany, on November 16, 1895; died December 28, 1963. In opposition to his parents, he left home at age 11 to pursue a musical career and earned a living in cafe and dance bands. He was a concert violist. In 1927 he was appointed professor at the Berlin High School for Music but left because of Hitler. In 1929 he gave the first performance of Walton's Viola Concerto in London. He toured the USA and settled there permanently in 1939. In 1942 he became chairman of the Music Department at Yale University.

Works

"Wir bauen eine Stadt," game for children (Robert Seitz) for children's voices and instruments (1930)

Schulwerk

No. 1: Nine pieces in the first position for beginners, first and second violins

No. 2: Eight canons in the first position for slightly more advanced players, first and second violins with third violins or viola

No. 3: Eight pieces in first position for more advanced players, first and second violins, viola, and cello

No. 4: Five pieces in first position for more advanced players for string orchestra

SOLO

"Three Easy Pieces" (For cello and pianoforte, 1938)
Sonata for Flute (1937) (For oboe, 1939; for bassoon, 1939)
Sonata for Clarinet (1949) (For horn, 1940; for trumpet, 1940)
Sonata for English Horn (1942) (For trombone, 1942)
"Echo for Flute" (1944)

BAND

Symphony in B-flat for Band

HOLST, GUSTAV

Born in Cheltenham, England, in 1874; died in 1934. His great-grandfather, a musician, had emigrated from Sweden to England in 1807. Gustav's mother, formerly a concert pianist, taught the boy to play the piano. This instruction was supplemented with lessons on the organ, and soon Gustav was able to officiate as organist in the local church. In 1893 he went to London for intensive music study, enrolling at the Royal College of Music, where, after two years, he won a scholarship in composition. As a conservatory student he wrote the music for an operetta which reflected his enthusiasm for Sir Arthur Sullivan. But a much more important influence on Holst was that of Wagner, whose style he emulated in several early works.

The Golden Goose (Ballet, 1927)
Quintet for Piano and Strings (1896)
Suite in E-flat Major (1900)
Two Psalms (Chorus, strings, and organ, 1912)
"Ode to Death" (Chorus and orchestra, 1919)
Choral Symphony
Walt Whitman Overture (1899)

"The Mystic Trumpeter" (Soprano and orchestra, 1904)
St. Paul's Suite for String Orchestra (1913)
The Planets (Suite for large orchestra and voices, 1916)
Fugal Overture (Flute, oboe, and strings, 1923)
Concerto for Two Violins and Orchestra (1929)

"Pacific 231" (Orchestra; musical description of a modern locomotive—1924)
Le Roi David (Oratorio)
Incidental music, radio and film music, and choral works (See Grove's Dictionary)

ORCHESTRA

Prelude to Maeterlink's Aglavaine et Selysette (1917)
"Le Chant de Nigamon" (1917)
"Danse macabre" (1919)
Pastorale d'été (For chamber orchestra, 1920)
"Horace victorieux" (1920)
"Marche funèbre" (1921)
Prelude to Shakespeare's Tempest (1923)
Mouvement symphonique No. 1: "Pacific 231" (1923)
Mouvement symphonique No. 2: "Rugby" (1928)
Symphony No. 1 (1930)
Mouvement symphonique No. 3 (1932-33)
Nocturne (1936)
Prelude, arioso et fugue (on BACH, 1936)
"La Construction d'une cité" (With Milhaud, 1937)
Suite, Jour de fête suisse (Seven parts, 1943)
1943)

"Serenade à Angelique" (For small orchestra, 1945)

SOLO, INSTRUMENTS, ORCHESTRA

Entrée, nocturne, et berceuse (Pianoforte and chamber orchestra)
Concertino for Pianoforte (1925)
Cello Concerto
Concerto de camera (Flute, English horn, and strings)

CHAMBER MUSIC

String Quartet No. 1
Sonatina for Two Violins
"Trois contrepoints" (For flute, English horn, violin, and cello)
"Prelude et blues" for Harp Quartet
Sonatina for Violins and Cello
"Petite suite" (For saxophones and pianoforte; for two flutes; for violin, clarinet, and piano)
String Quartet No. 2
String Quartet No. 3
"Rhapsodie" for two flutes, clarinet, and pianoforte
"Hymne" for ten string instruments

SOLOS WITH PIANOFORTE

"Danse de la chèvre" (flute, no piano)

Violin Sonatas Nos. 1 and 2 and *Cadence
from "De Boeuf sur le toit"*
Viola Sonata

Violoncello Sonata
Clarinet Sonatina

INGHELBRECHT, DÉSIRÉ-ÉMILE

French conductor and composer. Born in Paris, September 17, 1880; died February 14, 1965. He studied at the Paris Conservatory. He became the conductor of the Théâtre des Arts in 1908 and the Théâtre des Champs-Elysées in 1912. In 1925 he became the musical director of the Opéra Comique in Paris. He was music leader and conductor of the Radio Broadcasting Corporation in Paris from 1939.

Works

"Le Diable dans le beffroi"
**Pour le jour de la première neige au
vieux Japon** (Symphonic poem)
Automne (Symphonic sketch)
Rhapsodie de printemps

"El Greco, évocations symphoniques"
"Trois poèmes danses"
"La Metamorphose d'Eve"
"La Légende du grand St. Nicolas"

ISAAC, MERLE J.

Born in Pioneer, Iowa, on October 12, 1898. American Music Educator, Public School Administrator, composer, arranger, and conductor. He was educated in Chicago Schools. In 1951 he was principal of Talcott Elementary School of Chicago. He is an organist and pianist and has compiled and edited solos and albums for various band and orchestral instruments. His music is especially good for elementary instrumental work. He has done extensive arranging of music for elementary and junior high school levels.

Works

BAND *(Some in collaboration with
C. P. Lillya)*

"Great Grand Dad"
Concert Overture in G minor
"Gremlins' Patrol"
"Summer Evening Serenade"
Russian Chorale and Overture (Fischer)
"Deep South"
Latin American Fantasy

ORCHESTRA

Mexican Overture (Fischer)
Gypsy Overture

"Our School March"
"Segend"
"Siesta"
"Silken Fan"
Two Chorales

FOLIOS AND METHOD BOOKS

Activity Orchestra Folio (C. Fischer)
Achievement Orchestra Folio (C. Fischer)
Advancement Orchestra Folio (C. Fischer)
Attainment Orchestra Folio (C. Fischer)
String Class Method, Books 1 and 2
(Good class method book if used as
supplementary material)

JACOB, GORDON (Percival Septimus)

Born in London, July 5, 1895. English composer, conductor, and teacher. He began his career by teaching theory and composition. He is a specialist in instrumentation and has written a textbook on scoring and transcription, *Orchestral Technique*, 1931.

Works

ORCHESTRA

Variation on an Air by Purcell (Strings, 1930)

William Byrd Suite (1924)
"Flag of Stars"
"An Original Suite"

Viola Concerto (1925)
Concerto for Oboe and Strings (1933)
Concerto for Bassoon, Strings, and Percussion (1947)
Concerto for Horn and Strings (1951)

MILITARY BAND

Suite (1924)
Serenade for the 1951 Festival of Britain (1950)

ARRANGEMENTS FOR ORCHESTRA

William Byrd Suite (Revised, 1939)
Holst, *Suite in E Major* (1940)
Orlando Gibbon Suite (1943)
Concertino for Clarinet and Strings (Tartini) (1945)
Schumann, **Carnival** (1931)
Holst, *Suite in F Major* (1943)
Holst, *Mooreside Suite* (1944)

JENKINS, JOSEPH WILCOX

Contemporary American composer, born in Philadelphia in 1928. He is a graduate of Eastman. He has been a staff arranger for the U.S. Army Chorus. He was a Ford Foundation winner in 1959. Presently he is on the faculty of music at Duquesne University in Pittsburgh, Pennsylvania.

Works

BAND

"Three Images for Band"
"Cumberland Gap"

Arioso for Band
Charles County Overture
American Overture for Band
"Purcell Portraits"

JUREY, EDWARD B.

Supervisor of instrumental music for the Los Angeles Public Schools, he has written several string literature pieces for elementary string players, published by Mills. Materials are generally of very good quality.

First, Second, and Third Program Albums
  (Mills)
Gateway Album
"Praise Ye the Lord of Hosts" (Elementary
  orchestra and two-part chorus)

"Psalm of Praise" (Full orchestra)
"Cavatina and Air"
"Dixie Showboat"

KALMUS, EDWIN F.

Edwin F. Kalmus is an American music publisher who specializes in miniature orchestra scores. Among the composers featured are Bach, Beethoven, Berlioz, Bizet, Borodin, Brahms, Bruckner, Chabrier, Corelli, Debussy, Dvořák, Dukas, Franck, Glière, Grieg, Handel, Haydn, Kalinnikov, Liadov, Liszt, Mahler, McKay, Mendelssohn, Mozart, Moussorgsky, Nicolai, Prokofiev, Rachmaninoff, Rimsky-Korsakov, Rossini, Saint-Saëns, Schubert, Schumann, and many others. This is a highly recognized firm with an excellent offering.

KAY, ULYSSES S.

Born January 7, 1917, in Tucson, Arizona, this Black American composer was a student of Howard Hanson and Bernard Rogers at the Eastman School of Music and also of Paul Hindemith at Yale University and the Berkshire Music Center. While in the U.S. Navy between 1942 and 1945 he played various instruments in bands and orchestras and did some notable arranging and composing. Over a period of years he became the recipient of a Ditson Fellowship at Columbia University, a Julius Rosenwald Fellowship, a Prix de Rome, a Fulbright Scholarship, and a grant from the American Academy of Arts and Letters and the National Institute of Arts and Letters. His music has won several prizes, among them the Broadcast Music, Inc., First Prize for his Suite for Orchestra; the Gershwin Memorial Prize for "A Short Overture"; and an American Broadcasting Company Prize for "Of New Horizons." In 1953, Kay became editorial advisor for Broadcast Music, Inc., in New York. His music is said to disclose lyric talent and a firm command of form, a strong contrapuntal vein, and bold harmonic imagination.

Works

Two operas
Nine works for orchestra
Five works for string orchestra
One ballet
Fourteen works for chorus

Two works for solo voice with
  accompaniment
Two works for band
Fourteen chamber works
One work for organ
Two works for piano

KINDLER, HANS

Born January 8, 1892, in Rotterdam; died in 1949. Cellist and conductor. As a soloist, he concertized in the U.S. and Europe. He founded the National Symphony Orchestra in Washington, D.C., and served as permanent conductor.

17th Century Dutch Tunes (Orchestra)   Handel, *Prelude and Fugue in D minor*
Frescobaldi, *Toccata*   (High school orchestra)

KINYON, JOHN (LeRoy Jackson)

Specializing in works for young bands, Kinyon, through Bourne Publishers, has produced many compositions.

Works under "John Kinyon"

"Song of the Sahara"   "Tangotoon"

Works under "LeRoy Jackson"

"Ballad for Bambi"   "Bendemeer's Stream"
"High Barbary"   Little Irish Suite
"John Peel"   "Jubilee"
Little English Suite   Little Scotch Suite
Three Classic Miniatures   Three Songs of Colonial America

LANG, PHILLIP J.

Born April 17, 1911, in New York City. He attended St. Agnes Academy and Oceanside High School, in New York, and Ithaca College (B.S. 1932); he took graduate study in canon and fugue at Juilliard (1933) and studied privately with Felix Devo, Brooklyn (1935). He became a member of the WOR radio staff under Alfred Wallenstein, an arranger and assistant conductor for Morton Gould, and arranged orchestrations for Broadway musical shows. He is presently arranging and composing for publication.

Works

ARRANGEMENTS   ORIGINAL

"Sea Medley"   "Jay Walk"
Gavotte (From Prokofiev's *Classical*   "The Hare and the Hounds"
  Symphony)   "Plymouth Rock"
"El relicario"   "Dixi Polka"
Polka and Dance ("Shostakovich's Golden "Promenade"
  Age")   "Bric-a-Brac"
"Gay Nineties Medley"   "I've Been Dreaming"
"Christmas Fantasy"   "Sheepshead Bay March"

LARSSON, LARS-ERIK

Born in Okarp, Sweden, on May 15, 1908. A Swedish composer, he studied on piano-forte, violin, and organ. Qualifying as an organist, he entered the Stockholm Conservatory to study counterpoint and composition with E. Ellgerg. He studied at Vienna and Leipzig, was coach of the Royal Theatre (1933-37) and conductor of the Swedish Radio Service, and was selected as a member of the Academy of Music in 1943 and the High School of Music in 1947. He is noted for his opera and orchestral compositions.

Works

Symphony
Sinfonietta for String Orchestra
Concerto for Saxophone
Piano pieces
Songs

Divertimenti for Chamber Orchestra
Serenade for Stringed Instruments
Chamber music
Opera, **Prinsesson av Cypern**

LATHAM, WILLIAM

American composer, born in 1917 in Shreveport, Louisiana. He studied at Cincinnati Conservatory and at Eastman with Eugene Goossens and Howard Hanson. Is now on the faculty of the University of North Iowa.

Works

Two symphonies (1950 and 1953)
Symphonic poem, **Lady of Shalott** (1941)
Fantasy for Violin and Orchestra (1946)
Flute Sonatina
Ballad for Baritone and Orchestra, "River to the Sea" (1942)
Cantata, **The Ascension of Jesus** (1952)
Three string trios (1938-39)
Violin Sonata (1949)
Suite for Trumpet and String Orchestra

BAND

"Court Festival"
"Plymouth"
Three Chorale Preludes
"Three by Four"
"Il pasticcio"
"Proud Heritage"

LEIDZEN, ERIC

Born March 25, 1894, in Stockholm, Sweden. He came to the U.S. in 1915. He was head of the Theory Department at Ernest Williams School of music and was arranger for the world-famous Goldman Band about 1933. He is the author of An Invitation to Band Arranging (1950).

Works

BAND

First Swedish Rhapsody
Second Swedish Rhapsody
Dixie Rhapsody
Folksongs for Band
Doxology

Holiday Overture
Two Pieces for Band
"Storm King"
"Once Upon a Time" (Overture fantasy)
Many other overtures and brass ensemble works

EDITED WORKS

Beethoven, *Ecossaise and Polonaise*
Mendelssohn, *Funeral March, op. 103*

Wagner, *Trauersymphonie*
Bruchner, *Apollo March* and *March in E-flat*

McKAY, GEORGE FREDERICK

American composer, born in Harrington, Washington, on June 11, 1899. He studied at the University of Washington at Seattle and at the Eastman School of Music in Rochester with Palmgren and Sinding. He graduated in 1922 and joined the faculty at the University of Washington in 1941.

A *violin concerto*
A suite on Negro folksongs for strings called **Port Royal**
Fantasy on a Western Folksong
To a Liberator (Symphonic poem)
A Prairie Portrait
American Street Scenes (For clarinet, trumpet, saxophone, bassoon, and piano)
A *cello concerto*

ORCHESTRA

Symphonette in D (Galaxy)
Variants on a Texas Tune (G. Schirmer)
"Scenes from the Southwest" (Remick)
"The Big Sky" (Boston)
Suite on Old Fiddler's Tunes (Fischer)

"A Sketch of the West" (Summy-Birchard)
"Burlesque March"
"Caricature Dance Suite"
"Folk Song Variants" (Boston)
"From Foxen's Glen" (Barnhouse)
"The Forty-niners" (Presser)
"Jubilee"
"The Plainsmen" No. 4 (Boston)
"The Railroaders" (Five pieces) (Presser)
"Three Street Corner Sketches" (Schirmer)
"Western You"
"Wake Me Up for the Great Jubilee" (Presser; arr.)

MENNIN, PETER

Born in Erie, Pennsylvania, May 17, 1923. He has been studying and writing music since he was seven years old. He wrote several works while still in his teens at Oberlin College. He studied with Normand Lockwood until he entered the air force in 1942. After his release from the service, he entered Eastman School of Music at Rochester and studied with Howard Hanson and Bernard Rogers. In 1945 he received his B.A. and M.A. in composition, and that same year he won the first annual Gershwin Memorial Award for his second symphony. This number was performed by Leonard Bernstein and the New York Philharmonic Orchestra.

Works

Symphony No. 1 (1942)
Symphony No. 2 (1944)
Symphony No. 3 (1946)
Concerto for Flute, Strings, and Percussion
  (1945)
Concerto for Orchestra (1944)
Folk Overture (1945)

Sinfonia for Chamber Orchestra (1946)
String Quartet No. 1 (1941)
Pianoforte pieces and songs

BAND

"Canzona" (Fischer)

MILHAUD, DARIUS

Born September 1892 in Aix-en-Provence, France; died in 1974. He studied violin privately from childhood and graduated from the Paris Conservatory in 1909. He studied orchestral playing under Dukas and composition under Widor and Gedalge. He received prizes in violin playing, fugue, counterpoint, and composition. During World War I he went to Brazil with Claudel, and later, during World War II, he came to the U.S., where he was appointed to the faculty of Mills College. He returned to France in 1947. The leading French composer after the death of Ravel, he used popular and folk idioms of both the new and the old worlds. In later works he showed great skill in using ultramodern techniques, such as polytonality.

Works

Eight symphonies (Orchestra)
Suite française (Band)
Two marches (Band)
Eighteen string quartets (One more than
  Beethoven)
West Point Suite (Band)
Suite Provençal (Orchestra)
"Saudades do Brasil" (Orchestra)

"Le Bal Martiniquais" (Orchestra)
Two concerti for violin and orchestra
Three ballets
Protée—Symphonic Suite No. 2
  (Orchestra)
Four concerti for piano and orchestra
Two concerti for cello and orchestra

MOELHMAN

An American contemporary arranger, Moelhman is known chiefly for his band arrangements to Bach's preludes and fugues.

Works

"St. Francis of Assisi"
St. George Overture

ARRANGEMENTS

Bach, Prelude and Fugue in B-flat Major

Bach, Prelude and Fugue in D minor
Bach, Prelude and Fugue in F minor
Bach, "If Thou Be Near" (Chorale)
Mozart, **Titus** Overture
Hasse, "Canzona"

MOORE, DOUGLAS

Born in Cutchogue, New York, August 10, 1893; died July 25, 1969. American composer, music educator, and administrator. He was a MacDowell Professor of Music at Columbia University, head of the Department of Music 1940-62 (retired 1962), and conductor of the Columbia University Orchestra.

CHAMBER MUSIC

String Quartet
Music for violin and piano
Quintet for Woodwinds and Horn
Quintet for Clarinet and Strings

OPERAS

Operetta for high school, **The Headless**

ORCHESTRA

Village Music (Presser, designed for school use)
"A Farm Journal" (Fischer)
"Four Museum Pieces" (Originally for organ)
"Pageant of P. T. Barnum"
Moby Dick (Symphonic poem)

instruments at Columbia Training College 1933-38. Since 1938 he has been bandmaster at Tulane University—U.S. Army Special Officer (Major) 1942-46.

Works

BANDSTRATIONS

American Weekend (Suite)
"Bamboula" (Bayou tune)
Carnival Day in New Orleans (Suite)
Cathedral Echoes (Suite)
"Green Acres" (Overture)
"Hoopla" (Flute solo)
"Main Street, U.S.A."
"Martinique" (Beguine)
Overture for Band
"Pioneer Days"
"So Long Song" (Novelty)

"Chachuca" (Samba)
"Caribbean Fantasy"
French Quarter (Suite)
"Hey Pedro" (Novelty)
"Interlude" (Clarinet solo)
"Maracaibo" (Beguine)
"Nocturne" (Baritone solo)
"Papaya"
"Skyline" (Overture)
"Song for Trombone"
"Waltz for Band"
Three Sketches (Suite)

NIELSEN, AUGUST CARL

Born on Island of Fiinen in 1865; died in 1931. Eminent Danish violinist, conductor, and composer. He joined a military band at 14 and trained at Copenhagen Conservatory and in Paris and Italy.

Works

Saul and David (Opera, 1903)
"Hymnus amoris" (Choral)
Six symphonies
Three string quartets
Violin Sonata

Violin Concerto (1911)
Clarinet Concerto (1928)
"Serenata in vano" (For clarinet, bass, horn, cello, and bass, 1914)
Maskeraden (Opera, 1907)

"An den Schaf" (Choral)
Suite for Strings
Violin Romanza (With orchestra)
Fantasia for Oboe and Clarinet
Flute Concerto (1926)

Piano pieces and songs
Quintet for Flute, Oboe, Clari-Bassoon,
  and Horn (1922)
Allegretto (For two recorders, 1931)

OXFORD UNIVERSITY PRESS

Established as a result of the printing of six volumes of the *Oxford History of Music*, edited by W. H. Hadow. Oxford has published many notable scholastic books on music (Tovey, Bellowes, Scholes, Dent, and Terry). It began publishing choral music (*Oxford Choral Songs*, 1923), and established a general music publications department in 1924. Its organ music catalog is extensive (original English works and new editions of classical music). It is a very reliable publisher, with worldwide distribution.

PERSICHETTI, VINCENT

American composer, born in 1915. He studied composition with Russell King Miller and Roy Harris; he also studied at Curtis. He is now a member of the faculty at Juilliard School of Music. He has won many awards for composition and has written a music theory book, *Twentieth-Century Harmony*. His works include six symphonies, some vocal works, and numerous piano works.

Works

ORCHESTRA

"Dance Overture"
"Hollow Men" (For trumpet and string
  orchestra)
Symphony for Strings
Two string quartets
Serenade No. 5

BAND

Divertimento
Psalm for Band
"Three Bagatelles"
Chorale, "So Pure the Star"
Pageant
Symphony No. 6
Serenade for Band

PETERS, C. F.

German music publishing house founded at Leipzig by Carl Friedrich Peters, who in 1814 bought the *Bureau de Musique* of Hoffmeister and Kühnel, established in 1800, and greatly improved the business. Complete editions of Bach and Haydn were among the firm's early projects. Peters editions are known throughout the world and are very reliable. On his death in 1827 Peters was succeeded by C. G. S. Boehme, who was succeeded in 1855 by Julius Friedlander. Max Abraham joined Friedlander in 1863 and infused new life into the business, developing the now famous "Peters Edition" and opening the Peters Library to the public in 1893. C. F. Peters Corporation now operates in New York City and is partly affiliated with the Frankfurt and Leipzig firms.

PIERNÉ, GABRIEL HENRI CONSTANT

Born in Metz, France, August 16, 1863; died in Ploujean, Finistère, July 17, 1937. French composer and conductor, who took refuge with his musical family in Paris when the

Franco-Prussian War broke out. He won his first medal for solfège in 1874, for pianoforte in 1879, for organ in 1882, for counterpoint and fugue in 1881, and the Prix de Rome in 1882 with his cantata *Edith*. Pierné became deputy conductor at the Colonne concerts and was conductor of the same in 1910–32. He wrote numerous selections for solo instruments and orchestra, chamber music, music for one instrument and pianoforte, pianoforte solos and duets, selections for organ and for harp, and numerous songs.

Works

OPERAS AND BALLETS

BAND

"March of the Little Leaden Soldiers"

ORCHESTRA

"Overture symphonique" (1885)
"Marche solennelle" (1889)

Thirty symphonies
Oratorios (Best: **La Nativité**)

PRESSER PUBLISHING COMPANY

Of Philadelphia, Pennsylvania. Founded by Theodore Presser, a talented musician who opened an office to publish a music paper, the *Etude*. Attempting to meet the needs of music teachers, he provided new music in his magazine. This led him to publish music. Presser died in 1925 and James Francis Coake, editor of the *Etude*, became president of the company. The Presser Company then purchased the John Church Company in 1930 and the Oliver Ditson Company one year later. Presser founded the Music Teachers National Association, the Presser Home for Retired Music Teachers, and, in 1916, the Presser Foundation, which awards scholarships to music students.

PROKOFIEV, SERGEI SERGEEVICH

Russian composer, born in 1891 and died in 1953. At 7 years of age he played the piano well and had already begun to compose. After studying under Glière, he entered the St. Petersburg Conservatory, where he studied under Rimsky-Korsakov. In 1914 he left the conservatory with the highest prize awarded to pianists. He settled in America in 1918, and in 1921 the Chicago Opera Association produced his four-act opera *The Love for Three Oranges*. Also that year his ballet *The Buffoon* was produced in Paris. In 1922 he made his home in Paris, but in 1927 he moved again to Russia, where he remained. He wrote seven operas, six ballets, and twenty symphonies.

Works

Classical Symphony (His most widely
  known work)
Andante for Strings
Suite for Orchestra
Romeo and Juliet (Ballet)
Violin Concerto

BAND

Gavotta (Arr. Gardner)
"Troika" from **Lieutenant Kije** (Arr.
  Walters)
March and Scherzo (Arr. Cailliet)

OPERA

War and Peace

PURCELL, HENRY

Born in London about 1658; died in London November 21, 1695. A natural genius, he began composing at an early age. He was educated at Chapel Royal, London, and was a composer and organist for Westminster Abbey. His official duties led him to compose much church music, some grave, some light and rhythmically simple. A catalogue of Purcell's chief works can be found in *The International Encyclopedia of Music and Musicians*. *Purcell* by J. A. Westrup (London, 1937) contains unusually comprehensive and critical discussion of every branch of Purcell's work. His instrumental music includes fresh and delightful (if simple) harpsichord suites, sonatas for two violins, cellos, and harpsichord, and very beautiful string fantasies and a march and canzona for four trombones.

Works

STRING ORCHESTRA

The Virtuous Wife *Suite* (Arr. Dunhill)
  (Boosey & Hawkes)
Tunes and Dances from **Dioclesian** (Arr.
  Weston) (H. Elkan)
Suite from **Dido and Aeneas** (G.
  Schirmer)
Five Selected Pieces (Arr. Akon)
  (Associated)
Four Pieces from **Musick's Handmain**
  (Arr. Hunt) (C. Fischer)
Suite from the **Dramatic Music** (Oxford)
Chaconne in G minor (Arr. Whittaker)
  (Oxford)

ORCHESTRA

Trumpet Voluntary (Arr. Gardner) (Staff)
March in G (Arr. Jurey) (Mills)
Trumpet Tune and Air (Arr. Perry)
  (Boosey & Hawkes)
"Purcelliana" (Arr. Akon) (Associated)
Trumpet Voluntary (Arr. Wood)
  (Chappell)

BAND

Trumpet Voluntary (Arr. Gray) (Marks)
Courtly Festival (Arr. Gordon) (Mills)

REED, H. OWEN

Born June 17, 1910, in Odessa, Missouri. He was educated at the University of Missouri (1929-33), Louisiana State University (B.M. 1934, M.M. 1936, A.B. 1937) and Eastman School of Music (Ph.D. 1939). He studied composition at Louisiana under Helen Gunderson, composition and orchestration at Eastman under Howard Hanson and Bernard Rogers, conducting with Paul White, composition with Bohuslav Martinu (summer of 1942), and composition under Roy Harris (summer of 1947).

A Workbook in Harmony 1943)   *A Workbook in the Fundamentals of Music* (1947)

Works

ORCHESTRA

Evangeline (1938)
Symphony No. 1 (1939)
Overture (1940)

BAND

La fiesta mexicana (Folk song symphony)
"Spiritual for Band"

A prolific composer, born in Prague, February 26, 1770, and died in Paris, May 28, 1836. He was a flutist in the Electoral Orchestra in Bonn at the time Beethoven played the viola in the same orchestra. They became good friends. In 1818 he became professor of composition at the Conservatoire in Paris. His pupils included Liszt and Gounod. He wrote the *Art of Composition.*

Works

Several operas
One overture
Two symphonies
Scènes italiennes (For orchestra)

CHAMBER MUSIC

Twenty string quartets
Twenty-four quintets for woodwinds
Twenty-four horn trios
Piano sonatas

RESPIGHI, OTTORINO

Italian composer, born in 1879 and died in 1936. He studied at the Liceo Musicale from age 12 until age 20, when he received a diploma in violin. He then went to Russia, where he studied with Rimsky-Korsakov and received a diploma in composition. Later he studied composition with Max Bruch in Berlin. He began his career teaching piano and later became professor of composition at Saint Cecilia Academy, where he was appointed director in 1923. He was nominated to the Royal Academy of Italy in 1932. In 1935 he made his first American appearance as a pianist.

Works

Fountains of Rome (Orchestra)
Old Airs and Dances for the Lute (Transcribed for orchestra)
Concerto Gregoriano (Violin and orchestra)

Huntingtower (Band)
Pines of Rome (Band and orchestra)
Roman Festivals (Symphonic poem)
The Birds (Orchestral suite)

RICORDI, G.

Founded in Milan in 1808, this publisher has branches worldwide, publishing opera, choral, vocal, and piano works, and instrumental, symphonic, and band music. Publications number over 120,000, including the greater modern Italian works. Most of its music is on rental only.

RIEGGER, WALLINGFORD

Born in Albany, Georgia, in 1885; died April 2, 1961. American composer and teacher. He studied at the Institute of Musical Arts in New York, where he specialized in cello, composition, counterpoint, and conducting. In 1910 he was cellist in the St. Paul Symphony Orchestra. He taught at Drake University and the Ithaca Conservatory. At Ithaca he was head of the Theory Department. Later he taught cello at the Institute of Musical Art. He received the Paderewski Award in 1921.

Works

Sonatina for Violin and Piano
"Rhapsody" (Orchestra)
American Polonaise (Orchestra)
Lyric Suite (Orchestra)
"Dichotomy" (Orchestra)
Scherzo (Orchestra)
"Study in Sonority" (Orchestra)

Fantasy and Fugue
"New Dance"
Canon and Fugue for Strings
Passacaglia and Fugue (Band)
Funeral March (Band)
"Dance Rhythms"

ROUSSEL, ALBERT

A French composer, born in 1869 and died in 1937. In 1884 he entered the Collège Stanislas in Paris to prepare for a naval career. He studied organ for a short time and then, while on duty in the French Indochina area, he tried his hand at composing. A fellow musical officer suggested he show the composition to Edouard Colonne and to the director of the Conservatory of Roubaic. Favorable comments from them led to Roussel's resignation from the navy and return to Paris to study with Gigout, and in 1896 he became one of Vincent d'Indy's pupils. His first success, two madrigals for four voices, was in 1898. His first large-scale orchestral work was Le Poème de la forêt. His influence was gradually felt worldwide. He continued the vividness he had learned from d'Indy and crossed it with the impressionism of Debussy. A sophisticated composer, he used the tritone and the major 7th and absorbed oriental scales into an orchestral texture of great brilliance. His four symphonies have taken their place among the most considerable symphonic works of the present day.

Works

ORCHESTRA

"Resurrection" (Symphonic prelude after Tolstoy, 1903)
Symphony No. 1, **Le Poème de la Forêt** (Four movements)
Pour une fête de printemps (Symphonic poem)

Symphony No. 2 in B-flat Major
Suite en fa (Three parts)
Concerto for Small Orchestra
Petite Suite (Three parts)
Symphony No. 3 in G minor
Sinfonietta for Strings
Symphony No. 4 in A Major

Rhapsodie Flamande
Suite for Flute, Strings, and Drums

Fanfare pour un sacre païen (Brass and drums)
"A Glorious Day" (Military band)

ROWLEY, ALEC

English pianist, organist, and composer. Born March 15, 1892, in London; died there January 10, 1958. At the Royal Academy of Music he was a pupil of Corder, Richards, and Lake. He graduated from the Royal Academy of Music and became a teacher and examiner.

Georgian Suite (Orchestra)
"Phyllis and Corydon" (String quartet)
"From Faerie" (String quartet)
"Little Jesus" (Voice, piano, and string quartet)
Cantatas

…, violin, and cello)
"Three Little Trios" (Piano, violin, and cello)
"The Puppet Show"
"Four Contrasts"
A Short Suite
Piano pieces for children or teaching music for children

SAEVERUD, HARALD

Born April 17, 1897, in Bergen, Norway. A Norwegian composer, he began to compose as a boy and in 1912 conducted a program of his works in Bergen. He studied with Holmsen at the Bergen Music Academy and with F. E. Koch at the Berlin Hochschule für Musik. His works, influenced by Norwegian folk music, have attracted widespread attention because of their unusual and highly individual orchestral coloration and freshness of inspiration.

Works

Eight symphonies
Psalm *Symphony* (1944-45)
Minnesota *Symphony* (1958)
Cello Concerto (1930)
Oboe Concerto (1938)
Divertimento (Flute and strings, 1939)
Slatter (Norwegian folk dances)
"Canto ostinato" (1934)
"Festa campestre" (Danza sinfonica, 1942)
"Fifty Small Variations"
"Her Last Cradlesong" (Strings)

"Orchestral Fragments" (1949)
Overtura appassionata (1920)
Peer Gynt (Incidental music for Ibsen's play, for theater orchestra)
Peer Gynt *Suite No. 1* (After Shakespeare's poem **The Rape of Lucrece**; 1936)
"Twelve Pieces" (1947)
"Vade mors" (1956)
"Romanza" (Violin and orchestra, 1942)
"Rondo amoroso" (1939)
Shepherd's Tune Variations (1941)

SAINT-SAËNS, CHARLES CAMILLE

Composer, pianist, organist, and conductor. Born in Paris October 9, 1835; died in Algiers on December 16, 1921. One of the founders of the Société Nationale de Musique (1871). He received many honors during his lifetime, and he was active as a conductor and performer right up to his death. He holds a very important position in French music. He was violently opposed to "modern" music and looked askance at Debussy. The chief characteristics of his music are instrumental elaboration, fullness of sonority in orchestration, and a certain harmonic saturation. A prolific composer.

Works

ORCHESTRA

"Praise Ye the Lord of Hosts" (Arr. Jurey) (Mills)
"Bacchanale" from **Samson et Dalila** (Fox)
Marche militaire française (Arr. Isaac) (C. Fischer)

Danse macabre (C. Fischer)
Carnival of the Animals

BAND

Chorale from Organ Symphony (Staff)
Pavane (G. Schirmer)
Symphony No. 1 in E-flat (Witmark)

SCHIRMER, G.

This has been the largest music publishing firm in America. It is self-contained in that it has its own engraving and printing plant. Gustav Schirmer (1829-93) established this firm in New York. It publishes *The Musical Quarterly*, which was first edited by O. G. Sonneck. The firm is known as being generally reliable, but not all its material can be classified as good for bands and orchestras. It publishes works of Harris, Bloch, Loeffler, S. Barber, and W. Schuman.

SCHMITT, FLORENT

Born September 28, 1840; died August 17, 1958, in Paris. A French composer, Schmitt began the study of music at Nancy in 1887 and studied harmony under Massenet and Fauré at the Paris Conservatory. In 1900 he won the Grand Prix de Rome. He composed many songs and piano pieces. He cultivated all forms of musical composition except opera, and won for himself a leading place among contemporary French composers. 1922-24 he was director of the Lyons Conservatory. Since then he made his residence at St. Cloud, near Paris. He has written in many periodicals and was a member of the Institute de France. In Rome he wrote a monumental setting of Psalm 47 for soprano solo, chorus, organ, and orchestra. His impressive piano quintet (1908) and the Psalm 47 setting are considered among some of the finest of his time.

SCHOTT, B., AND SOHNE

German music publisher founded in 1773 by Bernhard Schott and carried on by his descendants to the present. Branches are in the main cities of Europe and in New York. It is a most reliable publisher and promoter of music.

SCHUMAN, WILLIAM

American composer and cultural leader, born in 1910. He graduated from Columbia in 1935 and 1937 and studied composition with C. Haubiel and Roy Harris. He has written for all fields of music. He is a teacher of music and director of the publications for a publishing house. He has been president of Juilliard and has won many awards for composition. At present he is head of the Lincoln Center for the Performing Arts in New York. His works include eight symphonies.

Works

ORCHESTRA

BALLET

"Chester"
"When Jesus Wept" (Prelude for band)
"George Washington Bridge"
"Newsreel in Five Shots"

CHAMBER MUSIC

Three string quartets
Steeltown (Music for film)

SHOSTAKOVICH, DMITRI

Born September 25, 1906, in St. Petersburg; died in 1975. A well-known Soviet composer, Shostakovich studied harmony and counterpoint with Nikolaeff and composition with Steinberg at the St. Petersburg Conservatory. He began composing at an early age, and at 13 wrote a scherzo for orchestra. In 1923 and 1925 he graduated in piano and composition respectively. The first public performance of his music was in 1926, when his Symphony No. 1 in F minor was performed in Leningrad. It was composed when he was 19 years old and is considered the most durable and successful of his works. His music is characterized by lively, almost boisterous, themes to lyric, meditative, and undisguised sentimentality. He regards Beethoven as a model to true "people's music" and applies Beethoven's fundamental qualities of drama, humor, and sentiment to the new uses. In his works he also shows contemporary technique of writing used by Schönberg, Krenek, Hindemith, and Alban Berg. Shostakovich has received many awards and prizes of 100,000 rubles each for his Quintet and his 7th Symphony.

Works

CHAMBER WORKS

Cello Sonata
String Quartet
Piano Quintet

8th Symphony (In five movements; $10,000 paid by Columbia Broadcasting Company for American rights of first performance)

Fourteen pieces for theater
Fifteen symphonies
Twenty-seven pieces for orchestra
Thirteen chamber works

Six string quartets
One concerto for piano and orchestra
Sixteen songs
Seven piano pieces

SIEGMEISTER, ELIE

Born in 1909, he became bored with the piano when he started at age 9, but his father awakened in him a strong love for music by having him attend concerts and operas. He first became interested in composition at Columbia University where he earned his Phi Beta Kappa pin in 1927. He studied with Seth Bingham and Wallingford Riegger, worked under Nadia Boulanger in Paris, and in 1935 received a Juilliard fellowship in conducting. He strove to achieve a direct and personal contact with many people who did not generally go to concerts. Compositions such as "American Holiday," "Lincoln Walks at Midnight," and *Created Equal* (WPA musical play) were composed for children and amateurs. Aunt Molly Jackson aroused in him interest in American folklore. He traveled collecting folk tunes, and collections such as the following resulted.

Works

A Treasury of American Songs (412 pp.)
Work and Sing (Songs that built America)
Singing down the Road
Sing Out, Sweet Land
Music Lover's Handbook
Ozark Set (Life of people in the Ozarks)
"Prairie Legend"
Western Suite (Based on cowboy tunes)

"Strange Funeral in Braddock" (Solo and orchestra)
"Elegies for García Lorca"
Wilderness Road (Traditions of midwest)
"Sunday in Brooklyn" (Five parts)
Funnybone Alley (Song cycle for kids)
"John Henry" (For concerts in empty lofts)

SMETANA, BEDRICH

Born March 2, 1824, in Bohemia; died May 12, 1884, in Prague. A vigorous promoter of Bohemian music, he came to be father of the Czech Nationalist School. His great interest in politics had a marked effect upon his music. His greatest success was a comic folk opera *The Bartered Bride.* Other national operas include "Dalibor" (1868), and "Libussa" (1871). Smetana lost his hearing in 1874 and ten years later in 1884 was admitted to an insane asylum, where he died.

Works

"The Moldau"
"Wallenstein's Camp"
Trio in G minor

String Quartet No. 2 in D minor
Má vlast
Quartet No. 1 in E minor (**From My Life**)

SOUSA, JOHN PHILIP

The march king of the world was born in 1854 and died in 1932. His marches are still the most popular the world over. He was leader of the United States Marine Corps Band in 1880. In 1892 he organized his own band, which later made European tours and a world tour in 1910-11. He composed many marches, light operas, orchestra suites, and songs. Some of his most celebrated marches are:

"The Stars and Stripes Forever"
"El capitán"
"The Washington Post"
"The High School Cadets"

"Thunderer"
"Semper fidelis"
"Manhattan Beach"
"King Cotton"

STAMITZ, KARL

Born May 7, 1745, in Mannheim; died November 9, 1801, in Jena. Violinist and composer and one of the sons of Johann Stamitz. He was well known as a virtuoso on the viola and did considerable touring with this instrument.

, ... ILUUNUVICH

Born in Oranienbaum, near St. Petersburg, June 17, 1882; died April 6, 1971. He studied law until he was 23 and then became acquainted with Rimsky-Korsakov. Rimsky-Korsakov and Diaghiev encouraged him to continue in his music, and in 1910, when Stravinsky was 28, his *Firebird* was performed in Paris. He came to the U.S. and became a citizen.

Works

Symphony in E-flat Major, op. 1 (1907)
Song Cycle, **Farm and Shepherdess**

ORCHESTRAL WORKS

Fireworks
Firebird
"Fantastic Scherzo"

BALLET

The Rite of Spring (1913)
The Soldier's Tale
Pulcinella
Oedipus Rex (Orchestral style of Bach or Handel)
Petroushka
The Nightingale
The Wedding (Cantata)

INSTRUMENTAL WORKS

Symphonies of Wind Instruments (1920; 23 wind instruments)

Ensemble music
Pianoforte music
Some string works

CHORAL

Symphony of Psalms (Choral symphony, 1930)

SMALL ORCHESTRA

Ragtime (1918)

ORCHESTRAL TRANSCRIPTIONS

Berceuse from **The Firebird** *Suite* (Arr. Gardner-Wilson) (Presser)
"Danse russe," from **Petroushka** (Marks)
Suite No. 1 for small orchestra (Chester, rental)
Suite No. 2 for small orchestra (Chester, rental)

Berceuse from **The Firebird** (Arr. Gardner) (Presser)
Dance Infernal" (Arr. Gardner) (Staff)
"Circus Polka" (Associated)
Ebony Concerto

Berceuse and Finale from **The Firebird** (Arr. Goldman) (Marks)
"Danse infernale," from **The Firebird**
Themes from **Petroushka** (Arr. Gardner) (Staff)

TELEMANN, GEORG MICHAEL

German composer and grandson of Georg Phillip Telemann, born in 1748 and died in 1831. He became accompanist to a Hamburg church choir. He studied theology in 1773 but changed to music in 1775. He became cantor and director of music at Riga and wrote theoretical and didactic works.

Works

Two hymn books
Book of trio sonatas
Six organ preludes

Choral work
Six violin sonatas

TELEMANN, GEORG PHILLIP

A self-taught German composer, born in 1681 and died in 1767. He wrote an opera at 12 and conducted the music in the Roman Catholic Church at Hildesheim when 14. In 1701 he entered Leipzig University and studied law and modern languages. In 1721 he became music director of the five principal churches at Hamburg, posts which he retained until his death. He was a very prolific composer, better known than Bach in his time, but subsequently suffered an eclipse. He wrote 3,000 works for orchestra and organ, over 600 overtures (French), many serenades, marches, trio sonatas, and other chamber music.

Works

Gavotte (Arr. Wilson) (Carlin)
Violin Concerto
Trio Sonata in E-flat (Reimann's, Collegium Musicum)
Symphony in Scherings Perlen ater Kammermusik

Concerto for Four Violins (Ed. Dameck)
Oboe Concerto (Ed. Stein)
Flute Quartet by Ermeler
Musique de table (Instrumental suites; ed. Seiffert)

VAUGHAN WILLIAMS, RALPH

English composer of world renown, born in 1872 and died in 1958. He was educated in music at Trinity College, Cambridge, and the Royal College of Music. He studied with Ravel. A very prolific composer, he composed in all mediums and made use of folk song material. His outstanding works include *London Symphony* (1914), "Fantasia on a Theme by Thomas Tallis," and much theater music, to mention only a few.

ORCHESTRA

Fantasy on Sussex Folk Tunes (For cello
  and orchestra, 1930)
Concerto accademico (For violin, 1925)
English Folk Song Suite
"Sine nomine"
Prelude, "49 Parallel" (Arr. Douglas)
Prelude, "Hyfrydol" (Arr. Foster)
Prelude, "Rhosymedre"

STRING ORCHESTRA

Concerto Grosso
The Charterhouse Suite
Fantasia ("Greensleeves")
"Five Variants of Dives and Lazarus"
Hymn Tune on Song 13 (Oxford)

BAND

... degree in 1934 from the University of Minnesota and later took courses with
Aaron Copland at Tanglewood, Roy Harris at Colorado College, and Frederick Jacobi
at Juilliard School of Music. He taught at Hamline University (1934-42) and at Mount
Holyoke College (1942-46). He also served as editor for G. Schirmer, Inc. (1947-48). In
1948 he was appointed instructor at the University of Washington.

Works

ORCHESTRA

Symphony for Young Orchestra
Symphony No. 1
Portrait of Man (Symphonic Suite)
Symphony No. 2
Violin Concerto
"Dark Night of Saint John"
Variations on an Ancient Tune"
Portrait of Saint Christopher (Symphonic
  poem)

OPERAS

The Cowherd and the Sky Maiden
The Wedding Knell
Three Blind Mice
Plainsmen
Christmas Fantasy (With chorus)

BAND MUSIC

"A Northern Overture"
"Sinfonia festiva"
"Holiday Mood"

VILLA-LOBOS, HEITOR

Foremost Brazilian composer, born in Rio de Janeiro in 1887. In 1907 he entered the
National Institute of Mexico, and in 1912 he traveled in Brazil. Artur Rubenstein
became an admirer of his. In 1932 Villa-Lobos was made superintendent of musical
and artistic education in Rio de Janeiro. He gathered Brazilian folk music and organized huge choruses of school children. Brazilian song material is the exclusive source
of his thematic inspiration. An exceptionally prolific composer, he has written operas,
ballets, symphonies, chamber music, choruses, piano pieces, and songs. His compositions exceed 2,000.

VOXMAN, HYMIE

Chairman of the Music Department of the University of Iowa. He has been editor for Rubank Publishing Co. He is an accomplished clarinetist and does a great deal of arranging for woodwinds. He has also written method books for woodwinds.

WALTON, SIR WILLIAM TURNER

Born in Oldham, England, March 29, 1902. At the age of ten he entered the Christ Church Cathedral Choir School at Oxford. He received some help from good teachers but was virtually self-taught. He entered undergraduate school at age sixteen, getting some advice from Ansermet and Busoni. While there he wrote a number of his choral works. He also composed some radio, film, and stage music.

Works

The Quest (Ballet, 1943)
Macbeth (Incidental music, 1941)
Troilus and Cressida (Opera, 1954)
Belshazzar's Feast (With baritone solo, orchestra, and two brass choirs—his best choral work)

ORCHESTRA

"Siesta" (1926)
Suite No. 1, *Façade* (1926)
   1. Polka
   2. Valse
   3. Swiss Yodeling Song
   4. Tango—Pasodoble
   5. Tarantella sevillona
Coronation March, "Crown Imperial" (Oxford)
Suite No. 2, *Façade* (Six movements)
Music for Children (Oxford)

Two Pieces for Strings from Henry V (Oxford)

SOLO INSTRUMENTS WITH ORCHESTRA

Sinfonia Concertante (Orchestra and pianoforte)
Viola Concerto
Violin Concerto
Chamber Music for Violin and Pianoforte, **Façade**
Trio for Two Cats and a Trombone
Duets for children and numerous songs

BAND TRANSCRIPTIONS

"Crown Imperial" (Arr. Duthort) (Boosey & Hawkes)
"Orb and Sceptre" (Arr. Richardson) (Boosey & Hawkes)
"Festaleta Overture" (Belwin)

WARD, ROBERT

American composer, born September 13, 1917, in Cleveland. He studied at the Eastman School of Music with Howard Hanson and Bernard Rogers. At Juilliard School he studied composition with Frederick Jacobi and conducting with Albert Stoessel, and he studied with Aaron Copland at the Berkshire Music Center. He served in the U.S. Army, graduated from the Army Music School at Fort Myer, Virginia, and was bandleader in the infantry. He graduated from the Juilliard School and taught there and at Columbia University. In 1955 he became president of the American Composers Alliance and vice-chairman of the American Music Center. He is a board member of the league of composers—ISCM, Composers Recordings, Inc., and the Henry Street Music School Settlement. Jazz and American folksong influence Ward's music. His style is melodic, rhythmic, and rich in texture and harmonies. His works include three operas and a number of pieces for orchestra.

OPERA

Pantaloon
He Who Gets Slapped
The Crucible

ORCHESTRA

"Fatal Interview" (Soprano and orchestra)
"Ode"

"Jonathon and the Gingery Snare" (For narrator, small orchestra, and percussion)
Symphony No. 3
"Fantasia" (For brass choir and timpani)
"Euphony"

CHAMBER MUSIC

WEAVER, RICHARD

A contemporary American arranger, Weaver is known chiefly for his orchestral arrangements of the Rosamunde Overture and other works good for high school orchestras.

WEBER, CARL MARIA FRIEDRICH ERNST VON

The founder of the German romantic school, Weber was born in Eutrin, Oldenburg, Germany, on November 18, 1786, and died in London, England, on June 5, 1826. Constanze Weber, Mozart's wife, was Carl's father's niece, and Carl was Mozart's first cousin by marriage. Carl's father belonged to a traveling theatrical troupe, and it was here that Carl got his knowledge and experience of the stage. He studied piano with Fritz (a pupil of Haydn) and J. P. Heuschkel. He studied counterpoint under Michael Haydn, singing under Valesi, and composition under Ralcher. He was composing at age 13. After learning engraving from Aloys Senefelder, he engraved his Variations for Piano, op. 2, in 1800. He became *musik intendant* to Duke Engen of Wurttemberg in Silesia. After several undertakings, he went to Dresden and worked for the King of Saxony, in charge of the German Opera Theater. He wrote *Der Freischutz* in 1820, after three years' work, and then the opera *Oberon* in 1826. He opened the era of musical romanticism.

Works

Die drei Pintos (1821); unfinished, but completed by Gustav Mahler and produced in 1888)
Many other works—operas, vocal selections, cantatas, masses, etc.

INSTRUMENTAL

Jubel Overture
Der Freischutz Overture
Oberon Overture
Euryanthe Overture
Invitation to the Waltz
Peter Schmoll Overture

WILLIAMS, CLIFTON

A contemporary American teacher at the University of Texas, and a very popular band composer. His music is excellent for public schools, grades III-IV, and is found in the selectives list. Summy-Birchard publishes most of his band work.

Works

BAND

Fanfare and Allegro
Academic Procession (For graduation)
"Festival"
"America"
"Revolutionary Fantasy"
Symphonic Suite
Symphony in C, Movements 1 and 2
Variation Overture
Concertino for Percussion and Band
"Solemn Fugue"

Symphony in C minor
"Hill Country Ballad"
"Ariosa"
"Pastorale"

ORCHESTRA

Chorale from Sinfonia Concertante
Chorale from Sinfonia Concertante (String orchestra)
March from Symphonic Suite

ADDENDUM

9

Guide to Publishers

This guide represents a combination of orchestra, band, chamber, woodwind, brass, and string publishers. The basic abbreviations are similar to the ones used by the American Society of Composers, Authors and Publishers and are the ones used throughout this guide. Although companies and addresses change, and although complete, up-to-date street addresses were occasionally unavailable in preparing this list, it will be a valuable reference.

Ab	Abington Press, 201 8th Ave. S., Nashville, Tenn. 37202
AB	Verlag Anton Boehm & Sohn, Augsburg, Germany
ABr	Alexander Broude, 1619 Broadway, New York, N.Y. 10019
ABR	Associated Board of the Royal Schools of Music, London, England. In USA, Belwin-Mills Publishing Corp., 25 Deshon Dr., Melville, N.Y. 11746
ACA	American Composers Alliance, 2121 Broadway, New York, N.Y. 10019
Acc	Accura Music, Box 887, Athens, Ohio 45701
ADF	Alphons Dreissen, Fa., Leidsegracht 11, Amsterdam C, Holland
Adv	Advanced Music Corp., Warner Brothers Publications, Inc., 75 Rockefeller Plaza, New York, N.Y. 10019
AdverMuInc	Advertiser's Music Inc., 54 W. Randolph St., Chicago, Ill. 60601
AE	Autograph Editions, c/o Atlantic Music Supply, 152 W. 42nd St., New York, N.Y. 10036
AGADU	AGADU (Asociación General de Autores del Uruguay) Calle Canelones No. 1130, Montevideo, Uruguay

AhnSimrock   Ahn & Simrock, Meinekestr. 10, 1 Berlin 15, West Germany

AKM   AKM (Staatlich Genehmigte Gesellschaft der Autoren, Komponisten und Musikverleger), Baumannstrasse 8, Vienna 3, Austria

AL   Alcove Music, c/o Western International Music, 2859 Holt Ave., Los Angeles, Calif. 90034

Alf   Alfred Music Co., 75 Channel Dr., Port Washington, N.Y. 11050

Alkor   Edition Alkor, GMBH., Heinrich-Schutz-Allee 29, 35 Kassel-Wilhelmshohe, West Germany. In USA, Joseph Boonin, Inc., P.O. 2124, S. Hackensack, N.J. 07606

Alm   Almitra Music Co., c/o Kendor Music, Delevan, N.Y. 14042

Alsbach   G. Alsbach & Co., c/o C. F. Peters Corp., 373 Park Ave. S., New York, N.Y. 10016

Alte & NeueK Alte & Neue Kunst Verlag, Rheingaustr. 3, 1 Berlin 41, West Germany

AmaMus.Co.   Ama Music Co., Suite 301, 1650 Broadway, New York, N.Y. 10019

Amb   Amberson Enterprises, c/o Boosey & Hawkes, Inc., 30 W. 57th St., New York, N.Y. 10019

AmerMusEd   American Music Edition, 258 E. 7th St., New York, N.Y. 10019. Now Carl Fisher, Inc., 56-62 Cooper Sq., New York, N.Y. 10003

Am. Mu. Ctr. American Music Center, Suite 15-79, 2109 Broadway, New York, N.Y. 10023

Amp   Amphion, c/o Belwin-Mills Publishing Corp., Melville, N.Y. 11746

AMP   Associated Music Publishers, Inc., 866 3rd Ave., New York, N.Y. 10022

AMSCO   AMSCO Music Publishing Co., c/o Music Sales Corp., 33 W. 60th St., New York, N.Y. 10023

Ande   Edition Andel Uitgave, c/o Henri Elkan Music Publisher, 1316 Walnut St., Philadelphia, Pa. 19107

Andraud   Albert J. Andraud, Wind Instrument Music Library, c/o Southern Music Co., 1100 Broadway, P.O. Box 329, San Antonio, Tex. 78206

AndrieuFr.   Andrieu Frères, c/o M. Gérard Billaudot, 21 avenue Mozart, Paris 16, France. Now Andrieu et Leblanc, Southern Music Co., 1100 Broadway, San Antonio, Tex. 78206

Anglo   Anglo-Canadian Music Co., Ltd., 58 Advance Rd., Toronto 18, Ontario, Canada

Ann A   Ann Arbor Publishers, 711 North University, Ann Arbor, Mich. 48104

AP   Autopress Publications, c/o Autograph Editions, 152 W. 42nd St., New York, N.Y. 10036

App   Appleyard Publications, Box 111, Durham, N.H. 03824

APRA   APRA (Australasian Performing Right Association, Ltd.), Box 4007, GPO Sidney, Australia

AR   Ar Publishing Co., 756 7th Ave., New York, N.Y. 10019

Arco   Arco Music Publishers, c/o Western International Music, 2859 Holt Ave., Los Angeles, Calif. 90034

Arg   Argee Music Press, Box 436, Greencastle, Ind. 46135

ArM	Artransa Music, c/o Western International Music, 2859 Holt Ave., Los Angeles, Calif. 90034
Arranger	(Name of individual), c/o ASCAP, 575 Madison Ave., New York, N.Y. 10022
Art	Artia, c/o Boosey & Hawkes, 30 W. 57th St., New York, N.Y. 10019
Asc	Ascherberg, Hopwood & Crew, 16 Mortimer St., London W1, England
Ascher	Emil Ascher, Inc., 745 5th Ave., New York, N.Y. 10022
Ash	Ashdown, 19 Hanover St., London, England
ASTA	American String Teachers Association, 1201 16th St. N.W.,

...	Avant Music, c/o Western International Music, 2859 Holt Ave., Los Angeles, Calif. 90034
AW	Addison-Wesley Publishing Co., Reading, Mass. 01867
Bärenrtr	Bärenreiter-Verlag, Heinrich-Schütz-Allee 31-37, 35 Kassel-Wilhelmshohe, West Germany. In USA, Joseph Boonin, Inc., P.O. Box 2124, S. Hackensack, N.J. 07606
Bak	John Baker, 5 Royal Opera Arcade, Pall Mall, London, England
BAM	British American Music Co., 19 W. Jackson, Chicago, Ill. 60604
B&C	British & Continental Music Agencies, 64 Dean St., London, England
B&F	Bayley & Ferguson, c/o G. Schirmer, 866 3rd Ave., New York, N.Y. 10022
B&vanP	(Broekmans & van Poppel) C. F. Peters Corp., 373 Park Ave. S., New York, N.Y. 10016
Bar	C. L. Barnhouse Co., Oskaloosa, Iowa 52577
Baron	M. Baron Co., P.O. Box 149, Oyster Bay, N.Y. 11771
BB-AMP	Edition Bote & Bock, Associated Music Publishers, Inc., 866 3rd Ave., New York, N.Y. 10022
B.-Barclay	Barger & Barclay, 1325 Orange Isle, Ft. Lauderdale, Fla. 33315
BCMD-Elk	Belgian Centre of Music Documentation, Brussels, Belgium
BD	Byron-Douglas Publications, Belwin-Mills Publishing Corp., 25 Deshon Dr., Melville, N.Y. 11746
BDA	British Dental Association, 64 Wimpole St., London, England
Be	M. P. Belaieff, c/o C. F. Peters Corp., 373 Park Ave. S., New York, N.Y. 10016
BE	Gustav Bosse Verlag, Regensburg, Germany

Beekman	Beekman Music, Inc., c/o Theodore Presser Co., Presser Place, Bryn Mawr, Pa. 19010
Belmont	Belmont Music Publishers, P.O. Box 49961, Los Angeles, Calif. 90049
Belwin	Belwin-Mills, Inc., 25 Deshon Dr., Melville, N.Y. 11746
Ben	Anton J. Benjamin, c/o Associated Music Publishers, 866 3rd Ave., New York, N.Y. 10023
Benn	Benn Co., c/o W. W. Norton & Co., 55 5th Ave., New York, N.Y. 10003
Bennefeld	Bennefeld Mvlg., Schopenhauerstr. 23, 1 Berlin 38, West Germany
Ber	Berandol Music Ltd., c/o Associated Music Publishers, 866 3rd Ave., New York, N.Y. 10023
Berb	Edizioni Musicali Berben, Theodore Presser Co., Presser Place, Bryn Mawr, Pa. 19010
Berk	Berklee Press Publications, Frank Music Corp., 119 W. 57th St., New York, N.Y. 10019
BFW	B. F. Wood Co., 1619 Broadway, New York, N.Y. 10019
Big 3	Big 3 Music Corp., 1540 Broadway, New York, N.Y. 10036
Bill	Editions Billaudot, c/o Theodore Presser Co., Presser Place, Bryn Mawr, Pa. 19010
Birchard	C. C. Birchard & Co. (now Summy-Birchard), 1834 Ridge Ave., Evanston Ill. 60205
Bloch	Bloch Publishing Co., 31 West 31st St., New York, N.Y. 10001
BMI-AMP	Broadcast Music Inc., c/o Associated Music Publishers, 866 3rd Ave., New York, N.Y. 10023
BMP	Brightstar Music Publications, c/o Western International Music, 2859 Holt Ave., Los Angeles, Calif. 90034
BMP-AMP	Bomart Music Publications, c/o Associated Music Publishers, 866 3rd Ave., New York, N.Y. 10022
Boelke-Bo.	Boelke-Bomart, Inc., Associated Music Publishers, Inc., 866 3rd Ave., New York, N.Y. 10022
Bo. Hawkes	Boosey & Hawkes, Inc., 30 West 57th St., New York, N.Y. 10019
Bos	Bosworth & Co., 45 rue de Ruysbroeck, Brussels, Belgium
Boston	Boston Music Co., 116 Boyleston St., Boston, Mass. 02116
Bourne	Bourne Co., 1212 Avenue of the Americas, New York, N.Y. 10036
BP	The Brass Press, 159 8th Ave. N., Nashville, Tenn. 37203
BRH-AMP	Breitkopf & Hartel, Weisbaden or Leipzig, Germany. In USA, c/o Associated Music Publishers, 866 3rd Ave., New York, N.Y. 10023
Brockhaus	Brockhaus Mvlg., Oskar-Grether-Str. 13, 785 Lorrach, 3, West Germany
Brodt	Brodt Music Co., 1409 N. Independence Blvd., Charlotte, N.C. 28201
Broe-Pet	Broekmans, Netherlands. In USA, c/o C. F. Peters Corp., 373 Park Ave. S., New York, N.Y. 10016
Brog	Editions Musicales Brogneaux, c/o Henri Elkan Music Publisher, 1316 Walnut St., Philadelphia, Pa. 19107

Broude	Broude Bros., 56 W. 45th St., New York, N.Y. 10019
Brown	Wm. C. Brown Co., 135 S. Locust St., Dubuque, Iowa 52001
Bru	Aldo Bruzzichelli, c/o Associated Music Publishers, 866 3rd Ave., New York, N.Y. 10022
Bruckner	Bruckner Verlag, c/o C. F. Peters Corp., 373 Park Ave. S., New York, N.Y. 10016
BS	Band Shed, Petal, Miss. 39465
BUMA	BUMA (Het Bureau Voor Muziek-Auteursrecht), Marius Bauerstraat 30, Amsterdam 17, Holland
Buvst	Mme Vve B....

Canadian	Canadian Music Sales Corp., Ltd., 58 Advance Rd., Toronto 18, Ontario, Canada. In USA, Brodt Music Co., 1409 N. Independence Blvd., Charlotte, N.C. 28201
CanMusCtr	Canadian Music Centre, 559 Avenue Rd., Toronto 7, Ontario, Canada
CAP	Composers Autograph Publications, Box 7103, Cleveland, Ohio 44128
CAPAC	CAPAC (Composers, Authors and Publishers Association of Canada, Ltd.), 1263 Bay St., Toronto 5, Ontario, Canada
Cap. Press	Capital Press, c/o Mr. Ralph Herman, Music Department, American Broadcasting Co., 7 W. 66th St., New York, N.Y. 10023
Car	Carisch, c/o Boosey & Hawkes, 30 W. 57th St., New York, N.Y. 10019
CAR	Carlin Music Publishing Co.
Carlvi	Carlvi Music co., Apt. 403, 511 S. Mariposa Ave., Los Angeles, Calif. 90005
CBDM	Centre Belge de Documentation Musicale, c/o Henri Elkan Music Publisher, 1316 Walnut St., Philadelphia, Pa. 19107
C-Bettony	Cundy-Bettony Co., Inc., Carl Fischer, Inc., 56-62 Cooper Sq., New York, N.Y. 10003
CBP	Claude Benny Press, Box 461, Milton Jct., Wis. 52654
CC	Cleveland Chamber Music Publishers, c/o Atlantic Music Supply, 152 W. 42nd St., New York, N.Y. 10036
CdM	Le Chant du Monde, MCA Music, 445 Park Ave., New York, N.Y. 10022
Cen	Century Music Publishing Co., 263 Veterans Blvd., Carlstadt, N.J. 07072
CF	Carl Fischer, Inc., 56-62 Cooper Square, New York, N.Y. 10003
CFE	Composers Facsimile Edition, 170 W. 74th St., New York, N.Y. 10023
CFP	C. F. Peters Corp., 373 Park Ave. S., New York, N.Y. 10016

Cha	Chandos Music, 41 Charing Cross Rd., London WC1, England
Chappell	Chappell & Co., Inc., 810 70th Ave., New York, N.Y. 10019
Charling	Charling Music Corp., c/o Edwin H. Morris & Co., Inc., 31 W. 54th St., New York, N.Y. 10019
Che	J. & W. Chester, Eagle Court, London, England
C. H. Hansen	Charles H. Hansen Music Corp., c/o Walter Hofer, 221 W. 57th St., New York, N.Y. 10019
Choudens	Editions Choudens, c/o C. F. Peters, Inc., 373 Park Ave. S., New York, N.Y. 10016
Church	The John Church Co., Bryn Mawr, Pa. 19010
Cim	Cimino Publications, 436 Maple Ave., Westbury, N.Y. 11590
CL-AMP	BMI-Canada, Ltd., c/o Associated Music Publishers, 866 3rd Ave., New York, N.Y. 10022
CML	Chamber Music Library, c/o Sam Fox Publishing Co., P.O. Box 850, Valley Forge, Pa. 19482
CMP	Concert Music Publishing Co., c/o Bourne Co., 136 W. 52nd St., New York, N.Y. 10019
Coar	Birchard Coar, Rt. No. 1, Box 91c, Sarasota, Fla. 33577
Cole	M. M. Cole Publishing Co., 251 E. Grand Ave., Chicago, Ill. 60611
Colf	Colfranc Music Publishing Corp. c/o G. Schirmer, 866 3rd Ave., New York, N.Y. 10023
Colin	Charles Colin, New Sounds in Modern Music, 315 W. 53rd St., New York, N.Y. 10019
Columbia	Columbia Pictures Music Corp., 666 5th Ave., New York, N.Y. 10019
ComNaCulBA	Comisión Nacional de Cultura, Avenida Alvear 1690, Buenos Aires, Argentina
Composer	(Name of individual), c/o ASCAP, 575 Madison Ave., New York, N.Y. 10022
Con	Concordia Publishing House, 3558 S. Jefferson Ave., St. Louis, Mo. 63118
Concord-ELK	Concord Music Publishers, c/o Henri Elkan Music Publisher, 1316 Walnut St., Philadelphia, Pa. 19107
Congress	Congress Music Publications, 410 N.E. 17th St., Miami, Fla. 33132
Consolidtd	Consolidated Music Publishers, Inc., 33 W. 60th St., New York, N.Y. 10023
Consonant	Consonant Music, Inc., 224 W. 49th St., New York, N.Y. 10036
CoP	Conservatory Publications, 18 Van Wyck St., Croton-on-Hudson, N.Y. 10520
Cor	Cor Publishing Co., 67 Bell Place, Massapequa, N.Y. 11758
Cost	Editions Costallat, Paris, France, c/o M. Baron Co., P.O. Box 149, Oyster Bay, N.Y. 11771. Or c/o Southern Music Co., 1100 Broadway, San Antonio, Tex. 78206

Cousins	Editions Cousins, M. René Defossez, 116 avenue Franklin Roosevelt, Brussels 5, Belgium
CPC	Crown Music Press, 4119 N. Pittsburg, Chicago, Ill. 60634
C. Press	The Composers Press, Inc., 4941 Ambrose Ave., Los Angeles, Calif. 90027
Cramer	J. B. Cramer & Co., Ltd., 99 St. Martin's Lane, London WC2, England. In USA, c/o Brodt Music Co., 1409 E. Independence Blvd., Charlotte, N.C. 28201
Cranz	Albert Cranz, 22 rue d'Assaut, Brussels 1, Belgium. Or 1740 Broadway, New York, N.Y. 10019

..., ᴮᴼˣ 1932, Santa Monica, Calif. 90406

Ded	Dedrick Bros., c/o Kendor Music, Delevan, N.Y. 14042
DEG	Deg Music Products, Lake Geneva, Wis. 53147
Del	Delrieu & Cie, c/o Galaxy Music Corp., 2121 Broadway, New York, N.Y. 10019
De Wolfe	De Wolfe, Ltd., 80-82 Wardour St., London W1, England
D. Gornston	David Gornston, 117 W. 48th St., New York, N.Y. Or P.O. Box 850, Valley Forge, Pa. 19482
Dis	Disney Music Co., 550 S. Buena Vista, Burbank, Calif. 91505
Ditson	Oliver Ditson Co., Presser Place, Bryn Mawr, Pa. 19010
DN	Dick Noel Enterprises, c/o Educulture, Inc., Box 1932, Santa Monica, Calif. 90406
Dn-Pet	Donemus, Netherlands. In USA, c/o C. F. Peters Corp., 373 Park Ave., New York, N.Y. 10016
DOB-AMP	Ludwig Doblinger, Verlag, Vienna, Austria. In USA, c/o Associated Music Publishers, 866 3rd Ave., New York, N.Y. 10022
Dorian	Dorian Music Publishers, Inc., 501 Madison Ave., Suite 1802, New York, N.Y. 10022
Dow	Dow Publishers, Inc., P.O. Box 176, Oyster Bay, N.Y. 11771
D. Rahter	D. Rahter, c/o Associated Music Publishers, 866 3rd Ave., New York, N.Y. 10023
Duc	Duchess Music Corp., c/o MCA Music Corp., 455 Park Ave., New York, N.Y. 10022
Dur	Durand et Cie., c/o Theodore Presser, Presser Place, Bryn Mawr, Pa. 19010
DVM	Deutscher Verlag für Musik, c/o Associated Music Publishers, 866 3rd Ave., New York, N.Y. 10023

Earl	Earl Music Co., c/o Mr. Earl S. Shuman, Suite 3-B, 111 E. 88th St., New York, N.Y. 10028
Earlham Col	Department of Music, Earlham College, Richmond, Ind.
ECS	E. C. Schirmer Music Co., 600 Washington St., Boston, Mass. 02111
EdArgent	Editorial Argentina de Musica Internacional, Lavalle 1494, Buenos Aires, Argentina
EdB	Editions Braun, c/o Theodore Presser, Presser Place, Bryn Mawr, Pa. 19010
Ed. Lyche	Harald Lyche & Cos., Forlag, c/o Henmar Press, Inc., 373 Park Ave. S., New York, N.Y. 10016
Ed Mex	Ediciones Mexicanas, Mexico City, Mexico. In USA, c/o Leeds Music Corp., 322 W. 48th St., New York, N.Y. 10019
EdP	Editions de Paris, 14 rue du Faubourg Poissonnière, Paris, France
Eds. Fran.	Editions Françaises de Musique, 116 avenue du President Kennedy, Paris 16, France
Eic	Eichenkreuz Verlag, Kassel-Wilhelmshohe, Germany
EK	Edition Kneusslin, c/o C. F. Peters Corp., 373 Park Ave. S., New York, N.Y. 10016
Elkan, H.	See H. Elkan
EM	Edition Musicus, 333 W. 52nd St., New York, N.Y. 10019
EMB	Editio Musica Budapest, c/o Boosey & Hawkes, 30 W. 57th St., New York, N.Y. 10019
EMC	Easton Music Co., c/o Robert King Music Co., 112A Main St., North Easton, Mass. 02356
EMS	Educational Music Service, 905 Gaffield Place, Evanston, Ill. 60201
EMT-Pr	Editions Musicales Transatlantiques, c/o Theodore Presser Co., Presser Place, Bryn Mawr, Pa. 19010
Engstrom	Engstrom & Sodring, c/o Henmar Pres, Inc., 373 Park Ave. S., New York, N.Y. 10016
Enoch	Enoch & Cie., 27 boulevard des Italiens, Paris 11, France
Ens	Ensemble Publications, Box 98, Buffalo, N.Y. 14222
EO	Editions Ouvrières, c/o Galaxy Music Corp., 2121 Broadway, New York, N.Y. 10023
Erdmann	Erdmann Musik-Verlag, Adolfsallee 34, 62 Weisbaden, West Germany
Erica	Erica Music, Inc., 35 W. 53rd St., New York, N.Y. 10019
ESC	Editions Max Eschig
Eulenburg	Ernst Eulenberg, Ltd., c/o Henmar Press, Inc., 373 Park Ave. S., New York, N.Y. 10016
EV	Elkan-Vogel Co., Inc., Presser Place, Bryn Mawr, Pa. 19010
Fab	Faber & Faber Music, c/o G. Schirmer, 866 3rd Ave., New York, N.Y. 10022
Fanfare	Fanfare Music Co., 1337 No. Orange Dr., Hollywood, Calif. 90028

Fazer	Edition Fazer, Aleksanterinkatu 11, Helsinki, Finland
F. Colombo	Franco Colombo, Inc., 16 W. 61st St., New York, N.Y. 10023
FDH	Francis, Day & Hunter, Ltd., London, England. In USA, c/o Robbins Music Corp., 1540 Broadway, New York, N.Y. 10036
Feist	Leo Feist, Inc., 1540 Broadway, New York, N.Y. 10036
Fer	G. Ferrario, Milan, Italy
Fillmore	Fillmore Music House, c/o Carl Fischer, Inc., 56-62 Cooper Sq., New York, N.Y. 10003
Finale	Finale Buhnen und Musikverlag, Schwalbeneck 13, 89 Augsburg, Germany

	ged Music Co., c/o Chantry Music Press, Inc., 32-34 N. Center, Springfield, Ohio 45501
G&C	G&C Music Corp., c/o Chappell & Co., Inc., 810 7th Ave., New York, N.Y. 10017
G&T	Goodwin & Tabb, Ltd., 36038 Dean St., London W1, England
Gate	Gate Music Co., 117 W. 48th St., New York, N.Y. 10037
Gehrmans	A. B. Carl Gehrmans Musikforlag, Posfack 505, Stockholm I, Sweden
GEMA	GEMA (Gesellschaft Fur Musikalische Aufführungs und Mechanische Vervielfaltigungsrechte), Herzog-Wilhelm Strasse 28, Munich 2, Germany
General	General Music Publishing Co., Inc., Box 267, Hastings on Hudson, New York, N.Y. 10709
Gerig	Musikverlag Hans Gerig, Cologne, Germany. In USA, c/o Robbins Music Corp., 1540 Broadway, New York, N.Y. 10036
Gershwin	Gershwin Publishing Corp., 609 5th Ave., New York, N.Y. 10017
Gervan	Edition Gervan, Mlle Germaine Blaton, 496-F chaussée de Waterloo, Brussels 6, Belgium
Gor	Gordon Music Co., 2680 Cherokee Way, Palm Springs, Calif. 92262
Gray	H. W. Gray Co., Inc., 159 E. 48th St., New York, N.Y. 10017
Gras	Editions Gras, 36 rue Paper Carpentier, La Flèche, France
Gro	Musikverlag Grosch, Osthofen, Germany
GR-Pet	Grahl, Germany. In USA, c/o C. F. Peters Corp., 373 Park Ave., New York, N.Y. 10016
G. Schirmer	G. Schirmer, Inc., 866 3rd Ave., New York, N.Y. 10022
GSco	G. Scott Music Publishing Co., c/o Western International Music, 2859 Holt Ave., Los Angeles, Calif. 90034

Guild Cal   Guild Publications of California, Inc., 3929 Fredonia Dr., Hollywood, Calif. 90028

GV Thompson   Gordon V. Thompson, Ltd., 32 Alcorn Ave., Toronto 7, Ontario, Canada. In USA, c/o Big 3 Music Corp., 729 7th Ave., New York, N.Y. 10019

HA   Henry Adler, c/o Belwin-Mills Publishing Corp., Melville, N.Y. 11746

Hae   Haenssler Verlag, c/o C. F. Peters Corp., 373 Park Ave. S., New York, N.Y. 10016

Hal   Musikverlag Wilhelm Halter, Karlsruhe, Germany

Han   Hansen Publications, 1842 West Ave., Miami Beach, Fla. 33169

H&G   Hullenhagen & Griehl, Loogestr. 28, 2 Hamburg 20, West Germany

Hansen   Wilhelm Hansen Musikforlag, Copenhagen, Denmark. In USA, c/o G. Schirmer, Inc., 866 3rd Ave., New York, N.Y. 10022

Hansen, C. H.   *See* C. H. Hansen

Hargail   Hargail Music Press, 157 W. 57th St., New York, N.Y. 10019

Harmonia   Harmonia-Uitgave, c/o Henmar Press, Inc., 373 Park Ave. S., New York, N.Y. 10016

Harms, Inc.   Harms, Inc., 488 Madison Ave., New York, N.Y. 10022

Harms, T. B.   *See* T. B. Harms

Harrison   Harrison Music Corp., c/o Sidney K. Russell, 6300 Orion Ave., Van Nuys, Calif. 91401

Hawlik   Friedrich Hawlik, Neubaugasse 7, Vienna 7, Austria

HB   Harold T. Brasch, 2707 S. June St., Arlington, Va. 22202

HBP   Harold Branch Publications, 42 Cornell Drive, Plainview, N.Y. 11803

Heer & Zn.   Joh. de Heer & Zoon, Jensiusstraat 58, Rotterdam, Holland

Hein   Heinrichshofen, c/o C. F. Peters Corp., 373 Park Ave. S., New York, N.Y. 10016

Helena   Helena Music Corp., c/o Mr. Joe Darion, 420 Riverside Dr., New York, N.Y. 10025

Helios-Dow   Helios Music Edition, c/o Dow Publishers, Inc., P.O. Box 176, Oyster Bay, N.Y. 11771

H. Elkan   Henri Elkan Music Publisher, 1316 Walnut St., Philadelphia, Pa. 19107

Hen   Henderson, c/o Roche-Thomas Co., 3508 N. Sierra Way, San Bernardino, Calif. 92405

Henle   G. Henle Verlag, c/o Carl Fischer, Inc., 62 Cooper Square, New York, N.Y. 10003

Henmar   Henmar Press, Inc., 373 Park Ave. S., New York, N.Y. 10016

Henn   Editions Henn, 8 rue de Hesse, 1200 Geneva, Switzerland

Hie   Musikverlag Max Hieber, Munich, Germany

Highland   Highland Music Co., 445 Park Ave., New York, N.Y. 10022

HiN   High Note Studios, Box 429, Hollywood, Calif. 90028

Hin-Pet	Hinrichsen Edition, London, England. In USA, c/o C. F. Peters Corp., 373 Park Ave. S., New York, N.Y. 10016
Hio	Heinrich Hiob, c/o Verlag von Paul Zschocher, Hamburg, Germany
HL	Hal Leonard Music Pointer Publications, 8112 W. Blue Mound Rd., Milwaukee, Wis. 53213
H-McCreary	Hall & McCreary Co., 527 Park Ave., Minneapolis, Minn. 55415
HN	The Hornists Nest, 229 Bernhardt Dr., Buffalo, N.Y. 14226
Hof	Friedrich Hofmeister, Frankfurt am Main, Germany. In USA, c/o Presto Music Service, 300 Franklin St., Tampa, Fla.
Hug	Hug & Co., c/o Henmar Press, Inc., 373 Park Ave. S., New York, N.Y. 10016
Hulpiau	Gabrielle C. M. Hulpiau, 122 rue de la Clinique, Anderlecht-Brussels, Belgium
Humphries	Bruce Humphries, c/o Boston Music Co., 116 Boylston St., Boston, Mass. 02116
Hun	Hunter, c/o Belwin-Mills Publishing Corp., 25 Deshon Dr., Melville, N.Y. 11746
Huni	Musikhaus Huni, Helbling & Co., Haus Melodie, 8604 Volketswil, Switzerland
Huntzinger	R. L. Huntzinger, Inc., 440 Main St., Cincinnati, Ohio 45201. Or c/o Willis Music Co., 7380 Industrial Rd., Florence, Ky. 41042
HWG	H. W. Gray Co., c/o Belwin-Mills Publishing Corp., Melville, N.Y. 11746
IBM	International Business Machines, 590 Madison Ave., New York, N.Y. 10022
IIM	Instituto Interamericano de Musicologia, c/o Southern Music Publishing Co., 1740 Broadway, New York, N.Y. 10019
IMC	Ivy Music Company
IMP	Israeli Music Publications, c/o Alexander Broude, Inc., 225 W. 57th St., New York, N.Y. 10019
Imu	Musikforlaget Imudico, Colbjornsensgade 19, 1652 Copenhagen V, Denmark
InFrAthens	Institut Français d'Athènes, Athens, Greece
Ins	The Instrumentalist, 1418 Lake St., Evanston, Ill. 60204
Integrity	Integrity Music Corp., Apt. 14-A, 1050 5th Ave., New York, N.Y. 10028

Interlochen	Interlochen Press of the National Music Camp, Interlochen, Mich. 49643
Internatl.	International Music Co., 509 5th Ave., New York, N.Y. 10017
Islandia	Islandia Edition, Freyjugata 3, Rykjavik, Iceland
Isr-Leed	Israel Music Publications, Tel Aviv, Israel. In USA, c/o Leeds Music Corp., 445 Park Ave., New York, N.Y. 10022
IUK	Izdanje Udruzenja Kompositora, c/o Edition Ka We, Brederodestraat 90, Amsterdam 13, Netherlands
Janfred	Janfred Music, c/o Mr. George Kleinsinger, Hotel Chelsea, 222 W. 23rd St., New York, N.Y. 10011
JASRAC	JASRAC (The Japanese Society of Rights of Authors and Composers), Tameike Meisan Bldg., No. 30, Akasaka Tameike-cho, Minato-ku, Tokyo, Japan
JM	John Markert & Co., 141 W. 15th St., New York, N.Y. 10011
Job	Société des Editions Jobert, 44 rue du Colisée, Paris, France. In USA, c/o Theodore Presser Co., Presser Place, Bryn Mawr, Pa. 19010
J. Oertel	Johannes Oertel, Prinzregenten Str., 64, 8 Munich, West Germany
Josef Marx	Josef Marx Music Co., 408 2nd Ave., New York, N.Y. 10010
Jungnickel	Ross Jungnickel, Inc., 1619 Broadway, 11th Floor, New York, N.Y. 10019
KAH-AMP	C. F. Kahnt, Leipzig, Germany. In USA, c/o C. F. Peters Corp., 373 Park Ave. S., New York, N.Y. 10016
Kalmus	Edwin F. Kalmus, 154 W. 57th St., New York, N.Y. 10019
K&S	Fr. Kistner & C. F. W. Siegel, Postfach 101, 5 Cologne 7, West Germany
Kelton	Kelton, Inc., 66 Mechanic St., New Rochelle, N.Y. 10801
Kend	Kendor Music, Delevan, N.Y. 14042
KeysMusCal	Keystone Music Co. of California, 9615 Helen Ave., Sunland, Calif. 91040
Kimberly	Kimberly Music Corp., 211 W. 58th St., New York, N.Y. 10019
Kjos	Neil A. Kjos Music Co., 4382 Jutland Dr., San Diego, Calif. 92117
K-K	Kay & Kay Corp.
Kli	Musikverlag Johann Kliment, Leipzig, Germany
K. Neufert	Kurt Neufert, Oppelner Str. 9, 69 Heidelberg-Kircheim, West Germany
KN-Pet	Kneusslin, Switzerland. In USA, c/o C. F. Peters Corp., 373 Park Ave. S., New York, N.Y. 10016
KODA	KODA (Selskaber Til Forvaltning af Internationale Komponistrettigheder), I Danmark, Kronprinsessegade 26, Copenhagen K., Denmark
Kof	Koff Music Co., Box 1442, Studio City, Calif. 91604
KP	Keith Prowse Publishing Co., c/o Sam Fox Publishing Co., 1540 Broadway, New York, N.Y. 10036

Kul	Kultura, Budapest, Hungary. In USA, c/o Boosey & Hawkes, 30 West 57th St., New York, N.Y. 10019
Kulma	Kulma Music Corp., Apt. 2-J, 300 West 53rd St., New York, N.Y. 10019
K We	Edition Ka We, Brederodestraat 90, Amsterdam 13, Netherlands
LaulMieh	Laulu-Miehet, Hietaniemenkatu 2, Helsinki, Finland
LAV	Lavell Publishing Co.
Law-Gould	Lawson-Gould Music Publishers, Inc., 866 3rd Ave., New York, N.Y. 10022
L. B. & Co.	Little, Brown & Co.

	..., Kenosha, Wis. 53140. Or c/o ... Music, 1100 Broadway, San Antonio, Tex. 78206
Leeds	Leeds, c/o MCA Music Division of MCA, Inc., 445 Park Ave., New York, N.Y. 10022
Lemoine	Henri Lemoine & Cie, c/o Elkan-Vogel Co., Inc., Presser Place, Bryn Mawr, Pa. 19010
Len	Alfred Lengnick & Co., 14 Berner St., London, England
LEO	Hal Leonard Music Company, 8112 W. Blue Mound Rd., Milwaukee, Wis. 53213
LeslieProd	Leslie Productions, Inc., c/o Mr. Paul Reif, 57 W. 58th St., New York, N.Y. 10019
Leuckart	F. E. C. Leuckart Musikverlag, c/o G. Schirmer, Inc., 866 3rd Ave., New York, N.Y. 10022
Lex	Lexicon Music, c/o Highland Music Co., 1311 N. Highland Ave., Hollywood, Calif. 90028
LGO	Edition le Grand Orgue, 476 Marion St., Brooklyn, N.Y. 11233
LH	Lyon and Healy Music Company, S. Wabash Ave., Chicago, Ill.
Lis	J. J. Lispet, c/o Henri Elkan Music Publisher, 1316 Walnut St., Philadelphia, Pa. 19107
Lit-Pet	Litolff, Germany. In USA, c/o C. F. Peters Corp., 373 Park Ave. S., New York, N.Y. 10016
LML	Luck's Music Library, 1744 Seminole, Detroit, Mich. 48214
LN-Pet	Lienau, Berlin, Germany. In USA, c/o C. F. Peters Corp., 373 Park Ave. S., New York, N.Y. 10016
L. Oertel	L. Oertel & Co., Karntner Platz 2, 3, Hanover-Waldhausen, West Germany
Lorenz	Lorenz Publishing Co., 501 E. 3rd St., Dayton, Ohio 45401

Lou	Louisville House, c/o Autograph Editions, c/o Atlantic Music Supply, 152 W. 42nd St., New York, N.Y. 10036
LS	Larry Shayne Music, c/o Cimino Publications, 436 Maple Ave., Westbury, N.Y. 11590
Ludwig	Ludwig Music Publishing Co., 557-59 E. 140th St., Cleveland, Ohio 44110
Lundquists	A. B. Abr. Lundquists Musikforlag, Beckombergavagen 11, Bromma, Sweden
Luth	Luther Publisher, Box 179, Ansonia Station, New York, N.Y. 10023
LUV	Luverne Publications
LY-Pet	Lyche, Norway. In USA, c/o C. F. Peters Corp., 373 Park Ave. S., New York, N.Y. 10016
Mag	Maggio Music Press, Box 9717R, North Hollywood, Calif. 91609
Magna	Magnamusic Distributors, Inc., Sharon, Conn. 06069
Mal	Malcolm Music, c/o Shawnee Press, Delaware Water Gap, Pa. 18327
Mannheimer	Mannheimer Musik-Verlag, GMBH, Richard-Wagner-Str. 6, 68 Mannheim, West Germany
Marbot	Edition Marbot, GMBH, c/o Southern Music Publishing Co., Inc., 1740 Broadway, New York, N.Y. 10019
Margery	Margery Music, Inc., c/o William W. Lazarow, Suite 1106, 119 W. 57th St., New York, N.Y. 10019
Marks	Edward B. Marks Music Corp., 1790 Broadway, New York, N.Y. 10019
Marl	Marlen Music Co., c/o Gordon Music Co., 2680 Cherokee Way, Palm Springs, Calif. 92262
Mau	J. Maurer, 7 avenue du Verseau, Brussels, Belgium
MaxwellWir	Maxwell-Wirges Publications, c/o Shawnee Press, Inc., Delaware Water Gap, Pa. 18327
MB	M. Baron Co., Box 149, Oyster Bay, N.Y. 11771
MBQ	Montreal Brass Quintette, c/o Montreal Music Supply, 1820 McGregor Ave., Montreal, Quebec, Canada
MBr	Mel Broiles, c/o McGinnis & Marx, Pietro Deiro, 133 7th Ave., New York, N.Y. 10014
MCA	MCA Music Corp., 445 Park Ave., New York, N.Y. 10022
McG	McGinnis & Marx, c/o Pietro Deiro, 133 7th Ave., New York, N.Y. 10014
Melomusic	Melomusic Publications, Inc., 1619 Broadway, New York, N.Y. 10019
Men	Mentor Music, c/o Sam Fox Music Sales Corp., 11 W. 60th St., New York, N.Y. 10023
Mercurio	Mercurio, S.R.L., Via Stoppani 10, Rome, Italy
Mercury	Mercury Music Corp., c/o Edwin H. Morris & Co., Inc., 31 W. 54th St., New York, N.Y. 10019

Meridian	Société des Nouvelles Editions Meridian, c/o Southern Music Publishing Co., Inc., 1740 Broadway, New York, N.Y. 10019
Merr	Merrymount Music Press, c/o Theodore Presser Co., Presser Place, Bryn Mawr, Pa. 19010
Mers	Merseburger, c/o C. F. Peters Corp., 373 Park Ave. S., New York, N.Y. 10016
Met	Editions Metropolis, c/o Henri Elkan Music Publisher, 1316 Walnut St., Philadelphia, Pa. 19107
M-F	M-F Music Co., Box 351, Evanston, Ill. 60204
MfP	Music for Percussion, 17 W. 60th St., N.Y.

	, Deston Dr., Melville, N.Y. 11746. Now Belwin-Mills.
MiS	Michigan State University Press, Box 550, E. Lansing, Mich. 48823
MJQ	MJQ Music, Sam Fox Publishing Co., P.O. Box 850, Valley Forge, Pa. 19482
MM	Merion Music, c/o Theodore Presser Co., Presser Place, Bryn Mawr, Pa. 19010
MMC	M. M. Cole Publishing Co., 251 E. Grand Ave., Chicago, Ill. 60611
MMP	Michigan Music Press, 117 S. Main St., Ann Arbor, Mich. 48108
Modern	Edition Modern, Hans Wewerka, Franz-Josef-Str. 2, 8 Munich 13, West Germany
Moeck	Moeck, c/o Magnamusic Distributors, Inc., Sharon, Conn.
Mole	Molenaar, c/o Henri Elkan Music Publisher, 1316 Walnut St., Philadelphia, Pa. 19107
Morris	Edwin H. Morris & Co., Inc., 31 W. 54th St., New York, N.Y. 10019
Moseler	Moseler-Verlag, Hoffman-von-Fallersleben-Str. 8, 334 Wolfenbüttel, West Germany
MP	Media Press, Box 895, Champaign, Ill. 61820
MPH	Music Publishers Holding Corp., 488 Madison Ave., New York, N.Y. 10019
MR	Musica Rara, c/o Pringsheim, Gt. Marlborough St., London W1, England
MRP	MRP Publishing Co., c/o Pietro Deiro, 133 7th Ave., New York, N.Y. 10014
MSP	MS Publications, Box 171, East Lansing, Mich. 48823

MT-Pet	Mitteldeutscher, Germany. In USA, c/o C. F. Peters Corp., 373 Park Ave. S., New York, N.Y. 10016
Musikk-HU	Musikk-Huset A/S, Karl Johans gate 45, Oslo 1, Norway
MusKonFor	Musikaliska Konstforeningen, Jan Carlstedt, Floragat 15 B, Stockholm, Sweden
Mus. Press	Music Press, c/o Theodore Presser Co., Presser Place, Bryn Mawr, Pa. 19010
Muz	Muziekbeurs, Amsterdam, Netherlands
Muz. Fonds	Het Muziekfonds Uitgave, 45 Prinsesstraat, Antwerp, Belgium
Nagel	Adolph Nagel, c/o G. Schirmer, Inc., 866 3rd Ave., New York, N.Y. 10022
Natl. Cath.	National Cathedral in Washington, Mt. St. Alban, Washington, D.C.
Nau	Naukaiizkustvo, c/o Edition Ka We, Brederodestraat 90, Amsterdam 13, Netherlands
Neue Oper.	Die Neue Operette, Kurt Neufert Verlag, Oppelner Str. 9, Heidelberg-Kircheim, West Germany
NewEngMuCr	New England Music Center, 9 Park St., Boston, Mass.
New Mus. Ed.	New Music Edition, c/o Theodore Presser, Co., Presser Place, Bryn Mawr, Pa. 19010
New World	New World Music Corp., c/o Warner Bros. Publications, Inc., 75 Rockefeller Plaza, New York, N.Y. 10019
NM	New Music Orchestra Series, c/o Theodore Presser Co., Presser Place, Bryn Mawr, Pa. 19010
Noack	Walter Noack Verlag, Moselstr. 20, 62 Wiesbaden-Schierstein, West Germany
Noe	Otto Heinrich Noetzel Verlag, c/o C. F. Peters Corp., 373 Park Ave. S., New York, N.Y. 10016
Noel	Pierre Noel, Editeur, 24 boulevard Poissonnière, Paris, France. In USA, c/o M. Baron Co., Box 149, Oyster Bay, N.Y. 11771
Noetzel	Noetzel Mvlg., c/o Henmar Press, Inc., 373 Park Ave. S., New York, N.Y.
Nordiska	A. B. Nordiska Musikforlaget, Fack 8, Stockholm Tull, Sweden
Norsk Mfl.	Norsk Musikforlag A/S, Karl Johans gate 39, Oslo 1, Norway
Norsk Ntk.	Norsk Notestik & Forlag A/S, Schonings gate 43, Oslo 3, Norway
North	North & Son Music, 666 5th Ave., New York, N.Y. 10019
Northern	Northern Music Corp., c/o MCA, 445 Park Ave., New York, N.Y. 10022
Note	6 Note Publishing Co., c/o Harold T. Brasch, 2707 S. June St., Arlington, Va. 22202
Nov	Novello & Co., London, England. In USA, c/o British American Music Co., 19 W. Jackson, Chicago, Ill.; or c/o 1221 Avenue of the Americas, New York, N.Y. 10020
NTS	National Trumpet Symposium, Lamont School of Music, University of Denver, Denver, Colo. 80210

NWM	New Wind Music Co., London, England
Oberon	Edition Oberon, Roosevelt-Platz 8, Vienna 9, Austria
OBV-AMP	Oesterreichischer Bundesverlag, c/o Associated Music Publishers, 1 W. 47th St., New York, N.Y. 10036
ODC	Oliver Ditson., c/o Theodore Presser, Presser Place, Bryn Mawr, Pa. 19010
Oertel, J.	*See J. Oertel*
Oertel, L.	*See L. Oertel*
Okr	Okra Music Corp., 177 E. 87th St., New York, N.Y.
Old	F. E. Ol

..., Press, inc., 200 Madison Ave., New York, N.Y. 10016

PABrussels	Palais des Académies, Brussels, Belgium
PacPub	Pacific Publications, University Station 8, Provo, Utah 84601
Pacific	Edition Pacific (Inh. Michael Wilke), Herzog-Wilhelmstr. 27, 8 Munich 2, West Germany
Pan	Panton, c/o Edition Da We, Brederodestraat 90, Amsterdam 13, Netherlands
Par	Verlag Paul Parey, c/o C. F. Peters corp., 373 Park Ave. S., New York, N.Y. 10016
Paramount	Paramount Music Corp., c/o Mr. Sidney Herman, 1501 Broadway, New York, N.Y. 10036. Or c/o Famous Music Corp., 1 Gulf & Western Plaza, New York, N.Y. 10023
Pat-CF	Paterson Publications, Ltd., London, England. In USA, c/o Carl Fischer, 56-62 Cooper Square, New York, N.Y. 10013
PAU	Pan American Union, c/o Southern Music Publishing Co., 1740 Broadway, New York, N.Y. 10019
Pax	Paxman Musical Instruments, 14 Gerrard St., London W1, England
P. C. Cabot	Paul C. Cabot, Boston, Mass.
Peer	Peer International, c/o Southern Music Publishing Co., 1740 Broadway, New York, N.Y. 10019
Peg	Pegasus, c/o C. F. Peters Corp., 373 Park Ave. S., New York, N.Y. 10016
Pel	Musikverlag Zum Pelikan, Zurich, Switzerland
Phil	Editions Philippo, c/o Theodore Presser Co., Presser Place, Bryn Mawr, Pa. 19010
Piedmont	Piedmont Music Co., Inc., 1790 Broadway, New York, N.Y. 10019

Plage, W.	*See* W. Plage
Pleasant	Pleasant Music Publishing Corp., 66 Mechanic St., New Rochelle, N.Y. 10801
PM	Pillin Music, c/o Western International Music, 2859 Holt Ave., Los Angeles, Calif. 90034
P. Maurice	The Peter Maurice Music Co., Ltd., 101 W. 55th St., New York, N.Y. 10019
P. Mus. Ltd.	"Pops" Music, Ltd., c/o Mr. Alfred Eisenstein, 94-30 59th Ave., Elmhurst, N.Y. 11373
PMV	Pro Musica Verlag, Leipzig, Germany. In USA, c/o Alexander Broude, Inc., 225 W. 57th St., New York, N.Y. 10019
PO	Pete Osterhoudt, 1376 S. Sherman, Denver, Colo. 80210
Pod	Podium Music, Valhalla, N.Y. 10595
Polfliet	J. Polfliet, Fa. van Rosmalen & Zn., Rosendaalselaan 18, Velp bij Arnhem, Holland
Prentice	Prentice-Hall, Inc., Box 903, Englewood Cliffs, N.J. 07632
Pres	Presto Music Service, 300 Franklin St., Tampa, Fla.
Pro-Art	Pro-Art Publications, Inc., Westbury, N.Y. 11590
Prov	Providence Music Press, Box 2362, Providence, R.I. 02906
PT	Pigott & Co., Ltd., London, England. In USA, c/o Belwin-Mills Publishing Corp., 25 Deshon Dr., Melville, N.Y. 11746
PWM	Polskie Wydawnictwo Muzycne, c/o Belwin-Mills Publishing Corp., 25 Deshon Dr., Melville, N.Y. 11746
PX	W. Paxton & Co., Ltd., c/o Belwin-Mills Publishing Corp., 25 Deshon Dr., Melville, N.Y. 11746
Pyr	Pyraminx Publications, 358 Aldrich Rd., Fairport, N.Y. 14450
PZ	Paul Zschocher, Hamburg, Germany
Queens	Music Dept., Queens College, 65-30 Kissena Blvd., Flushing, N.Y. 11367
RAH	Raymond A. Hoffman Co.
Rahter, D.	*See* D. Rahter
R&W	Ruehle & Wendling, Wiesbaden, Germany
RB	Rayner Brown, c/o Western International Music, 2859 Holt Ave., Los Angeles, Calif. 90034
R. B. Brown	Robert B. Brown Music Co., 1815 N. Kenmore Ave., Hollywood, Calif. 90027
RC	Redwin and Clark
Regaldi	Regaldi Music Co., 279 Warwick Ave., Teaneck, N.J. 07666
Regina	Regina-Verlages-Wrede, Schumannstr. 35-a, 62 Wiesbaden, West Germany
RejayMuPub	Rejay Music Publishers, 5052 Berkeley Ave., Westminster, Calif. 92683
Remick	Remick Music Corp., 75 Rockefeller Plaza, New York, N.Y. 10019

RH	Robert L. Haley, c/o Atlantic Music Supply, 152 W. 42nd St., New York, N.Y. 10036. Or c/o Criterion Music Corp., 17 W. 60th St., New York, N.Y. 10023
RH-Pet	Reinhardt, Switzerland. In USA, c/o C. F. Peters Corp., 373 Park Ave. S., New York, N.Y. 10016
Riccardo	Riccardo-Ton-Vlg., Drususgasse 7-11, 5 Cologne, West Germany
Richli	Edition Richli, Geneva, Switzerland. In USA, c/o M. Baron Co., P. O. Box 149, Oyster Bay, N.Y. 11771
Ricordi	G. Ricordi & Co., c/o Franco Colombo, Inc., 16 W. 61st St., New York, N.Y. Or c/o Belwin-Mills Publishing Corp., 25 Desh___ ___ ___ N.Y. 11746
	___, ___ Aldrich Rd., Fairport, N.Y. 14450
Ron	Rongwen Music, c/o Broude Bros., 56 W. 45th St., New York, N.Y. 10036
Ros	Roslyn Publications, Box 128, Malverne, N.Y. 11565
Rosarita	Rosarita Music, Inc., Room 808, 1650 Broadway, New York, N.Y. 10019
Row	R. D. Row Music Co., Inc., 56-62 Cooper Square, New York, N.Y. 10003
RR	Rideau Rouge, c/o Theodore Presser Corp., Presser Place, Bryn Mawr, Pa. 19010
RT	Roche-Thomas Co., 3508 Sierra Way, San Bernardino, Calif. 92405
Ru	Rubank, Inc., 16215 N.W. 15th Ave., Miami, Fla. 33169
Ruf	Rufer Verlag, Gutersloh, Germany
Ruhle	Ruhle-Vig., Am Biederstein 7, 8 Munich 23, West Germany
Rum	Rumson Music Co., c/o Dick Noel Enterprises, c/o Educulture, Inc., Box 1932, Santa Monica, Calif. 90406
Rytvoc	Rytvoc, Inc., 39 W. 54th St., New York, N.Y. 10019
SABAM	SABAM (Société Belge des Auteurs, Compositeurs et Editeurs), 61 rue de la Loi, Brussels, Belgium
SACEM	SACEM (Société des Auteurs, Compositeurs et Editeurs de Musique), 10 rue Chaptal, Paris, France
SAKOJ	SAKOJ (Savez Komzitora Jugoslavije), Misarska 12, Belgrade, Yugoslavia
Sal-Ric	Editions Salabert, Paris, France, c/o G. Ricordi & Co., 16 W. 61st St., New York, N.Y. 10023
Sam	Samfundet, Denmark. In USA, c/o C. F. Peters Corp., 373 Park Ave. S., New York, N.Y. 10016
Sam. French	Samuel French, Inc., 25 W. 45th St., New York, N.Y. 10036

San	Sansone, c/o Southern Music Co., 1100 Broadway, San Antonio, Tex. 78206
S&B	Stainer & Bell, c/o Galaxy Music Corp., 2121 Broadway, New York, N.Y. 10023
S&R	S&R Music Publishing Co., 6533 Hollywood Blvd., Hollywood, Calif. 90028
Santis	Edizioni de Santis, Rome, Italy
Saunders	Saunders Publications, Inc., 119 W. 57th St., New York, N.Y. 10019
SC	La Schola Cantorum, c/o Theodore Presser Co., Presser Place, Bryn Mawr, Pa. 19010
SCH-AMP	B. Schott's Sohne, Germany; Schott & Co., England. In USA, c/o Associated Music Publishers, 866 3rd Ave., New York, N.Y. 10022
Sche	Editions Musicales Scherzando, 14 rue Auguste Orts, Brussels, Belgium
Scherzando	Scherzando Uitage, M. Georges de Heer Follman, 41 Transvaal-Straat, Berchm Antwerp, Belgium
Schi	Schilke Music Products, 529 S. Wabash Ave., Chicago, Ill. 60605
Schl	Schlesinger, c/o C. F. Peters Corp., 373 Park Ave. S., New York, N.Y. 10016
Schott F. B.	Schott Freres, c/o Henmar Press, Inc., 373 Park Ave. S., New York, N.Y. 10016
Schuberth	J. Schuberth & Co., Schliessfach 1053, 62 Wiesbaden, West Germany
Schul	Carl B. Schulz Corp., 527 Ansborough, Waterloo, Iowa 50701
SCos	Silvio Coscia, c/o Robert King Music Co., 112A Main St., North Easton, Mass. 02356
ScudderPro	Mr. Wallace Scudder, Scudder Productions, Bondville, Vt. 05340
See	Seesaw Music Corp., 177 E. 87th St., New York, N.Y. 10028
SEI	Roland F. Seitz
Sel	Editions Selmer, 18 rue la Fontaine au Roi, Paris, France
SF	Sam Fox Publishing Co., P.O. Box 850, Valley Forge, Pa. 19482
SGAE	SGAE (Sociedad General de Autores de España), Calle Fernando VI, 4, Madrid, Spain
Shawnee	Shawnee Press, Inc., Delaware Water Gap, Pa. 18327
SHB	Shapiro, Bernstein and Co., Inc., 666 5th Ave., New York, N.Y. 10019
Shilkret	Nathaniel Shilkret Music Co., Inc., Box 38, Malverne, L.I., New York, N.Y. 11565
SHMc	Schmitt, Hall & McCreary, 110 N. 5th St., Minneapolis, Minn. 55403
Shubert-MPH	Shubert Music Publishing Corp., Music Publishers Holding Corp., 488 Madison Ave., New York, N.Y. 10022
SIAE	SIAE (Societa Italiana delgi Autori ed Editori), Via Valadier 37, Rome, Italy
SIB	Silver-Burdett Publishing Co.

Sid	Sidemton Verlag, Köln, Germany
Sie	Editions du Siècle Musical, Geneva, Switzerland
Sikorski	Sikorski Mvlg., c/o Franco Colombo, Inc., 16 W. 61st St., New York, N.Y. 10023
SIM-AMP	N. Simrock, A. Benjamin, and D. Rahter, Leipzig, Germany. In USA, c/o Associated Music Publishers, 866 3rd Ave., New York, N.Y. 10022
Sirius	Sirius-Verlag-Berlin (Inh. Margarita Katz), Wiclefstr. 67, 1 Berlin 21, West Germany
Skand&Bo.	Skandinavisk Musikforlag A/S, Borgergade 2, Copenhagen K, Denmark
Skidmore	
	Society for the Publication of American Music, Inc., c/o Yale University, New Haven, Conn. 06507
Spr	Spratt Music Publishers, 17 W. 60th St., New York, N.Y. 10023
SPR	Studio P/R, 224 S. Lebanon St., Lebanon, Ind. 46052
Sta	Staff Music Co., 17 W. 60th St., New York, N.Y. 10023
Ste	Richard Stegmann, 87 Wurzburg, Waldkugelweg 5a, Germany
Stev	Stevens-Costello, c/o Harold Branch Publications, 42 Cornell Dr., Plainview, N.Y. 11803
STIM	STIM (Société Suedoise des Compositeurs, Auteurs et Editeurs de Musique), Tegnerlunden 3, Stockholm C, Sweden
Suecia	Edition Suecia, Tegnerlunden 3, Stockholm C, Sweden
SUISA	SUISA (Société Suisse des Auteurs et Editeurs), General-Guisan-Quai 28, Zurich, Switzerland
SUM	Clayton F. Summy Co., Evanston, Ill. 60204
Summy-Bir	Summy-Birchard Publishing Co., 1834 Ridge Ave., Evanston, Ill. 60204
Sup	Editio Supraphon, c/o Frank Music Corp., 119 W. 57th St., New York, N.Y. 10019
SW	Southwestern, c/o Summy-Birchard Publishing Co., 1834 Ridge Ave., Evanston, Ill. 60204
Swiss M.L.	The Swiss Music Library, Madison Ave. and 69th St., New York, N.Y. 10012
Sym. House	Symphony House Music Publishers, c/o Paul Siegel Productions, Tauentizien Str. 16, Berlin W. 30, West Germany
Symphonia	Symphonia Verlag, A. G., c/o Franco Colombo Inc., 16 W. 61st St., New York, N.Y. 10023

SZ-AMP	Edizioni Suvini Zerboni, Milan, Italy. In USA, c/o Associated Music Publishers, 1 W. 47th St., New York, N.Y. 10036
T&J	Tischer & Jagenberg, Wilhelmshohenstr. 6-a, 813 Starnberg Obb, West Germany
T. B. Harms	T. B. Harms Co., 100 Wilshire Blvd., Ste 700, Santa Monica, Calif. 90401
Tem	Tempo Music Publications, Box 392, Chicago, Ill. 60690
Templeton	Templeton Publishing Co., Inc., c/o Shawnee Press, Inc., Delaware Water Gap, Pa. 18327
Ten	Tenuto Publications, c/o Theodore Presser Co., Presser Place, Bryn Mawr, Pa. 19010
TEOSTO	TEOSTO (Savaltajain Tekijanoikeustomisto Teosto), Hietaniemenkatu 2, Helsinki, Finland
Tier	Tierolff Muziekcentrale, c/o Henri Elkan Music Publisher, 1316 Walnut St., Philadelphia, Pa. 19107
TOR	Tor Music, Inc.
TP	Theodore Presser Co., Presser Place, Bryn Mawr, Pa. 19010
Transcon	Transcontinental Music Corp., 1674 Broadway, New York, N.Y. 10019
Translator	(Name of individual), c/o ASCAP, 575 Madison Ave., New York, N.Y. 10022
TRFMusInc.	T.R.F. Music Inc., 501 Madison Ave., New York, N.Y. 10022
Tritone Prs.	Tritone Press, c/o Mr. William Presser, 211 Hillendale Dr., Hattiesburg, Miss. 38401
Trom	Tromba Publications, 1859 York St., Denver, Colo. 80206
Troubadour	Troubadour Publishing Co., Suite 15-F, 345 W. 58th St., New York, N.Y. 10019
20th Cent.	Twentieth Century Music Corp., c/o Robbins Music Corp., 729 7th Ave., New York, N.Y. 10019
UBS	University Brass Series, c/o Cor Publishing Co., 67 Bell Place, Massapequa, N.Y. 11758
UE	Universal Edition, Vienna and London. In USA, c/o Joseph Boonin, Inc., P.O. Box 2124, S. Hackensack, N.J. 07606
UEE	Union Européene d'Editions, Monaco
UME-AMP	Union Musical Española, Madrid, Spain. In USA, c/o Associated Music Publishers, 866 3rd Ave., New York, N.Y. 10022
U. MiamiSO	University of Miami Symphony Orchestra, c/o Music Dept., University of Miami, Coral Gables, Fla. 33146
UMP	University Music Press, Box 1267, Ann Arbor, Mich. 48106
Universal	Universal Musical Instrument Co., 732 Broadway, New York, N.Y. 10003
Val	Valley Music Press, Sage Hall, Smith College, Northhampton, Mass. 01060
Varitone	Varitone, Inc., 545 5th Ave., New York, N.Y. 10017

VikingMfl.	Viking Musiforlag, Norrebrogade 34, Copenhagen N, Denmark
Volkwein	Volkwein Bros., Inc., 117 Sandusky St., Pittsburgh, Pa. 15212
Vriamont	M. George Vriamont, 25 rue de la Régence, Brussels 1, Belgium
VW-Pet	Vieweg, Berlin, Germany. In USA, c/o C. F. Peters Corp., 373 Park Ave. S., New York, N.Y. 10116
Wal	Wallan Music Co., 17 W. 60th St., New York, N.Y. 10023
War	Warner Bros. Music, 75 Rockefeller Plaza, New York, N.Y. 10019
Warock	Warock Corp., 39 W. 54th St., New York, N.Y. 10019
WashBalGld	Washington Ballet Guild
	...Co., c/o Mr. Felix C. Ziffer, 641 Lexington Ave., 22nd Floor, New York, N.Y. 10022
Western	Western Music Library, 615 N. LaSalle St., Chicago, Ill. 60610
Wil	Willis Music Co., 7380 Industrial Rd., Florence, Ky. 41042
Wild	Wilder Music, c/o Sam Fox Publishing Co., P.O. Box 850, Valley Forge, Pa. 19482
Wilhmiana	Wilhelmiana Musikverlag, Eschersheimer Landstr. 12, 6 Frankfurt-am-Main, West Germany
Williamson	Williamson Music Inc., 810 7th Ave., New York, N.Y. 10019
WIM	Western International Music, 2859 Holt Ave., Los Angeles, Calif. 90034
Wimbledon	Wimbledon Music Co., P.O. Box 1261, Grand Central Station, New York, N.Y. 10017
Wind	Wind Music, 1014 S. Goodman St., Rochester, N.Y. 14620
Witmark	M. Witmark & Sons, 75 Rockefeller Plaza, New York, N.Y. 10019
WL	Joseph Williams, Ltd., c/o Belwin-Mills Publishing Corp., 25 Deshon Dr., Melville, N.Y. 11746
W-Levant	Weaner-Levant, c/o Theodore Presser Co., Presser Place, Bryn Mawr, Pa. 19010
WLSM	World Library of Sacred Music, 2145 Central Parkway, Cincinnati, Ohio 45214
WM	Willy Mueller, c/o C. F. Peters Corp., 373 Park Ave. S., New York, N.Y. 10016
WN	Wynn Music
W. Plage	Dr. W. Plage, c/o GEMA, Herzog-Wilhelm-Strasse 28, Munich 2, West Germany

WPM	Wilshire Presbyterian Music Foundation, c/o Western International Music, 2859 Holt Ave., Los Angeles, Calif. 90034
WS	White-Smith
YE	Yorke Edition, c/o Galaxy Music Corp., 2121 Broadway, New York, N.Y. 10023
Y. Laulajat	Ylioppilaskunnan, Laulajat, Vanha Ylioppilastalo, Helsinki, Finland
ZA-Pet	Zanibon Edition, Padua, Italy. In USA, c/o C. F. Peters Corp., 373 Park Ave. S., New York, N.Y. 10016
Zau	David Zauder, 3365 Euclid Heights Blvd., Cleveland Heights, Ohio 44118
Zim	Wilhelm Zimmermann, c/o C. F. Peters Corp., 373 Park Ave. S., New York, N.Y. 10016

A. Harold Goodman, music department chairman and director of lyceums at Brigham Young University, brings to this book a wealth of experience in instrumental music. He has served as musical director and conductor of the Utah Valley Symphony Orchestra, the Utah Valley Youth Symphony Orchestra, the Northern Arizona Symphony Orchestra, and the Tucson Symphony Orchestra, and as director of bands and orchestras at Northern Arizona State University. He has conducted extensively both bands and orchestras in Canada and Mexico and throughout the United States, is a popular guest clinician, conductor, speaker, and adjudicator, and has been violin soloist for many church, school, and community recitals and concerts.

He received his B.A. from the University of Arizona and Master of Music and Ed.D. in music education from the University of Southern California. Dr. Goodman holds membership in Phi Mu Alpha, Kappa Kappa Psi, Phi Delta Kappa, Delta Epsilon, Phi Kappa Phi, and Pi Kappa Lambda, and is a life member of the Music Educators National Conference. In 1973 he was awarded the Karl G. Maeser Teaching Excellence Award at Brigham Young University.

He has served as president of the Utah Music Educators Association, vice-president of Arizona Music Educators, member of the Music Educators Research Council, and chairman of the BYU Faculty Advisory Council. For five years Dr. Goodman has been a board member of the National Association of Schools of Music and is actively engaged with the Young Audiences, American Federation of Musicians, and Central Utah Arts Council. He was recently elected president of the Western Division of the Music Educators National Conference.

Dr. Goodman has served on accreditation teams of the Northwest Accreditation Association, the National Association of Schools of Music, and the National Council Association of Teacher Education. He is the author of *Music Administration in Higher Learning* and of many articles in four international journals.

A member of The Church of Jesus Christ of Latter-day Saints, he has served as bishop, high councilor, stake president, member of the Sunday School general board, and chairman of the Church Music Department Executive Committee. Also active in community affairs, he has been president of the Flagstaff, Arizona, Lions Club and assisted in preparing two city charters.

These experiences have won Dr. Goodman recognition in various publications: *Outstanding Educators of America, Creative and Successful Personalities, Community Leaders and Noteworthy Americans, Personalities of the West and Midwest, Who's Who,* and *The World Who's Who of Musicians.*